BOOKS BY W. C. HEINZ

American Mirror

Once They Heard the Cheers

Emergency

Run to Daylight!
(with Vince Lombardi)

The Surgeon

The Fireside Book of Boxing
(Editor)

The Professional

American Mirror

W. C. Heinz

American

Mirror

1982
Doubleday & Company, Inc.
Garden City, New York

Major portions of this volume were previously published as follows:

"The Morning They Shot the Spies," in *True* magazine, December 1949, copyright 1949 by Fawcett Publications, Inc. Reprinted by permission of Lopez Publications, Inc.

"The Day of the Fight," in *Cosmopolitan* magazine, February 1947, copyright 1947 by Hearst Magazines, Inc. Reprinted by permission.

"The Fighter's Wife," in *Cosmopolitan* magazine, December 1949, copyright 1949 by Hearst Magazines, Inc. Reprinted by permission.

"So Long, Rock," as "Goodbye Graziano," in *Sport* magazine, March 1952, copyright 1952 by McFadden Publications, Inc.; copyright © 1980 by W. C. Heinz.

"D-Day Relived," as "I Took My Son to Omaha Beach," in *Collier's* magazine, June 11, 1954, copyright 1954 by The Crowell-Collier Publishing Company. Reprinted by permission.

"Punching Out a Living," in *Collier's* magazine, May 2, 1953, copyright 1953 by The Crowell-Collier Publishing Company. Reprinted by permission.

"The Rocky Road of Pistol Pete," in *True* magazine, March 1958, copyright © by Fawcett Publications, Inc. Reprinted by permission of Lopez Publications, Inc.

"Brownsville Bum," in *True* magazine, June 1951, copyright 1951 by Fawcett Publications, Inc.; copyright © 1979 by W. C. Heinz.

"Death of a Racehorse," in the New York *Sun*, July 28, 1949, copyright 1949 by the New York *Sun*. Reprinted by permission of Bell and Howell.

"Young Fighter," in *Esquire* magazine, July 1955, copyright © 1955 by Esquire, Inc. Reprinted by permission.

"The Man with a Life in His Hands," in *Life* magazine, January 20, 1961, copyright © 1961 by Time, Inc. Reprinted by permission.

"G.I. Lew," in *Argosy* magazine, November 1952, copyright 1952 by Popular Publications, Inc.; copyright © 1980 by W. C. Heinz.

"Great Day at Trickem Fork," in *The Saturday Evening Post*, May 22, 1965, copyright © 1965 by The Curtis Publishing Company. Reprinted by permission.

Library of Congress Cataloging in Publication Data

Heinz, W. C. (Wilfred Charles), 1915–
American mirror.

1. United States—Biography. 2. Courage. I. Title.
CT220.H43   920'.073
AACR2
ISBN: 0-385-12672-7
Library of Congress Catalog Card Number 80–723

Foreword

Jimmy Cannon was going to show Bill Heinz and me his new apartment on Central Park West. As we walked down the corridor, Bill was talking about Ben Hecht, who at the time was host of a nightly TV talk show.

"It tickles me," Bill said, "the way, no matter what the subject is, he inevitably gets around to asking, 'And what about the Germans with their watery eyes, thick necks, and no ankles?'"

"He's talking about Marlene Dietrich," Jimmy said, fumbling for his keys.

Like Miss Dietrich, though for different reasons, Bill Heinz is a walking contradiction of the stereotype of the phlegmatic Teuton. He is emotional and demonstrative. He can sink into depressions so deep they would give a sandhog the bends. His highs are several stories high. As cityside reporter, war correspondent, sports columnist, freelance journalist, and novelist, he was and is a dedicated craftsman and a penetrating observer who never gives half measure.

"Bill," his doctor once told him, "if you don't stop trying to be the greatest writer in the world, you're going to kill yourself."

"I'm not trying to be the greatest writer in the world," Bill said, "I'm only trying to be the best writer I can be."

Visiting Bill and Betty in their mountainside home in Vermont, my wife and I arrived the day after he had shipped the manuscript of his third novel to his publisher. I suppose I expected to find him exultant, or at least buoyant with relief. Instead, he was drained.

"When you spend three years trying to write better than you can," he said, "it takes something out of you."

Somebody has said that a prejudiced witness is all right, so long as you know his prejudices. This may be an excuse for permitting me to write this foreword, for I am deeply prejudiced in favor of Bill Heinz and his work, and this is no new state of mind. My admiration for his work is older than our friendship, which can be dated only with carbon 14.

Besides scrupulous accuracy, a mark of a good reporter is the ability to put the reader on the scene, which demands a visual and auditory memory for details—early morning in the village of Herve with steam rising from a bucketful of scrubwater poured in the gutter and the breath of villagers showing as they walk to work. Every time I read "The Morning They Shot the Spies" I feel the cold—and the fear.

Going further, the superior reporter enables the reader to know the subject of the piece personally, maybe even to think as the subject thinks and feel as the subject feels, as in "The Man with a Life in His Hands," that superb narrative that describes not only an operation for cancer but the beginnings, the training, the technique, and the aspirations of the great thoracic surgeon who was in real life Dr. J. Maxwell Chamberlain. It is the same sensitivity of the writer that enables the reader of "The Fighter's Wife" to understand the unspoken anguish of suspense suffered by Norma Graziano while Rocky was in the ring.

Reading about Norma trying to relieve her tension at the ironing board reminded me of Bobby Thomson's mother the day he hit The Home Run. It was the last of the ninth inning of the third and deciding game between the New York Giants and Brooklyn Dodgers in a play-off for the 1951 National League pennant. With the Dodgers leading, 4–2, two Giants on base and one out, Thomson hit the most theatrical home run in baseball history, winning the game, 5–4, and bringing the championship to the Giants.

Thomson lived with his little old Scottish mother on Staten Island. She followed the game by radio until the eighth inning when the Dodgers took their comfortable lead. Then, depressed, she shut the sound off.

All of a sudden, as she told it later, neighbors were clamoring at her door crying, "Bawbby hitt a home rrrrun! Bawbby hitt a home rrrrun!"

Mrs. Thomson got so excited she rushed downstairs and scrubbed the basement floor.

Perhaps once in a lifetime if he is very good and very lucky, a writer will see a piece of his accomplish tangible results, as Grant-land Rice's story covering the Army–Notre Dame football game of 1924 created an image for the Four Horsemen of Notre Dame— Jimmy Crowley, Harry Stuhldreher, Elmer Layden, and Don Miller —that was larger than life and endured as long as they lived.

In 1954, Bill Heinz escorted Colonel James Earl Rudder back to Pointe du Hoc, the towering cliff between Omaha Beach and Utah Beach on the Normandy coast where Allied forces had invaded France on D-Day, June 6, 1944. Rudder, taking what General Omar N. Bradley described as the most difficult assignment he ever gave a soldier, led three companies of Rangers up the sheer face of that cliff under murderous fire from above.

He won the D.S.C., the Silver Star, the Bronze Star with cluster, the Purple Heart with cluster, the Croix de Guerre, and the Légion d'Honneur, but his reputation never spread far outside his home-town of Brady, Texas (pop. 5,338), until *Collier's* published "D-Day Relived" as a cover story celebrating the tenth anniversary of the invasion.

Rudder had served as mayor of Brady after the war and was working as vice-president of a small airplane parts plant when the story came out. Now the governor of Texas sought his friendship. He became president of Texas A&M University, his alma mater in College Station, and then president of the statewide A&M system. After his death, a $10 million J. Earl Rudder Conference Center with a twelve-story memorial tower was built on the College Station campus. Rudder always gave Bill Heinz credit for the change in his fortunes.

"Old Bill," Rudder was telling him once, "I don't know how I can ever thank you for all that article of yours meant to me."

"Oh, sure," Bill said. "I took a lot of risks writing that story ten years later. On D-Day, all you did was land in the water up to your shoulders with the Germans firing down on you from the top of the cliff."

Bill Heinz was born in Mt. Vernon, New York, and grew up

there, a skinny kid wanting to be either Jack Dempsey, Babe Ruth, or Red Grange, or all three. When he learned early, through personal experience, that a punch on the nose is not intended to improve the recipient's appearance nor a baseball bounced off one's skull to clarify his powers of thought, he turned to other role models. Reading the sports pages he discovered that sportswriters actually traveled with major league teams and lived with fighters in training camps, and the writer emerged.

His new heroes became Westbrook Pegler, Heywood Broun, and, ultimately, Frank Graham and Ernest Hemingway. Graham, whose newspaper prose was as pure and whose dialogue was as accurate as any appearing anywhere, taught many of us, and it so happened that he and I were visiting Hemingway at his Finca Vigia, just outside Havana, shortly after Bill's first novel, *The Professional*, had appeared.

Hemingway had praised the work as the only good book he'd ever read about a fighter and an excellent first novel in its own right. He was still living with it during lunch.

"Damn," he said, "but I didn't want Bill's fighter to lose."

"*You* didn't want him to lose?" I said. "How about Bill? When he started the book he knew how he had to end it, but after he wrote the first line leading into the fight he had to take a day off and walk in the woods to get up the courage to have his fighter knocked out."

Well, in this book are collected a few of the pieces Bill Heinz wrote over the years, mostly the years since the New York *Sun* set and he turned from daily sports columnist to freelance work. In my judgement they are far too few. I could list at least as many more that I think should be preserved between hard covers, but Bill himself made the choices and his standards are unreasonably high.

Red Smith
New Canaan,
Connecticut

Author's Note

A writer, unless he has his own printing press, is indebted to publishers and editors, and he might as well admit it. Now, in presenting these pieces, my own gratitude goes to those individuals who came up with the story ideas, or accepted mine, and especially to those who handled the copy as if it were their own. To Hugh O'Neill, at Doubleday, go my thanks for seeing the virtues of work much of which was turned out before his time, and for his guidance in putting together this package. I owe a particular debt to Bard Lindeman, my good friend and as good a reporter, who, on the Selma March, patrolled with me U.S. 80, and whose legwork, perceptivity, and tenacity were responsible for much that is in the last piece in this book.

". . . .To Red Smith, when he passed away on January 15, 1982, I owed thanks not only for his words of introduction to this volume, but for a friendship that had grown to span thirty-five years."

Contents

American Mirror

1

The Morning

They Shot

the Spies

We skirted Liége and turned east on the road that leads past the Belgian forts dug into the ground. It was cold. It was two days to Christmas. It was still early and the mist hung over the fields and, in some places, over the road. I remembered when we went through here with the tanks in September. The sun shone every day and it was warm then, and the Germans were running for the Rhine. It was hard to find Germans then, and when the Americans found them the Germans quit easy and it seemed that the war would be over by Christmas and maybe we would be home.

"Stay on here," I said to the driver. "After we go through Herve I'll tell you. I remember it's on the left-hand side of the road."

When we went through Herve the people were just starting the day. There were a few of them on the street—a woman in a shawl pouring a pail of steaming, cloudy water into the cobblestone gutter, and a couple of workers walking along the sidewalk, their breaths showing, the collars of their old jackets turned up and their hands in their pants pockets. They paid no attention to us.

"That's the place up on the left," I said to the driver. "I can remember it."

I could remember the wall along the road, and the opening in it. I could remember the low stucco barracks on the other three sides of the dirt quadrangle, and we drove past the guard at the gate and across the frozen yard. The driver put the jeep in with some others at the far end, and we got out, stiff from the cold, and walked back across the dry, hard dirt to what looked like the office.

There were some M.P. personnel working in there at desks behind a guard rail. There was a potbellied stove at the back, and we walked over to it, standing around it and taking the heat and talking about it until a young lieutenant came over and asked us if he could help us.

"We're here for this spy thing," I said.

"Oh," he said. "Then you go across there to the mess hall."

He pointed and you could see through the glass in the far door the building that he meant.

"What time is it coming off?"

"I'm afraid I don't know," the lieutenant said. "This place is in a mess. Just go over there. I'm sure that someone will tell you in plenty of time for you to see it."

We went out and walked across the quadrangle toward the building. The side showing on the quadrangle was made up almost entirely of wide sliding doors. One of them was open and, looking in, I could see some people who had driven down from the Ninth Army at Maastricht.

I judged this place had been a stable when the Germans had used it. Now the Americans were using it as a mess hall, and a couple of the people from Ninth Army were sitting on the benches, their backs to the long tables, while the others moved around, stamping their feet, their hands in their pockets. There was no heat in the place.

The Ninth Army people didn't know anything. I could tell from the way they talked that they didn't know the censors had put a stop on this, that you couldn't write about it, but I wasn't going to tell them.

2

In a few minutes a captain came in. He was quite young and freshly shaven, and he looked cleaner than anything else around the place. He was smiling and he went around introducing himself and shaking hands. He seemed to be trying to be the perfect host, and his enthusiasm and his friendliness made me a little annoyed with him.

"I suppose," he said, "that you gentlemen understand about the censorship of all pictures."

"We know all about it," one of the photographers said. "You don't have to worry about it."

"And I suppose you also understand," the captain said, "that nothing is to be written about this."

I felt a little sorry for the writers who had come down from Maastricht. It came to them as a surprise. They started to put up a real kick, but they must have known it was a waste of time to argue.

"But I thought they wanted a lot of publicity about it," one of them said. "I thought they wanted it to get back to the Germans so they'd stop this sneaking guys into our lines."

"I don't know anything about that," the captain said.

"Then why didn't they tell us?" somebody else said. "Why didn't they tell us before we wasted our time driving way down here in this cold?"

"I'm sorry," the captain said. "You know as much about it as I do."

Several of them said they would leave, talking about it among themselves, but they all stayed. To put an end to the argument someone asked the captain what he knew about the prisoners.

"All I know," he said, and you could see him thinking about what he had rehearsed, "is that they were picked up at night inside our lines in an American jeep. They were wearing American uniforms, and had a radio. They hadn't accomplished anything, as they had just entered our lines when they were picked up.

"One of them is an out-and-out Nazi. He's the short one. The other two, I believe, are innocent of any original intent of spying. One of them is a farm boy from Westphalia. He's quite simple and, I think, quite honest.

"The story he tells—and I'm inclined to believe it—is that several weeks ago, before this German counteroffensive started, a call went out for men who speak English. He volunteered, he said, because he thought it would be a soft job back at headquarters on propaganda or prisoner interrogation or something like that. The next thing he knew, he was in an American uniform and in an American jeep and heading for our lines. He said there was nothing he could do, and I don't suppose there was, because they always put one Nazi in with the weak ones to see that they keep in line."

We stood around the captain listening, and some of the Ninth Army people were taking notes. I thought the captain was very efficient. He was telling us all that he could.

"We've never done anything like this before," he said. "It's rather a messy thing, and we'll be glad to get it over."

"Then what are we waiting for? We were notified this thing would be at nine-thirty."

"I don't know," the captain said. "I imagine they may be waiting to see if there's any other word from SHAEF. I suppose they want to be sure SHAEF hasn't had a change of mind about it."

"Then how long do we have to wait?"

"I haven't found out," the captain said, "but it should be within a half hour."

"How about the prisoners? Can you tell us how they're taking it?"

"All right," the captain said. "The chaplain has been seeing two of them, but the Nazi wants nothing to do with him. We have some Wehrmacht nurses in the next cell, and last night the three asked that the nurses be allowed to sing some Christmas carols for them."

"Then they know they're going to be shot this morning?"

"Yes. The chaplain informed them last night."

"Was the request for the carols granted?"

"Of course."

"What carols did the nurses sing?"

"I don't remember exactly," the captain said, "because the only one I recognized was 'Silent Night.' We had to stop them after a while."

"Why?"

"Because they were disturbing our troops."

I wondered if the captain knew that "Silent Night" is an Austrian carol that the rest of us borrowed.

4

"We can go now," he said. "Keep together and follow me. When you get there, keep about twenty-five or thirty feet back. There will be an M.P. stationed there, and you are to keep behind that line. That goes for the photographers, too. Also, once you get there you will have to stay because no one will be allowed to leave."

"In other words," one of the Ninth Army people said, "if we want to back out, we have to back out now."

"That's right," the captain said, smiling.

I thought about backing out and I wished no one had mentioned it. I was starting to feel a fear, and we followed the captain out and across the quadrangle. We walked in a straggling group past the place where the jeeps were parked, and we took a path that ran along, on the left, the side wall of a low, gray stucco building. On the right there was a field, gray with frost, and the path was rough with frozen footprints. I wondered if the prisoners knew now how close they were to it.

The path we took led down into a field behind the stucco building. The field sloped a little away from the building, running down to a barbed-wire fence. Beyond that the ground dropped rather suddenly, and you could see into a valley, filled now with the mist. We walked maybe fifty feet into the field, the captain taking us around several M.P.s standing at ease in the field, and then we turned and faced the back wall of the building.

The wall was about eight feet high. About three feet out from it and spaced about fifteen feet apart were three squared posts stained brown. The postholes were new.

We stood there in a group, an M.P. to our left, looking at the posts. I looked at the ground, frost-white, the grass tufts frozen, the soil hard and uneven. I wondered if it is better to die on a warm, bright day among friends, or on a day when even the weather is your enemy. I turned around and looked down into the valley. The mist still hung in the valley, but it was starting to take on a brassy tint from the sun beginning to work through it. I could make out three white farm buildings on the valley floor—a little yellowed now from the weak sunlight—and I could envision this, in the spring, a pleasant valley.

This view I see now, I said to myself, will be the last thing their eyes will ever see. I looked at it intently for that reason. I thought

5

I watched them, thinking that these were among the last steps these prisoners would ever take. (*John Florea,* Life; © *Time, Inc.*)

of the human eye and of its complexity and its marvelous efficiency. I found myself thinking only of the farm boy, the Westphalian, for whom this would be the last room, the last view, and I turned back to the others.

That was when we heard the sound of marching feet. I turned and I saw them coming around the corner of the building, along the path we had taken.

There was, first, an M.P. officer. Behind him came the first prisoner and I knew at once that he was the one the captain had described as the farm boy from Westphalia. Behind him, in twos, marched eight M.P.s, then another prisoner, eight M.P.s, the third prisoner, and eight more M.P.s. The boots of the M.P.s shone with polish and on their helmets the lettering and bands were a fresh, new white. The prisoners wore American combat jackets over fatigue jumpers like those that garage mechanics sometimes wear—more green than khaki—and there was a stripe of light blue paint down the front of each leg.

So that technically they won't be shot in American uniforms, I thought. They had to give them something to wear.

It was difficult to march well over the rough, frozen ground. You could tell this by the way the tips of the rifles wavered in the lines. I watched them, thinking of the wonders of the walking process, of the countless steps we give away so cheaply for needless reasons until there are no more. Now the column seemed to be marching so quickly.

They had turned off the path and now moved across in front of us, between us and the wall. When they reached a point where the Westphalian was opposite the last post, the officer at the head shouted and the column stopped, the men marking time, the feet of the prisoners a part of the rhythm. Then he shouted again and the feet stopped and the column stood at attention. Both times that he shouted I noticed the Westphalian looked down and back nervously at the feet of the M.P.s behind him as he obeyed the orders.

He is a good soldier, I thought. At a time like this he is worrying about being in step, and he is afraid that he is not catching the commands. You have to give him something for that, I thought, and I looked at him carefullly. He was the one all right—tall, big-boned, long-faced, with long arms, his fingers red and just showing below the sleeves of the American jacket that fitted him poorly and made him seem all the more pathetic.

There was no doubt about the second one either. He was the one the captain had described as the Nazi. He was short, about five feet four, and he had a high, bulging forehead and flat, black hair and he wore black-rimmed glasses. He stood very erect, his face set as stiffly as his body.

The third one did not impress me. He was well built—by far the best looking of the three—and he had black, curly hair. In my mind he was something between the farm boy and the Nazi, and so I closed my mind to him.

I saw these things quickly, for the officer was shouting again and the M.P.s, the prisoners a split second behind them, were facing left. They were facing the wall and the three posts in front of it, and then two M.P.s were leading each prisoner to a post, and the column was turning and marching back toward us, then turning back again to the wall and standing in two rows, twelve men to a row.

The prisoners, standing in front of the posts, looked very pale now. I looked at their thin fatigues and their bare hands. I wondered if the Westphalian felt the cold. I should have liked to have asked him.

Now, while the squad and the rest of us waited, two M.P.s walked to the post where the Westphalian stood, and there were strands of yellow, braided rope in their hands. You could see how new and clean the rope was, and when one of the M.P.s took a strand of rope and bent down at the post the other took the Westphalian by the shoulders and moved him back an inch or two. The first M.P. wrapped the rope around the Westphalian's ankles and around the post, and as he started to do this the Westphalian looked down, his hair falling forward, and he shuffled his feet back, watching until the M.P. was done. After that the second M.P. took the Westphalian's arms and put them back, one on each side, behind the post. Then the first M.P. tied them there, and the Westphalian, turning first to one side and then the other, watched intently.

He is trying to help them, I said to myself. Even now he is trying to do the right thing. I wondered how he could do this, and I knew he was brave because he was very afraid. I wondered how a man could be that brave, and then I saw a photographer, disobeying what the captain had told us, kneeling a few feet in front of the Westphalian, focusing his camera on him. I saw the Westphalian staring right back at the photographer, his eyes wide, his whole face questioning, and for that moment he seemed about to cry.

They left the Westphalian and went to the one in the middle, the one the captain had described as the Nazi. He already stood very stiffly against the post, and he did not move when they tied his feet. When they tied his arms behind his post he thrust them back there for them, and he squared his head and shoulders against the post. He was looking over the heads of all of us, and his face was very stern.

They went, then, to tie the third prisoner, the unimportant one. I looked at the other two, tied to the posts, looking out over the heads of the firing squad. I remembered the view of the valley behind my back. That is the last thing, I thought again, that the Westphalian will ever see. I looked at his long, pale face and I wondered if he was seeing anything. I knew that someone would think of him presently, as they might be thinking of him now, wondering what he was doing. I thought of a farmhouse, like so many we had passed in this war, the whitened stone cottage, the flat fields, an old woman, a turnip heap, and, somewhere in the yard, a dung pile.

When they tied his arms behind his post he thrust them back there for them, and he squared his head and shoulders against the post. He was looking over the heads of all of us, and his face was very stern. (*John Florea*, Life; © *Time, Inc.*).

They had finished tying the third prisoner. The three stood rigid against the posts like woodcuts of men facing execution. There were M.P. officers, clean and erect and efficient, moving between them, inspecting knots and saluting one another and then a chaplain—a full colonel, helmeted, wearing a trench coat but with a black satin stole around his neck and hanging down his front—stepped out from beside the squad and walked slowly, a small black book held in his hands in front of him, to the post where the Westphalian was tied.

I saw him say something to the Westphalian and I saw the Westphalian look to him and stare into his face and nod his head. I saw the chaplain reading from the book, and once I saw the

Above, *the prisoners, standing in front of the posts, looked very pale now.* (John Florea, Life; © Time, Inc.)

Then two M.P.s . . . pinned over the heart of each prisoner a white paper circle . . . about the size of a large orange. (John Florea, Life; © Time, Inc.)

Westphalian's lips moving, his head nodding a little, and then the chaplain was finished and the Westphalian was staring into his face as he moved away.

The chaplain stopped beside the one in the middle, the one described as the Nazi. The prisoner shook his head without looking at the chaplain, but the chaplain was saying something anyway, and then he moved on to the prisoner at the end who listened as the chaplain spoke.

When the chaplain had finished he walked back to a point behind the firing squad. Then two M.P.s stepped forward and walked to the Westphalian and one of them had in his hand a band of black cloth. He stood in back of the post and he reached around the head of the Westphalian to fix the cloth across his eyes.

This now, I said to myself, is that last moment that he will see anything on this earth. I wondered if the Westphalian was thinking that thought.

They fixed the bands over the eyes of the others. Then two M.P.s stepped forward and, starting with the prisoner on the left, pinned over the heart of each prisoner a white paper circle. The circles were about the size of a large orange. So they won't miss, I thought.

I was very cold, now, in these few gray seconds in this field. There was some saluting among the M.P. officers, and there were the three prisoners, each alone, their eyes bound with black and the white circles over their hearts, waiting.

I will not look, I was saying to myself. I think I am afraid to look. It is so easy to turn away, I thought, and then I said that I had come to see this when I did not have to because I had wanted to study myself.

I heard then the M.P. officer at the right of the firing squad give a command, and I saw the first row of twelve men drop to one knee. I heard another command and saw the rifles come up and I heard the sound of the stocks rustling against the clothing, and then I heard the Nazi in the middle shouting, guttural and loud in the morning, and I caught the end of his sentence.

". . . *Unser Fuehrer, Adolf Hitler!*"

At that moment—with the Nazi shouting—I heard the command to fire and I heard the explosion of the rifles, not quite all together and almost like a short burst from a machine gun. I was watching the Nazi, whose cry had drawn me at the last second, and I saw

11

. . . I heard the command to fire and I heard the explosion of the rifles, not quite all together and almost like a short burst from a machine gun. (John Florea, Life; © *Time, Inc.)*

him stiffen in the noise and I saw the wall behind him chip and the dust come off it, and the Nazi flattened and rigid still against the post.

He's dead, I said to myself. They're all dead.

I looked, then, to the Westphalian, and as I looked I saw the blood on his front and I saw his head fall forward and then his shoulders and chest move out from the pole. I saw the Nazi standing rigid and the other prisoner beginning to sag out, and I was conscious again of the photographers. I remembered, now, seeing the one moving up to take pictures as they had prepared the prisoners, and now again he was kneeling in front of the Westphalian and shooting his camera at him and the others were moving about rapidly and shooting quickly, and I envied them their occupation.

I watched the weird dance, then, of the prisoners, dead but still dying. The Nazi stood firm against the post, only his head bent forward, but the one on the left sagged forward slowly, and then I saw the Westphalian go, first to his left and then, pausing, to his right, swaying. I saw him hang there for a moment, and then I saw him pitch forward, hung by his wrists, bent in the middle, his head down to his knees, his long hair hanging, the whole of him straining at the ropes around his wrists.

I saw him hang there for a moment, and then I saw him pitch forward, hung by his wrists, bent in the middle, his head down to his knees, . . . (John Florea, Life; © Time, Inc.)

13

He's not alive, I said to myself. He's really dead.

Two medics walked up to him then and the one, bending down, looked into his eyes and, with his fingers, closed the lids. Then the second, bending down, slid his hands under the Westphalian's armpits, lifting him so that the first could put a stethoscope to his chest. In a moment they dropped him, leaving him sagging and swaying a little, and they moved on to the Nazi in the middle.

The Nazi strained a little at the ropes but his body was still rigid. I saw them pausing longer at the Nazi, the two of them looking at him more carefully. I was wondering if they were really finding the Nazi harder to kill. They stood there, talking to each other, putting the stethoscope on him for the second time, and then they finally moved on. They found the other prisoner dead and they walked back to the group beside the firing squad. They saluted the officer in charge and I heard the officer's command to the squad and saw the squad, facing left, march back across the field and up the path.

"What he said," one of the Ninth Army men was saying, "means 'Long live our Fuehrer, Adolf Hitler.'"

We waited for the photographers to finish taking their pictures of the prisoners in their positions of death and of the two M.P.s cutting them from the poles. They cut the Westphalian down first and put him on a stretcher, and then two others came with a white mattress cover and they slid him, feet first, off the stretcher and into the mattress cover. They left the mattress cover in front of the post and they went on to the Nazi.

When the M.P.s were finished and we were ready to leave I looked for the last time at what was left. There was the wall, chipped behind each post, and among the marks the bullets had made were small splashes of blood. There were the three posts, spattered, and before each post a white mattress cover, filled with a body. There were the stretchers, blood-spattered, and on the frozen ground were strewn the things typically American—the black paper ends from the film packs, the flash bulbs, milky-white and expended, and an empty, crumpled Lucky Strike cigarette package. An M.P., a rifle on his shoulder, walked up and down.

We went back to the small office near the gate. Our fingers and hands were stiff and ached from the cold, and we stood near the potbellied stove. There was a G.I. working at a filing cabinet near the stove and he started to talk to us.

"I'm glad it's over," he said.

"I am, too," I said.

"Not as much as us," he said. "For three days this place has been on end. We haven't been able to get anything else done."

The captain who had led us to the field came in. I thanked him and told him I thought it had all gone very well.

"We should have used combat troops," he said. "This bunch was so nervous that—just between us—there were only three bullets in one of the bull's-eyes, only three out of eight."

"Maybe one had the blank," I said. "That would be three out of seven."

"I don't know," the captain said. "I don't know if they used one blank."

The chaplain who had pronounced the last rites came in. He stood talking with another officer who was, I judged, the chaplain attached to the M.P. battalion.

"Well," he said, sticking out his hand, "I think it was conducted very well."

"Thank you," the other said, taking his hand. "Come and see us again. We hope next time it will be under more pleasant circumstances."

We went out and found our driver and he wanted to know how it was. We said it was all right, and we drove back. By afternoon the weather had cleared and the Germans came over. They came in so low that I could see the black crosses on the first plane and they bombed the hell out of us. They killed Jack Frankish and three Belgians, and Colonel Flynn Andrew died later in the hospital.

Damn, I said to myself, I wish this war were over and I wish I were home. For such a long time in September we had all thought we might be home for Christmas.

The three posts are, of course, no longer there. The gray stucco wall, however, is still marked in three places, bullet-pocked. I do not know where the three Germans were buried, but if one stands where they last stood and looks across the valley now, and if the wind and the light are just right, one can see, where the ground rises gently at the far right, an American flag flying. It flies over the cemetery at Henri Chapelle where, their graves marked by the precise rows of crosses and Stars of David, are buried 7,900 Americans.

2
The Day
of the Fight

The window was open from the bottom and in the bed by the window the prizefighter lay under a sheet and a candlewick spread. In the other bed another prizefighter slept, but the first one lay there looking at the ceiling. It was nine-thirty in the morning and he would fight that night.

The name of the first prizefighter is Rocky Graziano, but you don't have to remember that. The thing to remember is that he is a prizefighter, because they said this was to be a piece telling what a fighter does, from the moment he gets up in the morning until the moment he climbs into the ring, on the day when he must fight.

"All right, Rock," Whitey Bimstein, his trainer, said. "If you don't want to sleep you can get up."

The suite is on the twelfth floor of a hotel in New York's West Eighties, off Central Park. In the other bedroom Eddie Coco, one of the fighter's managers, still slept. On the soiled striped sofa in the sitting room a young lightweight named Al Pennino lay on his right side, facing the room, a blanket over him and a pillow under his head.

"If he don't feel like sleepin'," Whitey said, "there's no sense of him lyin' there if he wants to get up."

(*UPI Photo.*)

He was walking around the sitting room, picking up newspapers and putting them on the table, fussing around the doors of the closetlike kitchenette. Graziano and Whitey had been living there in the long weeks Graziano had been training for this one. They do not let a fighter live at home when he is in training for a fight.

"What time is it?" Graziano said. He had come out of the bedroom and was standing just inside the sitting room. He was wearing a pair of brown checked shorts and that was all. There was sleep in his face and the black hair was mussed on his head.

"Nine thirty-five," Whitey said.

Pennino and Coco were awake and walking around now. The other fighter, Lou Valles, a welterweight, came out of the bedroom in a shirt and a pair of slacks.

"You sleep?" Coco said to Graziano.

"Yeah," Graziano said. "All right."

"We got a nice day."

Outside the window the sun shone a pale yellow and in the distance over the park there was a blue-gray haze. This one was to be held in Yankee Stadium and the weather is one of the things they worry about when they have an outdoor fight.

As they sat around the small sitting room now they said little, seeming reluctant to break the sleep that was still in their heads. Finally Valles got up and walked over to the table by the wall and picked up the morning newspapers. They were opened to the sports sections because Graziano was going to fight Tony Zale, the middleweight champion, and this one was an important fight.

"You see?" he said, showing one of the papers to Pennino. "That Rocky takes a good picture. Right?"

Graziano did not say anything.

"He's a good-looking guy," Pennino said.

"You know what I'm going to do if I win the title tonight?" Graziano said. "If I win the title, I'm gonna get drunk. You know what I mean by that?"

"Yeah," Whitey said. "I know what you mean. You remind me of another fighter I had. He said if he won the title he'd get drunk. He won the title and he had one beer and he was drunk."

"Who?" Graziano asked.

"Lou Ambers," Whitey said.

Graziano went to the bedroom and when he came out he had on a pair of gray sharkskin slacks, turned once at the cuffs, a basque shirt with narrow blue stripes, and over this a gray-blue sleeveless sweater. He had washed and his hair was combed back. At ten-thirty Jack Healey came in. He is another of Graziano's managers, a suave but nervous type they call "The Mustache."

"You all right?"

"Sure," Graziano said. "Relax. I'm all right."

They waited for Pennino and Coco to finish dressing and they sat around talking about Stanley Ketchel, Bob Fitzsimmons, and Joe Dundee, Healey and Whitey talking and the fighters gazing around the room and out the window.

They were ready to leave then because it was eleven-fifteen. At the door the maid, in a blue dress with white cuffs and collar, said she wished them luck, and the woman who ran the elevator smiled at them in a way implying that she knew it was a special day.

Graziano's car was waiting in front of the hotel. It is blue and buff, new, and on the front doors the small letters read "Rocky." They got in, Healey driving, Graziano in the middle, and Coco on the outside, Whitey and Pennino and Valles in the back.

When they reached Fifty-fourth Street they turned west and stopped in front of the side door to Stillman's Gym. They got out and left Pennino to watch the car and went upstairs and into the gym, gray and, but for Lou Stillman and a couple of others, deserted.

"Hey," Stillman said, coming across the floor from the front. "What you guys want anyway?"

"You know what we want," Whitey said.

"I'll punch you in the nose," Stillman said to Graziano. "I'll knock you out before tonight."

"You'll what?" Graziano said, feigning annoyance and taking a fighting pose.

"What's the matter?" Stillman said, smiling. "Can't you take a joke?"

They went back into a small partitioned room in the back. There was a scale and Graziano started stripping and they shut the door. In a couple of minutes they came out, Graziano fastening his belt.

"I'll bet you down there he'll weigh fifty-three and a half," Whitey said. "I'll bet you'll see."

"What did he weigh here?" Healey said.

"A little over fifty-four," Whitey said, "but he'll go to the toilet."

"He looks great," Healey said. "You can tell from his eyes."

In the car again they started around the block. Graziano shut off the radio which Pennino must have turned on while the rest were in the gym.

"You should listen to that," Healey said. "They might tell you about the fight."

Graziano said nothing. They drove west to the West Side Highway and south past the North River docks.

"Rock," Whitey said, "your old man still working down here?"

"No," Graziano said. "He's workin' down at the Fish Market instead."

It was 11:48 A.M. when they were looking ahead down the street to the mob around the rear entrance to the New York State build-

20

ing where Graziano and Zale would weigh in. There were about two hundred people there, men, kids, photographers, and even a few women standing on and around the steps.

"We'll park down in front of your grandmother's," Healey said.

He drove slowly across the intersection past the park and pulled up at the curb on the right in front of the building where Graziano, as a kid, had lived. This was his neighborhood, and when they got out of the car there was a cop standing there and he stuck out his hand to Graziano and shook his head.

"Well," he said, "you're still the same, aren't you?"

Graziano said something but by now some of the crowd, running, had caught up. They were men, young and middle-aged and a lot of kids, and one of the men had his left arm in a sling.

"You see this?" he was shouting at Graziano from the back and waving his right fist. "You see this? Think of this tonight."

"All right. All right," the cop was shouting. "Stand back."

They hustled the fighter, then, into the narrow doorway between two stores and, with the fighter leading, they climbed up three flights. He opened a door and there they followed him into the kitchen of an apartment.

"Hello," he said to the man standing there and then pausing and looking around. "Where's Grandma?"

"In the park maybe," the man, Graziano's uncle, Silvio, said. "Maybe shopping. She went out about half an hour ago."

Graziano sat on a chair by the window, his right elbow on the windowsill. He looked around the room and through the door and into one of the bedrooms and his uncle watched him.

"How you feel, Rocky?" Silvio said.

"I feel fine," Graziano said.

That was all they said. He sat there waiting, looking around occasionally, not saying anything to the others who had followed him in. The door to the hall was open and presently a couple of photographers came in.

"Do you mind, Rocky?" one of them said. "We'd just like to get a picture of you and your grandmother."

"That's all right," Graziano said. "She'll be in soon."

He looked out the window again and, leaning forward, at the street below.

"Here she comes now," he said.

An old woman hurried across the street carrying a brown paper

21

bag in one arm. She had been stout once and she had on a gray print house dress and a small black hat and when she came in, breathing heavily from climbing the stairs, she walked across the room, smiling, and took Graziano by the hands and the two of them stood there speaking in Italian and smiling.

Graziano took her then by the arms and led her to the chair by the window and she sat down and put her bundle on the floor and took off her hat. She sat there smiling at Graziano and looking occasionally at the others and nodding her head.

"Do you mind now?" the photographer said to Graziano.

"Oh," Graziano said, and then he turned to the old woman. "They want to take a picture for the newspapers of you and me."

"Picture?" the old woman said, and her face changed. "That's why you come?"

"Oh no," Graziano said, and his own face had changed and he was shaking his head. "Oh no. I'd have come anyway. They just came in."

"I put on black dress," the old woman said.

"No," the photographer said to Graziano. "Tell her no. We'll only take a minute. We haven't got time."

"No," Graziano said to her. "That dress is all right."

"I put on nice black dress," the old woman said.

They took several pictures, then, of Graziano showing his grandmother, in the house dress, his right fist, and then Graziano said good-by to her, taking her by the hands, and he and those who had followed him went downstairs where there was a crowd waiting.

They pushed through the crowd, kids grabbing at Graziano and trying to run along at his side, and men shouting at him, things like: "Hey, Rocky!" . . . "Good luck, Rocky!" . . . "Flatten him for me, Rocky!"

They swarmed, half-running, down the street and the bigger crowd around the steps of the State building shouted and pushed, the cops shoving them back, and the photographers' bulbs flashing and many in the crowd making fists. Inside they hurried into an elevator that was waiting. The room upstairs was a big one. It was crowded with men, some of them standing on chairs, and at the end of the room by the desk there was a scale and around that the crowd was tight-packed.

They pushed the fighter through, the crowd quiet, and when he got to the desk there was some milling around and conversation and then he started taking off his clothes and tossing them on the desk. The crowd stood back and watched him, and he stripped and took off even his wristwatch and his ring, and put on a pair of purple boxing trunks.

Mike Jacobs, the promoter, Nat Rogers, the matchmaker, Eddie Eagan, the chairman of the New York State Athletic Commission, Irving Cohen, another of Graziano's managers, Art Winch and Sam Pian, Zale's managers, Healey and Coco and Whitey—they all were there on the inside of the crowd. Outside of them were newspapermen and photographers and more commissioners, and then Graziano stepped on the scale and Eagan leaned forward and adjusted the weight on the bar and watched the bar settle slowly to rest.

"The weight," Eagan said, announcing it, "is exactly one hundred fifty-four. Graziano, one hundred fifty-four pounds."

Several of the newspapermen were crowding out to find telephones and there was the noise of conversation in the crowd.

"How much did Zale weigh?" Healey asked.

"A hundred and sixty," somebody said.

"Black trunks for Zale," Harry Markson, Jacobs' press agent, said, announcing it. "Purple trunks for Graziano."

Graziano sat on the desk and Dr. Vincent Nardiello, the commission physician, put a stethoscope to Graziano's chest. Then the doctor took the fighter's blood pressure and announced the heartbeat and blood pressure figures to the press.

"All right, Zale," Eagan said, raising his voice. "All right, Zale. Come out."

The other fighter, Zale, who would fight Graziano, came out through a doorway to the left of the desk. He was naked except for the black trunks and tan street shoes. The crowd moved back and he walked to the scales where Graziano stood. They did not look at each other.

"Take a pose. Make them pose," the photographers were hollering and Zale and Graziano faced each other, Graziano's arms cocked wide at the sides of his chest, Zale's arms drawn up in a fighting pose in front of his chest. They stood there holding the pose while the bulbs flashed again and their eyes met. Graziano smiled once and nodded; Zale smiled back.

The photographers were still working away, shouting for one

23

more, swearing at each other, when Eagan stepped between the fighters and moved them over beside the desk.

"Now, I understand you're both good rugged fighters," Eagan said, "but I want a clean fight. I want no hitting in the breaks and that's one rule I'm going to caution the referee to observe."

He talked with them for another moment and then he turned and Zale went back through the door and Graziano went back to the desk and they both dressed. When they were finished dressing they walked, each with his group around him, through the crowd down the hall to another office where, in separate corners of the room, they tried on the gloves and alternate sets of gloves. One of the commissioners marked with a pen each fighter's name on the white lining of his gloves.

"He's got a bad eye," someone said to Graziano, nodding toward Zale who was waiting while the commissioner marked his set. "It's his left."

"No," Graziano said, looking over at Zale. "I noticed that. It's his right, not his left."

There were crowds again in the hall and outside the building, running after him and shouting the same things, a few of them different things, but most of them over and over again: "Hey, Rock!" . . . "Good luck, Rock!" . . . "I prayed for you last night."

They hurried down the street, photographers running ahead of them, and pausing to snap them, and the crown pushed on behind. They passed the car parked at the curb and went into a small bar and restaurant on the right where a cop stood by the door to keep the crowd out.

They walked through the bar quickly into a small restaurant in the back. There were a half-dozen tables with red and white striped tablecloths on them and Graziano sat down at a table at the right. In the corner at the left there were two men and two women at a table, and one of the men said something to the others and they turned around quickly and watched Graziano as he sat there fingering a fork and waiting while the others, eight or ten, pulled up chairs around the table or stood in back.

"Look, Rock," Healey said, and he shoved a photograph of Graziano in a fighting pose across the table, "autograph this, will you?"

"Okay, Jack," Graziano said, looking at him and then reaching around for the pen someone handed him from in back. "Don't get excited. Relax."

"I know," Healey said, "I'm more excited than you are. I'll relax."

"Autograph it to Pete," someone said. "Pete is his first name. Pasca is the last. P-A-S-C-A."

Graziano wrote something on the photograph and Healey put another down in front of him.

"Sign that to Pat," he said. "P-A-T."

"What is it, a girl or a fella?" Graziano said.

"I don't know," Healey said. "Put 'Best Wishes, Rocky.' It don't matter. That covers it."

In the arched doorway they stood watching, about fifteen or twenty of them, and then the waitress came from the back, carrying on a tray a cup of tea with a slice of lemon on the saucer. She put those down and went away and when she came back she had toast and a soft-boiled egg broken into a cup.

Graziano sat there eating the egg and the toast, blowing on the tea and trying it. They had let those from the bar into the restaurant now and they stood, three and four deep around the table, not saying anything or speaking only in whispers, watching in almost complete silence the fighter as he finished the egg and toast.

There were the crowds outside again, then, shouting the same things and the cop had to clear a path through them to the car. There were many faces at the windows of the car, faces shouting and fists, and Healey pulled the car away from the curb and drove east and then north on Second Avenue and at Forty-ninth Street he turned west.

On Forty-ninth Street at Seventh Avenue they had to stop for a light. They sat there, not saying anything and waiting for the light to change, when a guy in a white shirt, in his twenties, came off the sidewalk and thrust his face into the open front window of the car where Graziano sat between Healey and Coco.

"Hey, Rock," he said, making a fist, "if you win I get married. If you lose she'll have to wait a couple more years."

He turned as if to leave the car and then he saw them inside starting to smile.

"I ain't kiddin'," he said, turning back and reaching into his pants pocket and coming our with a fist full of bills. "Fresh dough I just got from the bank."

Graziano said nothing. Healey drove over to Ninth Avenue where he had to swerve the car out to avoid a bus pulling wide from the curb.

"You see?" he said. "These bus guys think they got a license to do anything they want."

"Watch," somebody said. "He's gonna yap."

The bus driver was shouting out of the window at his side.

"Hey, Rock!" he was shouting. "Good luck tonight. I know you can flatten that guy."

"What do you make of that?" Healey said. "How do you like that?"

In front of the hotel they sat in the car waiting while Whitey went up to get a leather bag containing Graziano's robe, his boxing shoes, his trunks, and the other things he would need in the fight. While they waited Healey went across the street to a newsstand and came back with the afternoon newspapers. He tossed them down on the front seat and Graziano picked up the first one and turned to the sports page where the banner headline read: "Zale Picked to Knock Out Graziano in Eight Rounds."

"Look at this," he said to Healey, flatly, without emotion.

"That's okay," Healey said. "What a guy thinks, he should write."

They drove to Coco's house, which is in the Pelham Bay section of the Bronx. They parked the car in front of the house and walked down the concrete driveway to the back where there were eight or ten men and women and a couple of kids on the back porch.

"Rocky," Mrs. Coco said, "these are friends of ours from Utica. They'd like to meet you and they came down for the fight."

Graziano shook hands with them and they all smiled and tried not to look at him steadily. They studied him furtively, the way some men study an attractive girl on the subway. He sat there on the porch for a few minutes while the others talked around him and they took him downstairs for the dinner on which he would fight.

There is a bar at one end of the wood-paneled room and there was a long table set for twelve. He sat at the head of the table and some of the others sat watching him while they brought him his dish of spinach, his plate of lettuce, his toast, and his steak.

Graziano ate quickly, cutting large pieces, using his fork with his left hand, always holding the knife in his right. When he said he wanted some water, Whitey said he could have a little without ice.

He had some hot tea and lemon and then he said he did not want to eat any more, pushing away the plate on which there was still a small portion of steak.

"That's all right," Whitey said. "If you feel satisfied, don't force yourself."

He went upstairs, then, and sat on the porch while the others ate. When they had finished, a half hour later, it was four-twenty and Whitey said they would take a short walk before Graziano took a nap.

They walked—Graziano and Pennino in front and Whitey and Healey in back—down the street and across the street under the elevated to the park. They walked through the park until four-thirty and then Whitey told them it was time to turn back. They walked past a barbershop where they saw Coco sitting down for a shave. Whitey said he would stop in the drugstore down the block and that he would be right back. Graziano and Pennino went into the barbershop and Graziano sat down in the barber chair next to the one in which Coco sat.

"I'll get a trim, Eddie," he said. "Is it all right if I just get a trim in the back?"

"Sure," Coco said. "Why not?"

A couple of girls in their teens and wearing sweaters and skirts came in then and stood by the chair looking at Graziano as he looked back at them.

"Are you Rocky Graziano?" one of them said.

"Yeah," Graziano said. "That's right."

"I could tell by your nose," one of them said. "You gonna win to-night?"

"Sure," Graziano said, smiling. "Why not?"

By now Whitey had come back.

"What are you doin' in the chair?" he said.

"I'm gettin' a trim," Graziano said.

"A what?"

"A trim. A trim just in the back."

"Listen," Whitey said, "get up out of there. It's time for you to rest."

"Look, Whitey," Graziano said, "I'm restin' here."

"C'mon," Whitey said.

When they got back to Coco's house they sat in the living room.

27

At ten minutes to five Graziano went in the next room and phoned his wife and at five o'clock Whitey said it was time for Graziano to go upstairs and lie down.

"What difference does it make?" Healey said. "He'll flatten the guy anyway."

"I know," Whitey said, "but he goes upstairs and takes his nap."

Graziano and Whitey went upstairs then and Mrs. Coco showed them a small room with maple furniture and a single bed. When Mrs. Coco had turned the covers back she left and Graziano stripped down to his shorts and sat on the bed.

"See if they got any comic books, will you, Whitey?" he said. "Go downstairs and see, hey?"

Whitey went downstairs and came back with one comic book. Graziano took it and looked at the cover.

"Go out, hey Whitey?" he said, looking up. "Go out and get some others."

Whitey and Coco walked up the street to a candy store where they picked out ten books from the rack—"Buzzy" . . . "Comic Capers" . . . "Captain Marvel, Jr." . . . "Whiz Comics" . . . "Sensation Comics" . . . "Ace Comics" . . . "All-Flash" . . .

When they came back and opened the door to the bedroom Graziano was lying on his back under the covers reading the comic book and there was a towel over the pillow under his head.

"Hey!" Coco said. "What about that towel?"

"Yeah," Graziano said. "I got some grease on my hair."

"What of it?" Coco said. "We're gonna wash the sheets and pillow case."

They went downstairs, then, and left him. It was five-twenty and for the next hour and a half the men sat in the driveway at the back on chairs they had brought from the porch and the kitchen and they talked about fights.

At six-fifty Whitey got up and went into the house. He heard someone on the stairs and Graziano came into the kitchen, dressed, his hair combed back.

"Hey," Whitey said. "I was just gonna get you up. You sleep?"

"I don't know," Graziano said. "I think maybe I dropped off a little."

They went out into the back yard, then, and Graziano sat down on one of the chairs. Dusk was setting in, so one of them lighted the garage light so they could see a little better and they sat around waiting and not saying much. At seven twenty-five Whitey said they had to go.

The driveway, dark, seemed full of people. Some of them wanted to shake his hand and the rest kept calling the word "luck."

"If you hear any noise from section thirty-three," one woman yelled, "that's us."

"We've got an undertaker with us from Utica," another woman said, "so you don't have to worry and you can hit him as hard as you like."

"Excuse me, Rocky," Mrs. Coco said, "but this is my delivery boy and he wants to meet you."

"Sure. Hello," Graziano said.

They walked out the dark driveway and pushed through a lot of kids who had been waiting there all afternoon and got into the car. It took them twenty minutes to drive to Yankee Stadium. On the way Pennino, in the back seat, sang songs and Whitey told a couple of old jokes.

When they reached the Stadium, Healey pulled the car up in front of Gate Four and stopped.

"You can't stop here," a cop said.

"This is Graziano," Healey said.

"I can't help it," the cop said.

Healey did not argue with the cop but eased the car down a few feet in front of another cop. Now someone in the crowd had spotted Graziano in the front seat and the crowd stopped moving forward and started to gather around the car.

"This is Graziano," Healey said to the cop.

"You shouldn't stop here," the cop said.

"I know it," Healey said, "but we gotta stop somewhere. He's fightin' tonight."

"You better see the lieutenant," the cop said.

"C'mon," Whitey said. "Let's get out. Leave it here."

They got out and the cops were pushing the crowd back now and those in the crowd were calling the same things the other crowds had called before. The cops were clearing a way through and Whitey gave Pennino the bag and they pushed through to the gate.

Along the tunnel under the stands they led Graziano now into the clubhouse used by the visiting teams. It was divided lengthwise down the middle by a wood-framed partition covered with cheap lavender cloth. Just inside the door a half-dozen preliminary fighters were in various stages of preparation, getting into their ring clothes, having their hands taped, warming up. They led Graziano past them and, parting a heavy dark blue drape, into his own part of the room.

"What time is it now?" he said, looking around.

"Eight o'clock," somebody said.

He sat down on one of the folding chairs to wait. Whitey had opened the leather bag and was taking out the equipment—the ring shoes, the boxing trunks, the protective cup—and placing them on the rubbing table, when Commissioner Eagan and Commissioner Bruno came in. They shook Graziano's hand as he stood up and stood talking with him for a minute or so and then they left.

"You better warm up, Rock," Whitey said. "Just warm up a little."

Graziano moved around the room, clothed, throwing short punches for about five minutes, and then sat down again.

"Let's go," a voice outside said, calling to the preliminary fighters. "The first two bouts."

Graziano stood up again. He took off his sweater and his basque shirt and went to a locker and hung them up. He came back and sat down on the table, and took off his shoes and socks. He got off the table and put them in the locker and then he took off his trousers and shorts and hung them up. He came back and sat down, naked now, on the table, and Whitey handed him a new pair of white woolen socks. He put them on and then put on his boxing shoes. He started moving around the room again, throwing short punches, weaving and bobbing a little as he went. He did this for a couple of minutes and then Whitey called to him and he went over and tried on a pair of the purple trunks. He took them off and tried on another pair, which he seemed to like better.

Sol Bimstein, Whitey's brother, came in and walked over to the table and picked up a pair of the purple trunks.

"Ain't these a nicer color purple?" he said.

"I like these best," Graziano said.

"Whichever he likes best," Whitey said.

Graziano put on his basque shirt, then, and began shadowboxing around the room again. A couple of deputy commissioners came in to stand there and watch him and then Whitey took Graziano's robe—white with a green trim and with Graziano's name in green block letters on the back—and spread it over half the table. Graziano stopped the shadowboxing and took off his trunks and shirt and walked to the table and lay down on his back.

Whitey worked first over his upper body. He rubbed coco oil on Graziano's chest. Then he put a towel across Graziano's chest and Graziano turned over and lay facedown and Whitey rubbed the oil on his back. Then he sat up and Whitey went over his legs with rubbing alcohol. Whitey was sweating and he took off his own shirt. He worked hard on Graziano's legs and then he went back at his shoulders and chest. When he was finished Graziano got off the table and, once again stripped but for his shoes and socks, moved around throwing punches until Whitey stopped him and took him over to a corner where they talked together quietly and Whitey showed Graziano a move with his left. Then he told Graziano to sit down and put his feet up on the table and he put a towel across Graziano's back and another across his legs.

"What time is it?" Graziano said.

"Eight fifty-five," Sol Bimstein said.

"I thought it was later than that," Graziano said.

"How do you feel?" Whitey said.

"Tired," Graziano said.

At nine o'clock a couple of commissioners and Art Winch, one of Zale's managers, came in.

"Is it time?" Whitey said.

"Yes," Winch said. "We might as well get started."

Graziano got up, then, and Whitey helped him into the white and green satin robe. He sat on the table, his legs hanging over, and Whitey started bandaging Graziano's right hand, Winch and the commissioners watching. It took him about seven minutes to do the right hand. When he was starting the left hand Winch said something and Whitey raised his voice.

"Just what I'm allowed," he said. "No more. No less."

"All right. All right," Winch said.

They stood there watching until the job was done and then Sam Pian, Zale's other manager, came in.

"You stayin'?" Winch said.

"Right," Pian said. He sat down on a chair by the lockers and

Winch and the commissioners went out. Graziano, the tape and gauze a gleaming white on his hands now, started moving around, shadowboxing again.

"I'm spying," Pian said as Graziano passed near him.

"Yeah. Sure," Graziano said. "I know."

He stopped throwing punches.

"This tape stinks," he said, looking at his hands.

"I know it does," Pian said.

"It peels off," Graziano said. He started moving around again, the leather of his shoes squeaking in the quiet room, the satin of his robe rustling. Mike Jacobs came in and Graziano stopped and spoke with him and then Jacobs went out and Healey came in.

"You got half an hour," he said.

"All right," Graziano said. He walked out through the drape.

"Where's he goin'?" Pian asked.

"Some of the preliminary fighters want to see him," Healey said. "They can't come in so he went out to see them."

"Oh," Pian said.

"He's a nice kid, ain't he, Sam?" Healey said.

"Yes," Pian said. "I guess he's a nice kid."

He got up to follow Graziano as Graziano came back in. Healey started out, and put his head back in between the curtains.

"I'll see you after, Rock," he said.

"Scram," Graziano said, looking up from where he was sitting by the table, his feet on the table, his hands on his lap. "Get out."

"I'll punch you in the eye," Healey said. He threw a kiss and pulled his head out as Sol Bimstein came in. "Main bout next," Sol said. "There's two rounds to go in the semifinal."

"Is it warm out?" Graziano said.

"Just nice," Sol said.

Graziano sat there waiting and Whitey came over to him and rubbed a little Vaseline on Graziano's face. It was ten minutes to ten. Whitey said something to him and he got up and went out. In a minute he came back and Whitey helped him off with his robe. He helped him into his protector and his trunks and then Graziano stood there rotating his shoulders, bending at the waist. When he stopped Whitey gave him a short drink from the water bottle. Then Whitey rubbed Graziano's chest and his stomach and his shoulders and Graziano took several deep breaths. Then Graziano began pac-

Round six, Yankee Stadium, September 27, 1946, after the right to the body and the left to the head. (AP Photo.)

ing back and forth, throwing short punches, breathing hard through his nose. He was doing this when a couple of the commissioners came in.

"Hey, Rock," one of them said to him. "What are you going to do with all the dough you get? The place is packed."

"All right," a voice shouted in from outside. "Main bout. Main bout."

"All right, Rocky," Whitey said. He moved over to his fighter and put the towel around his fighter's neck, crossing the ends in front, and he helped him back into his robe. Somebody took the pail and Whitey had his first-aid kit and, with Pian still watching them and following them, they moved out.

In the tunnel there were special cops and a couple of preliminary fighters who shouted something at Graziano. They moved quickly through the tunnel and down the steps to the lower level. Whitey's hand was on Graziano's back. Graziano kept exercising his arms, jigging a little now and then. They were close around him and they moved quickly along the lower level and then up the steps of the dugout where they hit him with the sound.

There were 39,827 people there and they had paid $342,497 to be there and when Graziano's head came up out of the dugout they rose and made their sound. The place was filled with it and it came from far off and then he was moving quickly down beneath this ceiling of sound, between the two long walls of faces, turned toward him and yellow in the artificial light and shouting things, mouths open, eyes wide, into the ring where, in one of the most brutal fights ever seen in New York, Zale dropped him once and he dropped Zale once before, in the sixth round, Zale suddenly, with a right to the body and a left to the head, knocked him out.

3

The

Fighter's Wife

It was nine-thirty in the evening, and they would put on the fight shortly after ten. There were about a dozen people in the house, all but two of them women, but it was not noisy. They sat in the carpeted, lush living room on the ground floor of the red brick, two-family house. For an hour, on and off, she had taken part in their small talk, but now she went into the kitchen and got out the ironing board.

"I hope he should retire," her grandmother said. "I hope he should win and retire healthy. He must be healthy for his family. Allus I hope with my whole heart he should be healthy."

One day, when Norma Unger was seventeen years old, she and her friend Alice and Alice's friend Yolanda were sitting at a table in an ice-cream parlor on the corner of Seventh Street and Second Avenue. They were having sodas and talking about boys. Yolanda said her brother was coming out of the Army, and she reached into a pocket and came out with two snapshots of him.

"I think you'd like him," she said to Norma, while Norma looked at the pictures, "and I think he'd like you. I think it would be fun to arrange a blind date."

That was the first time Norma Unger ever heard of Rocky Graziano, the first time in her life.

"The last time he fought Zale," her mother said, "she had her portable radio, and was walking up and down the street, turning it on and off."

"Once she sat in the bathtub all through the fight," her grandmother said.

So they arranged a blind date for the next Saturday night. On Saturday, she found she wanted to do something else so, still early in the evening, she walked over to Yolanda's house. It was a walk-up on First Avenue, and she climbed the steps, rang the bell in the hallway, and waited. There was one bulb burning at the ceiling. After a while Yolanda came downstairs, and Norma explained to Yolanda. While she was explaining, she heard a noise at the top of the stairs, and there he was, hurrying down the stairs. She was embarrassed.

"Oh," Yolanda said, stopping him when he got to the foot of the stairs, "this is Norma Unger. Norma, this is my brother, Rocky."

"Hello," she said looking at him.

"Hello," Rocky said, and then he turned, "I'll see you." He left.

He was wearing a dark-blue suit, and he had on a gray hat, pork-pie style. He had nice eyes and a nice smile and a nice face—he looked nice altogether. That was the first time Norma Unger ever saw Rocky Graziano, the first time in her life.

"The time he won the title in Chicago," her mother said. "You remember how he was getting beaten, and she ran crying into the bedroom and locked the door. When she came out, he was middleweight champion."

"I don't know," her grandmother said.

"Every time she does something different," her mother said.

They used to see each other around the neighborhood after that. She saw him in the ice-cream parlor a few times. A couple of times they had sodas together. Alice used to go out with Terry Young, the fighter, and he was Rocky's friend, so the first date they had was a double date with Alice and Terry. That was when she found out he was a fighter, but nobody had ever heard of him, and she didn't think much about it. After that they went to the movies a lot. He was always in a happy mood, and he wasn't one of those guys who was always trying to kiss a girl good night, and that helped.

"I don't know," her grandmother said. "I wonder what she does tonight."

"I don't know," her mother said, looking around. "Where'd she go?"

It was the first they had missed her. A couple of her friends, one named Lucille and the other named Innocent, got up and walked out into the kitchen and found her ironing.

"So?" Innocent said.

"Oh," she said, "just a blouse for Audrey for school tomorrow. I thought I could sneak it in. You know, anything to keep busy."

"That's right," Lucille said. "That's why we should do the dresses."

It was nine thirty-five.

They were married after they had known each other for three months. For a while they had teased each other about getting married. One day Rocky met her and said Yolanda was getting married. He said Yolanda was going down for her blood test, and they ought to go along to see what it was like. When they got there with Yolanda, they decided to take the blood test themselves. Then, because they had had the blood test, they decided they should get married right away.

She was still only seventeen. They went to City Hall, but a man told them she would have to have her mother's consent. She was afraid to ask her mother or her grandmother, so they took the Hudson Tubes to Hoboken, New Jersey, and then took a bus to Bayonne. They walked along the street and asked some people until they found a place with big windows in the front. It looked sort of like a real-estate office, but it said "Justice of the Peace" on the window. The man said they would have to have the blood test in Jersey and stay there for a while before he could marry them, so they went home.

She doesn't remember exactly how they managed it. A few days later they started going around to buildings downtown. They went around to a hundred buildings, it seemed, and finally a man married them.

It was in an office. She had on a beige suit, and Rocky had on a dark-blue suit and a white shirt and dark-blue tie. There were a couple of detectives around the building, and Rocky gave them five dollars each to be witnesses. The ceremony seemed so short. She had never thought anything about a big wedding, because they didn't have the money, but still it seemed so short.

A funny thing—after Rocky became famous he was fighting in

*the Garden one night and after the fight, as he was coming out of
the ring, a man stopped him in the aisle.*

"Hey," the man said. "Remember me? I'm your best man."

"Who the hell are you?" Rocky said.

"Don't you remember?" the man said, and it was one of the detectives. "I'm the guy who stood up with you on the day you were
married, Rock."

She went into one of the bedrooms—quietly, because Audrey,
who is five, and Roxie, who is going on two, were sleeping.

When she came out, she had a pile of new dresses in her arms.
She dropped them on the table, found the sewing basket, and stood
there watching, smoking a cigarette, while Lucille and Innocent
began to sort the dresses. Each selected a dress, and began to turn
up its hem.

It was nine-forty.

"I'll take the radio in," Norma said. "I won't listen."

She went to a closet and took out a small radio and carried it,
with its electric cord dangling, to those sitting in the living room.
While she was gone the other two sat sewing, not saying anything.

"She's too nervous," Lucille said finally. "I told her to have some
brandy around."

"She doesn't drink," the one named Innocent said.

"She could have some brandy around."

When Norma came back they were silent. She stood, leaning on
the sideboard, smoking and watching them. She is twenty-three
now, slim, dark-haired. She had on a gray-and-green print dress,
with short sleeves and a flared skirt.

"I called up my husband," Lucille said, sewing, "and he said the
whole place is closed down. Everybody went to the fight. Even the
bartender went to the fight."

*She used to go to see him fight, but that was at first. One day,
while they were still just going together, he asked her to walk over
to the gym with him to watch him train. It was the gym on Fourteenth Street, and it was the first time she had ever seen any
fighters in a ring. She stood in the gray, dusty-looking gym with all
the men, watching Rocky box. Then he always wanted her to go
with him when he fought, to Fort Hamilton and the Broadway
Arena and the Ridgewood Grove. She liked it less and less, and the*

first Frankie Terry fight was the last she ever saw. It was such a bad thing to watch, because they were cursing and even kicking. It was a real free-for-all, and after that she wouldn't go any more, although for a while she used to stand outside the clubs and wait for him to come out.

At first, he couldn't understand it. Maybe he thought it meant something else, because he got mad about it once. When she wouldn't go with him for his fight with Leon Anthony, he wouldn't fight. They went to a movie together instead, and Rocky was suspended by the Boxing Commission because of it. After a while, though, she was able to explain it so he saw it, and now he understands why she doesn't even want to watch him train.

"What time is it?" the one named Babe asked.

"It's nine forty-five," Lucille said.

"You people sew so nice," Babe said. Babe was standing in the doorway, watching the two at the table. Then she walked into the kitchen and sat down on one of the high red and white stools.

"The sewing circle," Norma said. "Boys are so much easier."

"Don't say that," Babe said. "You should see my Joseph."

"They make clothes so nice now," Innocent said, sewing.

"I'm getting a nervous stomach," Norma said.

She left them and walked toward the bedrooms and the bath. It was nine-fifty by the kitchen clock.

Their first night they spent in a hotel on Fourteenth Street. Then they went to the flat where Rocky's people lived, on First Avenue between Eighth and Ninth streets. They had one bedroom and Rocky's parents had the other. There were only four rooms, so Rocky's brother Lennie slept in the living room, and his sister Ida slept in the kitchen. They lived like that for five months.

For two years after that they lived in Brooklyn with Norma's mother and stepfather. There were only three rooms, so they slept in the living room. When Audrey came a crib was moved into the living room, too.

"Norma," one of those from the living room said, "what's the number on that little radio?"

It was the one named Lee; she was standing in the doorway, leaning against the frame. Norma had come back into the kitchen and was watching the sewing.

"I don't know," Norma said, and the one named Lee left.

39

"Listen, Norma," Babe said. "He'll come out all right. You know what my husband said, 'We'll carry him home on our shoulders.' Tony says, 'I shouldn't go to the fight, because I get so nervous, but I'm goin' because Rocky is gonna win.'"

"Like my husband," Lucille said. "Dom was cryin' after the last one. Some fellas from Second Avenue found him and said, 'C'mon, we'll take you home.' So tonight he said he didn't care if he was to go or not."

They could hear them tuning in the radio in the living room. Music and then a man's voice came over the radio very loud, and then softer. It was just ten o'clock.

"Say," Norma said, "and what do you think you're doing?"

It was Audrey, standing in the doorway that leads to the bedrooms—a small, dark-haired child in a long white nightgown. She was just standing, blinking in the light, rubbing her eyes with the backs of her hands.

"Aah," Babe said.

"You're makin' too much noise," the child said, still rubbing her eyes, her voice small and whining. "You're makin' too much noise."

"Aah," Babe said. "C'mere."

She reached down and drew the child onto her lap. Audrey continued to rub her eyes.

"How do you like school?" Babe said, bending over to talk to the child.

"She won't be able to stay up," Norma said. "She has to get some sleep."

"She knows something is happening," Innocent said.

"You're makin' too much noise," the child said.

"What's happened?" Norma said, looking up. "You can't get it?"

It was Phil, Lee's husband. He was just standing there, dapper and looking at them and smiling.

"We got it," he said, smiling. "I'm goin' in now."

Now they could hear from the radio the voice of Bill Corum. It was Bill Corum all right, the voice just a little hard and sportslike.

"Bill Corum with Don Dunphy bringing you another major sports event for . . ."

"All right," Norma said softly, getting up and going to the child. She took the child from Babe then, and carried her out of the room.

After a minute, Norma came back. She stood in the doorway and watched the girls sew, and she lighted another cigarette.

"I don't even think it's ten o'clock yet," Lucille said.

"It's after ten," Norma said, "but they have to get the introductions out of the way."

Now, from the radio far off in the living room they could hear the voice of Johnny Addie, the ring announcer. His voice was very clear, but distant, the only sound in the house.

". . . popular middleweight from Cleveland, Chuck Hunter."

"My husband was like this all day," Babe said, moving her hands. "Back and forth, back and forth. He couldn't eat."

". . . middleweight contender from Brooklyn, Vinnie Cidone."

"If anybody wants to go in—" Norma said.

"No," the two at the table said together, shaking their heads.

"I have to go in," Babe said, sliding off the stool.

"If anybody else wants to go in," Norma said, "—because I'm gonna close this door."

"No," her mother, a rather short, trim woman, standing in the doorway, said. "Let's take a walk."

"Wait until it starts," Norma said.

". . . the welterweight king, Sugar Ray Robinson!"

"This is the worst part," Lucille said, "waiting through 'The Star-Spangled Banner.'"

"All right," her mother said. "Let's go."

". . . the ring officials are assigned here by the New York State Athletic Commission . . ."

Norma went to get a fresh pack of cigarettes, and then they hurried, the three of them, each one seeming almost to fall over the one ahead, through the dining room and through the living room. In the living room, those crowded around the small radio looked up and shouted something as the three hurried out the front door.

"We're going for a walk," Lucille said, shouting it back.

". . . from Irvington, New Jersey, wearing black trunks—Charley Fusari!"

It was the last thing she heard, as she rushed out of her own house and into the night.

She had never, at any time, thought marriage would be like this. When she was still so young that she had listened to the words of

41

Frank Sinatra's songs, she had known they were not the truth, and that it would never be like that. She had not thought about it much, just when she did get married it would probably be to some ordinary working guy, and they would live in a little apartment. She could never have known that it would be to a fighter, and that they would have two cars and live in their own house, and that, periodically, she would be driven from her own house by voices like this.

"It's an advantage I have when he fights in the warm weather," Norma said. "I can go for nice long walks."

They stood together for a moment under the tree in front of the house. It was a warm, rather humid evening and the street was busy with traffic, the cars' headlights flooding across the three women standing under the tree and lighting cigarettes and then starting to walk down the block.

"It's not so warm," her mother said. "I'm cold."

"It isn't really cold," Norma said, "but my teeth are chattering."

"Listen," Lucille said, "you can hear the fight even out here on the street. Look at them up there."

They could see them on a second-floor sun porch of one of the brick houses, men sitting around, shirt-sleeved, smoking. Through the open windows they could hear, faintly, the voice of Dunphy. They could tell he was calling the fight, but it was impossible to tell what he was saying, and they walked along under the trees, their heels making hard sounds on the pavement.

"Fusari's! . . ."

They heard that much as they started past another house, and when Lucille heard it she stopped, dropping back. Then she turned into a driveway, her head forward and stood motionless.

"Let's walk faster," Norma said.

"All I hear is 'Graziano, Graziano,'" her mother said.

"It isn't so much that he wins or loses," Norma said, "but that he doesn't get hurt. Of course, when you win it leaves a better taste, but it's just that he shouldn't get hurt."

Walking along, their heels clicking faster, they could hear Lucille running up behind them, breathing audibly.

"Your husband must be winning," Lucille said. "Your husband must have knocked Fusari down. I heard him say something about the middle of the ring."

"I don't want to hear it," Norma said, walking.

When they came to the corner they stopped for just a moment under the streetlight. Then they turned left and started walking again.

"Who said being a fighter's wife is easy?" Lucille said.

"It's like being in the ring," Norma said.

"She fights right in the ring with him every fight," her mother said, talking to Lucille.

"That's the trouble," Norma said. "You can't get in the ring with him."

"What could you do?" her mother said.

"Well," she said, "if they put Fusari's wife in the ring."

"He just said Fusari's in trouble," Lucille said quickly.

"You heard it?" Norma said.

"Yes."

"I don't know," Norma said. "It's too much."

"That's the funny thing," Lucille said. "Everybody seems to wait for tonight but you."

"I wait for the night after tonight."

They had reached another corner and turned left again. The radio was loud from the house on the corner, the whole first floor lighted beyond the stucco steps. They could hear the hysteria in Dunphy's voice, the crowd noises behind it.

"Shall I ask?" Lucille said. "I could ask here if somebody has been knocked out."

"No," Norma said. "Never mind."

She kept walking, but her mother and Lucille stopped. Lucille started up the steps, toward the loud and frantic radio. When she got to the top of the steps, a dog started to bark in the house, and then the door opened and the dog, wild-looking, stood there barking.

"No," Lucille said to the dog, holding up her hands and starting to back down. "Never mind."

A boy showed behind the dog, a boy of about twelve or thirteen. The boy grabbed the dog and the dog stopped barking.

"We wanted to know—" Lucille said, halfway down the steps, "we wanted to know if one of the fighters was knocked out."

"No," the boy said, "but Fusari is hurt bad. He's gettin' a beating."

"Norma!" her mother said, standing on the sidewalk and hollering it. "Rocky's winning."

"But when?" Norma said, stopping and turning and shouting it back.

The two were running down the block toward her now. They could see her dress, the light from a streetlamp falling on it through the trees.

"It's the fourth round," Lucille said, running up.

"All I hear," her mother said, "is 'a left by Graziano, a right by Graziano.'"

They lighted more cigarettes and started to walk again, Norma between them. A car went by and slowed as it approached the corner, and they could hear the car radio coming through the night.

"It's still going on," Norma said.

"All of a sudden it isn't cold any more," her mother said.

"It got warm," Norma said, trying to laugh.

"That's a funny thing," Lucille said. "Isn't that funny?"

This is a neighborhood of those two-family brick homes. There are small, neat lawns in front of the houses, and low hedges and concrete walks leading up to the front doors.

"We should have gone to a movie," her mother said.

"That's what I did for the Bummy Davis fight," Norma said. "I saw half a movie. You would think you'd get over it."

"Every fight it gets worse," her mother said. "At first we used to be able to go to the fights."

They were back in front of the house. They had slowed down and now they stopped. They could hear, although not distinctly, the radio in the house. They seemed reluctant now to leave the vicinity of the house, to start out on another walk. Suddenly, Babe came running out.

"What?" Norma said. "It's over?"

"No," Babe said, excited, "but Rocky's ahead. He can't seem to get the left, though. They say something on the radio that he can't seem to get the left." She was shaking her left fist.

"Was Fusari down?" Lucille said.

"No, but in one round the bell saved him, so we hear. Now it's four rounds for Rocky and three for Fusari or something, but Fusari's bleeding now."

"Is Rocky hurt?" the mother said.

"In the third round he was bleeding over his left eye, but it doesn't bother him now. You should hear it, because it seems—"

Norma was rocking a little, back and forth, one foot ahead of the other, smoking and looking at Babe and then down the block.

"You should look on it like any other business," Norma said.

"Whatever happens happens," her mother said.

"But you can't do it," Norma said.

Dunphy's excited voice came from the house again. Lucille turned and ran toward the house, and Babe followed her. Norma and her mother began to talk.

"Babe said that Rocky slipped, that he crossed his feet and slipped."

"He always does that," Norma said. "Clumsy."

"Once he fell off a ladder," her mother said.

"Yes, remember?" Norma said, a small smile starting. "Audrey was inside the house watching him through the window, and all of a sudden he disappeared. When he's introduced, he usually manages to fall into the ring."

"It seems such a long time," her mother said.

"Well, it takes forty minutes if it goes ten rounds. That's a long time."

"You're telling me."

"I should go to the dentist when he fights. That way I can't worry about him."

"Oh-oh, it's still on."

"I want to hear it, but I don't want to hear it."

"That's it. You want to hear the good part of it."

"It must be the tenth round pretty soon now."

". . . Fusari's down! . . ."

The phrase, from a car radio, came quickly and loudly, and then was gone. When they heard it they stopped, their feet poised to go on.

"Fusari's down!" her mother said.

"But did he get up?"

". . . a left hook by Graziano. A right by Graziano . . ."

It came from a house and they stood facing the house, their heads turned to hear it. Even then they could hear only some of it.

"Maybe he'll do what he did in the Cochrane fights," Norma said.

"Norma!" It was a scream from down the block. When they heard it, they turned quickly, and they could see figures running, through the light and shadow, out of the house.

"Norma! Rocky wins! He wins! He wins!"

They ran toward the house. As they ran, neighbors came tumbling out of houses, appearing at the low ledges along the sidewalk, shouting to them. The street was all noise now, and when she got to the house she was out of breath, and they were swarming around her, hugging her, kissing her, shouting at her, all of them trying to tell her at once.

Inside now, she hurried to the radio, where the rest were still gathered, and she knelt down in front of it, listening while Corum told again how it had happened. Now she could not get enough.

"What time will he get home?" somebody asked.

"I don't know," she said. "You never can tell."

After the last Zale fight, she couldn't help it. Even when she heard them bringing him into the house, she couldn't stop crying, because that was the first time he had ever really been knocked out like that.

The night in Chicago when he beat Zale was the other kind of night. When he came back to the hotel, with the mob around him, Rocky and she went into the bedroom together to wake Audrey and tell her that her father was the middleweight champion of the world. Audrey was three then, and when they woke her she stood up in the crib and looked at her father and saw the bandages over one eye and the other eye swollen and closed and the welts on his face.

"What happened, Daddy?" Audrey asked sleepily.

"You see what I said?" he said, bending over and pointing his finger at Audrey. "Now stay outta the gutter."

It was three hours before he got home. During those three hours more people had come. The neighbors came in and the men came back from the fight. They congregated in the kitchen, those who had been there and the newcomers, and they fought it all over again for her—swinging their arms, getting more and more excited. They said the same things over and over, and even those who had been in the house all evening, listening to the radio, kept repeating themselves.

"What happened, Daddy?" . . . *"You see what I said?* . . . *Now stay outta the gutter."* (UPI Photo.)

"When I was close to the radio," the one named Lee told her twice, "he was losing, and when I walked away he was always winning. I walked away, and Fusari was down. So I stayed away, and Rocky won the fight."

Norma stood out on the terrace for a long time, waiting. A couple of reporters came—Jim Jennings and Harold Weissman from the *Mirror*—and Weissman asked her questions about when she had last seen Rocky fight, and if she had been nervous. In the house, the phone rang again and again and someone finally answered it.

"You should go to bed," her grandmother said to Norma. "The baby will be up early."

At one forty-five a car pulled up, and the mob along the curb and

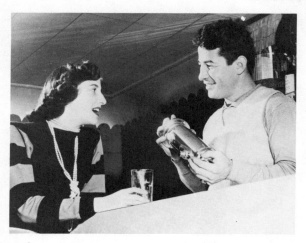

"I think a husband should do whatever work he likes to do. I think if a wife sees her husband happy, that's enough." (Photoworld.)

on the sidewalk pressed around it. It was Jack Romeo, and he pushed through them and came up the steps, handing her something in a paper bag.

"What is it?" she said reaching for it. "A bottle?"

"No," he said. "The gloves."

She heard them along the curb, then, calling and applauding. In what light there was, she could see him—in a white cap, a white towel around his neck. Then he had the towel in his hands, and he was pushing through them, acknowledging them in a thick voice, until he climbed the steps and saw her.

"Hello, honey," he said, going to her and kissing her quickly.

They walked into the house together, their friends around them. They stood for a minute in the middle of the crowd, Rocky answering Weissman's questions.

Rocky said, finally, "I'm gonna take a hot bath now, if you'll excuse me. I mean I'm all sweaty. You know? I gotta relax."

"Sure. Sure," they said.

She walked out with him, through the dining room and the kitchen and down the hall to the bathroom to run the water into the tub—to be glad again, finally—at two o'clock in the morning—that she is this fighter's wife.

The Fighter's Wife

"But don't you want him to retire?" a reporter said to her once. "I mean as soon as you get a little more money?"

She was sitting in a chair in the corner of the room and the reporter was sitting across the room from her.

"No," she said, "I mean that's not up to me. I think a husband should do whatever work he likes to do. I think if a wife sees her husband happy, that's enough."

4

So Long, Rock

We were sitting in the living room of a hotel suite in Chicago, and it was about nine o'clock at night. Rocky Graziano was sitting in an easy chair, with his legs over one of the arms. He had on slacks and a T-shirt, and he was sucking on a dry pipe and trying to spit small, almost-dry spit into a wastebasket over by the near wall.

There were a couple of sparring partners on the sofa, and Whitey Bimstein and Irving Cohen were sitting with a card table between them and Irving was counting through a batch of tickets. There was a small radio on the windowsill and the Cubs' game was on. The only noise in the room was the noise of the announcer.

I was watching the Rock. I was watching him sit there, sucking on the pipe and spitting and then staring straight ahead, and I had it all figured out for myself.

This is a guy, I was thinking to myself, who is not listening to a ball game. This is a guy who is twenty-five hours away, a guy in a ring fighting Tony Zale for the middleweight title for the second time and remembering the first time in Yankee Stadium when he had Zale down and beaten and Zale came out the next round, his legs wobbling, and pumped that right hand into the body so it brought this guy's right knee up and then followed it with the hook to the chin that knocked this guy out.

"It's a single over short going into left center field," the announcer said, his voice rising. "The runners on third and second will score, and here they come . . ."

50

"You see?" the Rock said suddenly, swinging his feet around onto the floor and taking the pipe out of his mouth and pointing it at us. "If they make that double play they get out of the inning and no runs score. You see?"

I am thinking of this now because on February 20 the Rock is going back into that same ring in Chicago, this time against Sugar Ray Robinson for that same middleweight title. This is just a guy out for the big paynight now, but when he had it he was the most exciting fighter of our time. Now they say this is where he gets off and that this will probably be the last magazine piece anybody will write about him for a long time.

"All right," Whitey said after a while. "You better get up to bed now, Rock. It's time you were in."

He got up from the chair and he stretched and he started out the door. Whitey motioned over his shoulder with his head and I followed them out.

We went down the hall and took the stairway up to the next floor. It was a two-room suite with three cots in one room for the sparring partners and two beds in the other room, one for Whitey and the other for the Rock.

"You better try those trunks on," Whitey said.

The Rock got undressed. He had been training for months and he was in great shape, and he tried on the two pairs of trunks, black with the red stripes, squatting down and standing up.

"The first ones are too tight," he said. "These are best."

He got, naked, into one of the beds then and he pulled the covers up. He put two pillows under his head, so he was half sitting up, and Whitey walked into the other room.

"So, I'll go now, Rock," I said.

"Okay," he said.

"You have to lick this guy, Rock," I said suddenly, bending over the bed. "If you ever had to win a fight, you have to win this one."

He knew what I meant. In New York they had revoked his license for failing to report the offer of a bribe he had never accepted for a fight that had never been fought. There were those of us who had gone day after day to the hearings, who had been able to see through this to the politics behind it, and we had been appalled that such a thing could happen in this country.

"I despise them for what they did to you," I said, "and you hate them, and there's only one way you can get even. If you lose tomorrow night, you're done, not only in New York but everywhere. You have to win, Rock."

"I know," he said.

"You have to stick it," I said. "You have to win the title, because when you win the title it's yours and they can't take it away from you outside the ring. You win it and they need it and they'll come crawling back, begging you on their hands and knees."

"I know," he said, lying there in the bed and looking right at me. "If I have to, I'll die in there, tryin'."

We shook hands and he snapped off the light over the bed and I left. I felt bad for having made a speech like that, because they make few better guys than Tony Zale and they make them no tougher inside the ropes, and where do you get off telling another guy he has to take those Sunday shots in the belly and on the chin while you sit at ringside feeling a lot but taking nothing and just looking up?

It was 120 degrees at ringside inside the Chicago Stadium that July night. They drew $422,918 for a new indoor record and had them hanging from the rafters. Suddenly the hot, wet, sweat-smelling air was still and the organ started "East Side, West Side" and a roar went up in the back and down the aisle came the Rock. He had the white satin robe with the green trim over his shoulders and Whitey and Irving and Frank Percoco were behind him. The noise was all over the place now and Whitey was rubbing his back under the white robe as they came and then, two steps from the stairs, he broke from Whitey and took the three stairs in one step and vaulted through the ropes, throwing his arms so the robe slid off.

"Yes," I said to myself, "he'll stick it all right."

He stuck it, and there were times when it looked like he'd have to die doing it. Over his right eye the brow swelled and came down and shut the eye, and when Zale cut the left eye the blood flowed into it so he was stumbling around blind or seeing only through a red haze. Zale pitched all his big stuff at him and he took it all. There were times in the third round when I said to myself that if this were just a fight, and not bigger than a fight, he would go down. I said to myself that he couldn't win it but at least he showed them he had guts. Then a funny thing happened.

Between the fourth and fifth rounds, Frank Percoco took the hard edge of a quarter and, pressing with it between his fingers, broke the skin of the swelling over the right eye. When the blood came out the swelling came down enough for the lid to pull up, and the Rock could see. For two bits they won the middleweight title and made maybe $250,000 and it was the beginning of all that would follow.

He had Zale helpless on the ropes now in the sixth round. Zale, collapsing, had his back to him and, in that frenzy that made him what only he and Dempsey were, the Rock climbed all over him, hitting him wherever he could find a place to hit him. Then the referee stopped it. And now he was standing in the shower stall, the right eye shut again, a clip holding the other cut closed, only a fireman in uniform with us, standing guard.

"Well," I said to him, "the world is a big place, and how does it feel to be the middleweight champion of it?"

"I don't know," he said, hurt and leaning back and resting one arm on the shower handles, trying to think and to talk. "I don't know. I mean . . . I mean as a kid I . . . I mean I was no good . . . I mean nobody ever . . . You know what I mean?"

He was standing, naked and cut and swollen, in this basement and holding his hands out to us. It was quiet but for the drip of the shut-off shower.

"I know what you mean, Rocky," the fireman said, out of nowhere. "You're giving a talk on democracy."

"I mean I never . . ." The Rock said, and then he turned to the fireman and he said, "You're a good guy. You're all right. You know what I mean?"

They came through the door then, a half-dozen newspapermen from the mob in the dressing room. They got him in a corner, all of them with their pencils and paper out.

"But how did you feel in there?" one of them shouted at him.

"I wanted to kill him," he said. "I got nothing against him. He's a nice guy. I like him, but I wanted to kill him."

That is the kind of a fighter he was, a special kind. I remember the night he fought Marty Servo in the Garden. Marty had just knocked out Red Cochrane for the welterweight title, and now Graziano had him against the ropes, holding Marty's head up with his open left glove, clubbing him with his right. He'd have killed

53

Marty if he had had a knife in there that night, and he would have been guilty of only one thing. He would have been guilty of giving himself over completely to that which they send two men out to do when they face each other in a ring.

Don't you know, too, that the Rock liked Marty and Marty liked the Rock? Marty was never a fighter again after that beating. He had to give up his welterweight title without ever defending it, and by that beating he lost the money he had counted on to give him security the rest of his life. I remember a night a couple of years later. The Rock was walking ahead of us and we were going out to eat.

"Where are we going?" I said.

"We're going to that place where Marty Servo tends bar," Irving Cohen said. "Rocky likes him and he always tries to bring business into the place."

We went into the place and Marty, in a white jacket, was standing behind the bar, leaning against the rack that holds the glasses in front of the mirror. When he saw us his face brightened and he leaned over the bar and shook hands. When he shook hands with the Rock, he smiled and faked as if to hook with his left. The Rock, leaning over the bar, stuck his left under Marty's chin as he had that night and faked to throw the right, and then the two of them dropped their hands and laughed.

"I'll be glad when that Graziano stops fighting," a guy said once in Stillman's. "It's gettin' so you can't even move in here."

When the Rock trained, they would stand packed, all the way back to the wall. They would be packed on the stairs and they would be packed in the balcony, too. In his dressing room, there was always a mob. There was one little guy there named Barney who always wore a dirty cap and who played the harmonica. He didn't play it by blowing on it with his mouth. He played it by blowing on it through his nostrils.

"Ain't he a good musician?" the Rock would say, sitting back in his robe and listening. "Did you ever see anybody do that before? I'd like to get this poor guy a job."

The guy would smile and then he'd play some more. He had three numbers. He'd play "Beer Barrel Polka," "The Darktown Strutters' Ball," and "Bugle Call Rag." All the time he was playing "Bugle Call Rag," blowing on the harmonica through his nostrils, he'd salute with his left hand.

"Ain't that great?" the Rock would say, and he would mean it. "Why can't I get this guy a job?"

The guy was satisfied. The Rock staked him. He staked a lot of them. One day I saw him give a guy the shirt he was wearing. The Christmas of the first year he made any money he bought a second-hand 1940 Cadillac and filled it with $1,500 worth of toys. He drove it down to his old neighborhood on the East Side and unloaded the toys on the kids and another $1,500 on their parents. He never mentioned it. It came out because a trainer from the gym who lives in the neighborhood saw it.

"Look, Rocky," Irving Cohen said to him. "It's nice to do things like that, but you haven't got that kind of money and you've got to save money. You won't be fighting forever."

"Sure, Irving," the Rock said, "but those are poor people. They're good people. They never done no wrong. They never hurt nobody. They just never got a break."

One day in Stillman's, the Rock walked up to Irving. He asked him for a touch.

"I've got fifty bucks," Irving said.

"Give it to me," the Rock said, "and hustle up another fifty for me."

Irving circulated and borrowed fifty and gave that to the Rock. The Rock walked away and Irving, who is a little, round guy, sidled after him.

As you come into Stillman's there are rows of chairs facing the ring. In one of the chairs there was a former fighter sitting. This one is still a young man, but he is blind. The Rock sat down next to him and talked with him for a while. Irving sidled up behind them, and then the Rock leaned over and slipped the rolled-up bills into the lapel pocket of the fighter's jacket.

"There's something in your pocket," he said, and he got up.

It is a shame we lied to a guy like this when we told him that, if he won the title that night in Chicago, he would be all right because they could never take it away from him outside the ring. We didn't tell it as a lie. It just came out a lie. It came out a lie because when he won the title he became big in people's minds. He was a name, and now they got it out of Washington that he had gone AWOL in the Army, had put in seven months in Leavenworth, and had a dishonorable discharge. They wanted to bar him from the ring.

I remember the night after he ran out on a fight in California. His disappearance made headlines, and finally he walked through the door into a suite at the Capitol Hotel across Eighth Avenue from the Garden. He had on a beautiful camel's hair polo coat, but there was the growth of several days' beard on his face, and under the coat he wore an old woolen shirt and dirty slacks and there were heavy running shoes on his feet.

"I'm with my friends," he said, and he held his hands out.

They were New York sportswriters called there on the promise that he would show up. Only some of them were his friends, but they all stood up when he came in and when he said that you could hear every breath.

"It's like I got a scar on my face," he said, staring through them and bringing his right hand up slowly to his right cheek. "Why don't they leave me alone or put me in jail?"

Of course, they took his title away outside the ring. They let him defend it against Zale in Newark on June 10, 1948, and they paid him for it, but he was no fighter then. The things they had done to him had taken out of him that which had made him the fighter he had been. He walked toward Zale as he was to walk toward those others in that hotel room another time, and Zale measured him and for two rounds gave him a terrible beating and in the third round knocked him out.

It is an odd thing, but once Rocky Graziano would have fought Ray Robinson for the fun of it. That would be four or five years ago, and he made Irving Cohen's life miserable with it.

"Get me Robinson, will you, Irving?" he would say, over and over again. "Believe me, Irving, I'll knock him out."

"Sure, Rocky," Irving would say. "Sure you will. But wait."

There were just those two things, you see, that the Rock had that made him what he was. He could take your head off your shoulders with that right-hand punch, and he fought with that animal fury that is the pure, primitive expression of the essence of combat.

He has not put those two things together in a ring since the night he won the title from Zale in Chicago and they pulled the Army on him. There is no evidence that they are any longer a part of him, and if that is so then this is the end of the road, the last big pay-night, the final chapter of a memorable book—and I can't find the one big sentence with which to end it.

Winning the middleweight title from Tony Zale in Chicago, July 16, 1947. The Rock could take your head off your shoulders with that right-hand punch, and he fought with that animal fury that is the pure, primitive expression of the essence of combat. (UPI Photo.)

Against Ray Robinson, in the third round that night in Chicago, he still put enough of that fury into one right-hand punch to drop Robinson. Then Robinson got up and, with that barrage that was typical of him, knocked him out.

Now the fighter and his wife live in a high-rise apartment in what is known as New York's fashionable Upper East Side, three miles north of where he was born and grew up. He is sixty-one years old, and they are grandparents.

"I just made The Big One," he told me fifteen years ago.

"The Big One?" I said. "What's that?"

"A million bucks."

"You're worth a million?" I said.

"Yeah," he said. "My accountant just told me. How about that?"

It started with his ring earnings, and it came from his autobiography, *Somebody Up There Likes Me*, from the movie they made from it, from his television and personal appearances, and from radio and television commercials. He visits schools and talks on juvenile delinquency, and when he told me that he had lectured at Fordham University I asked him what he had said.

"I spoke to all the kids who were graduatin'," he said, "and a lot of elderly people, like professors and priests."

"But what did you tell them?" I said.

"You know what it is," he said. "I start out, whether I'm talkin' about criminology or juvenile delinquency, and I say, 'You know, I'm so glad my father took the boat, because this is the best country in the world, and if there was another country like this one, I'd be jealous.'"

5

D-Day Relived

It was about ten o'clock in the morning when we reached the cross-road just west of Formigny. The mist was still blowing inland off the Channel, coming across the green field to the right and, where there were trees, coming between the trees.

Ten years had passed since the American had been here, but he remembered the crossroad very well—the calvary on the one corner and the battle monuments on the three others—and he turned the small gray Peugeot to the right and drove down the narrow winding blacktop, hemmed in between the thick bulk of the hedgerows, until it widened out, where the new road curves through the center of Vierville-sur-Mer.

"The Vierville church," he said now, measuring the words and standing there and looking up at it. "A lot of Americans who landed on the beach will remember the Vierville church."

Next to the church is the walled graveyard, built up above the surface of the road. The church itself is gutted still, the roof gone and only a few fragments of stained glass still sticking in the windows, but from the front a new steeple points up into the sky.

"The Vierville church," he said again. "Bud, that was one of the old landmarks we studied a lot in England before the invasion. We studied it over and over."

The boy said nothing. He is fourteen years old now, named after his father, and has brown, slightly wavy hair and blue eyes. He was wearing crepe-soled shoes and blue jeans, a blue plaid shirt and a red corduroy jacket, and all of his memories of the war are involved with the small white house with the big mulberry tree in the back yard on South Bridge Street in Brady, Texas.

There was a hut in the tree, and the small boy would play there and, in the mornings, he would stand in the front yard and watch the trucks filled with German prisoners heading out to the farms. In the late afternoons he would see them come back, and he remembers the machine guns on the trucks and the Germans neither laughing nor shouting but just standing in the trucks as they went by. Now the boy looked up at the steeple.

"You haven't any idea how that old church used to worry us," his father said.

"Why?" the boy said.

"Because of the observation it gave the Germans," his father said. "The Channel is only about a half mile down the road here, and the Germans used all these church steeples for observation. That's why we had to shoot the steeple down."

In 1932, James Earl Rudder had received his academic degree and his commission as a second lieutenant, Infantry Reserve, from Texas A&M. He had played center for Matty Bell, but that first summer, at the depth of the depression, he dug ditches. From 1933 to 1938 he coached football and taught at Brady High School. He was coaching at John Tarleton College, in Stephenville, Texas, when he went on active duty in 1941 at Fort Sam Houston.

"It's a funny thing," Rudder said. "We shoot down the steeple, and that's the first thing the French build back, even before they build the church."

He drove through the small intersection of the town. Two houses away from one corner two workmen were just starting to put back the stones that had lain in a pile for ten years, and as the car went by they stopped, turning to watch it. Then Rudder drove down a slight slope that bent around to the left between hedgerows, and as the car came out of the curve, still on the slope, you could see a large new yellow fieldstone house, still not completed, and, straight ahead, the gray-blue waters and the mist above them.

"There's your English Channel, Bud," he said.

"There?" the boy said.

"That's right, and that's where we came in, the men who didn't hit the cliff. A lot of American soldiers came up this road we're on now, because it was the main exit road for everybody who came in on this end of the beach."

The car was stopped in the middle of the sloping road, and the man and the boy just sat there looking down across the top of the two German concrete emplacements and at the tilted hulk of a hollow concrete floating pier that had been driven by a storm onto the shore. Then Rudder released the brake and the car rolled down the road toward the emplacements and then stopped on a wide, sweeping curve.

"And there's Omaha Beach."

He had known it was there, he said later, but still it came as a surprise. There it was, three and a half miles of deserted crescent, curving eastward, the blue-gray waters of the Channel on the left, the white waves rolling up onto the stretch of smooth, tan sand.

"What's this gun here?" the boy said.

The car was parked now on the rise behind the two concrete emplacements. The boy had run around to the front of the first of them, and was looking at the long, rusting barrel that pointed down the beach.

"That's an old 88," Rudder said. "You can see how it was set here to cover the beach."

"I wish we could go in this blockhouse," the boy said, "but there's this screen over the front of it."

"You can see they had direct hits from the Navy on it," his father said, "but they never could get that gun. That's why the soldiers had to come in and take it."

The boy had run now to the second emplacement, and his father walked after him. The father was wearing black shoes, gray sharkskin trousers, a reddish plaid shirt, a mixed-tan sport jacket, a covert-cloth topcoat, and a light tan fedora.

"Can I go in this one?" the boy said. "You can get in, and there's a big machine gun here."

"That was covering the beach, too," the father said and then he swept his hand below, "and right over there is where Frank Corder got hit. They were trying to make it up here."

Frank Corder was a young captain from Rock Springs, Texas, who had joined the Rangers late. Rudder had handpicked the 2nd Ranger Battalion at Camp Forrest, Tennessee, in July of 1943. The battalion had shipped to England in December of that year, and it was a month later, when he was in Northern Ireland recruiting volunteers to be used as a reserve after the invasion, that he signed up Corder, whom he had met before. After the war he and Corder went into the general-appliance and tire business in Brady. Now Corder has three children and is a livestock dealer.

"He lost his left eye and some of his teeth on this beach," Rudder said. "He still gets some pain, on and off, but I'll never forget one day I was trying to take him on a livestock deal, the way you will, and he squinted at me and he said, 'Colonel, remember this. I've still got one good eye.'"

Where the sand ends at the top of the beach the white, smooth, egg-shaped stones begin. There used to be about fifty feet of them, but now the French have built a six-foot sloping concrete and field-stone seawall that covers most of them. On top of the seawall there is a curbed sidewalk and a two-lane roadway that runs the length of the beach, for the convenience of sightseers.

"What's this?" the boy said. "A gas mask?"

They had walked along the sidewalk and then down one of the flights of stairs leading to the beach. They had crossed the stones and Rudder was just standing, looking east along the sand, when the boy ran up to him with the olive-drab rubber facepiece in his hand.

"An old American gas mask," Rudder said turning it over in his hands. "The old canister gas mask. I didn't think you'd find anything here."

He turned now, and started to walk slowly back toward the two concrete gun emplacements. Then he stopped, and with the toe of his right shoe he started to scuff into the smooth, tight sand.

"Can you imagine," he said, "some poor American kid trying to find cover in this?"

"It sure is pretty now, with the waves and everything," the boy said. "You'd never think there was any fighting here."

The late morning sun had finally started to eat through the haze, and you could begin to feel its warmth. It was quiet on the deserted beach, with just the soft rhythmic slur of the waves and the occasional cry of a wheeling gull.

"I want you to try to picture this, Bud," Rudder said, turning again to look along the length of the beach and sweeping it with his right arm. "A lot of American boys died here."

"Yes, sir," the boy said.

"You've got to picture this whole beach covered with all kinds of equipment, with boats and trucks and jeeps and tanks, a lot of them wrecked, and with American soldiers, and the Germans firing into them from the high ground and a smoke haze over everything."

"Yes, sir."

"You remember General Cota, Bud?"

"Yes, sir."

Major General Norman D. Cota, of Philadelphia, was assistant commander of the 29th Infantry Division and took the 116th Regiment into Omaha on the right flank of the 1st Infantry Division. Later he became commander of the 28th Infantry Division, and Rudder led the 109th Regiment, under Cota, through the Bulge and on to Germany.

"Here's where he did his good work, getting the boys up off the beach," Rudder said. "A lot of them just froze from the horror of it, and he got them up."

"Is he the one gave me that toy watch?" the boy said.

"His wife gave it to you."

"I remember."

They walked along the beach together, not saying anything, the boy swinging the mask at his side and watching the white waves slush up onto the sand. Then the father turned back toward the smooth white stones at the foot of the seawall and the boy followed him. When Rudder reached the stones he kneeled down. With one hand he began to pore among them, to the smaller stones underneath.

"Here," he said, handing three or four to the boy. "Put these in your pocket."

The boy, kneeling beside his father, took the stones and looked at them. Then he looked at his father. "Why?" he said.

"Take them back to Buddy and Elene and Mary Glenn," he said, speaking of Corder's children. "These stones are off the beach where their daddy was hit. They might want them."

We left the beach and drove back through Vierville and then turned right and followed the blacktop coastal road west toward Grandcamp-les-Bains. Looking down from the crest of the road we recognized the town at once, the red-tiled roofs that many an American Navy man will remember when he thinks of the little

63

fishing and bathing community of a couple of hundred houses that stood, by a miracle of war, almost untouched between Omaha Beach and Utah Beach.

We drove through the narrow, cobblestoned street, to the rectangular quay west of the town. In the basin below the quay the black-bodied fishing boats, side by side, were rising slowly with the tide, and on some of them nets were drying, strung from their masts and booms. On the quay a half-dozen fishermen were standing, and they turned and looked at us when we drove up and stopped the car.

"But it is not necessary to go by boat," one of them said, when I told them what we wanted to do.

"I know," I said.

"It is very easy to go with your car," he said, standing there on the quay in the sunlight and pointing. "You drive here through the village and five kilometers on the left you will see the road."

"But you do not understand," I said. "The day of the invasion, this gentleman here, was a colonel of the American Rangers. He was the first American to land at Pointe du Hoe."

An American Army cartographer made the error in reading the French maps— he mistook the "c" for an "e," and so in the American military annals it is "Pointe du Hoe," while to the French it is, of course, Pointe du Hoc.

"He landed at Pointe du Hoc?"

"Yes."

"He mounted the cliff?"

"Yes."

They looked at one another and then at Rudder. It was easy to read their minds. Rudder is forty-four years old now. His brown hair is graying at the temples. He has added four inches around the waist and about thirty pounds, and he was standing now, his topcoat open, trying to understand some of this.

"It was very difficult and very dangerous," one of them said, "what he did."

That is how we got the boat, an old, dirty-green, twenty-foot launch with the engine in the middle only partly housed, and the oily water slopping in the pit. There were three Frenchmen in it— the old man with a week's growth of gray beard who owns it and the two younger ones—and they sat in silence together near the

*James Earl Rudder before shipping overseas,
1942. (L.B. Smith, Courtesy of Mrs. James
Earl Rudder.)*

tiller and when, now and then, we looked back at them they would
smile and nod their heads.

The sun was bright now, so the Channel was very blue around
us, and when we had passed beyond the breakwater the old man
turned east. Now we could see it unfold, the sharp nose sticking
way out into the Channel and beyond the nose, the dark cliffs rising
seventy-five to one hundred feet straight up from the narrow beach.

"There it is," Rudder said quietly, leaning with his elbows on the
waist-high forward deck, with his son beside him. "Pointe du Hoe."

He had heard of "Pointe du Hoe" for the first time five months
before the invasion, in a second-floor room in London behind a
whitestone front, with the blackout drapes drawn and four of them
standing there with the maps and photos on the table. Rudder and
Max Schneider, a colonel out of Iowa who had trained the 1st
Ranger Battalion, had come up by train from Bude, in Cornwall,
and they got their D-Day assignment from Truman Thorson, the

65

tall, thin-cheeked colonel out of Birmingham, Alabama, who was G-3 for First Army, and from the officer who was Thorson's assistant.

"When we got a look at it," Rudder said, "Max just whistled once through his teeth. He had a way of doing that. He'd made three landings already, but I was just a country boy coaching football a year and a half before. It would almost knock you out of your boots."

The cliffs rise as high as a nine-story office building, and on the tableland above them the Germans had observation on the whole Channel area and had mounted and were casemating guns capable of firing onto both Omaha and Utah beaches. It was the Germans' strongest point and it had to be taken. It was what General Omar N. Bradley was later to describe as the most difficult assignment he had ever given a soldier in his military career.

Rudder and Schneider took the assignment back to Bude, put a twenty-four-hour guard on the door, and at night would get out the maps and the pictures and study them. Every time the Germans dug another trench or set another mine field the P-38 reconnaissance planes, skimming over the cliffs, got pictures of it. The French brought back samples of the soil and of the cliffs, and Rudder, in England, held the dirt in his hands and finally made the decision to scale the cliffs.

"Do you think," the boy said now, "we'll be able to climb it?"

The two of them, the father and the son, were leaning forward and studying the shaded face of the cliff. The old Frenchman was still taking the boat parallel to it about a quarter mile out, waiting for us to tell him to turn it in.

"No, son," Rudder said. "We won't."

"But you climbed it before."

"I was younger then, son, and we trained for it. We had the special equipment, too."

In the months before the invasion they had found, at Swanage, on the south coast of England, cliffs of almost exactly the same height and composition, and they climbed these, sometimes three times a day. They had ropes, affixed to steel grapnels to be propelled to the cliff top by rockets, and they also carried four-foot sections of tubular steel ladders and had mounted, on four DUKWs, one-hundred-foot extension ladders borrowed from the London Fire Department.

"It wasn't," the boy said, "a nice day like this, was it?"

"It was a good deal colder and rougher," his father said, "and early in the morning."

It had been 4:05 in the morning and still dark when the Rangers loaded into the British LCAs from the Amsterdam and the Ben Machree. They were ten miles from shore and there were 225 of them and they had to start bailing with their helmets almost immediately. Twenty-one men from D Company had to be rescued by launch. One supply craft sank with only one survivor, and another threw its packs overboard to stay afloat.

"Can you imagine," Rudder said now, "anybody going up that thing?"

"It's twice as high as I thought," the boy said.

Lieutenant General Clarence R. Huebner, of New York, commanding the 1st Division and mounting the Omaha assault, had forbidden Rudder to lead the three companies of Rangers in. "We're not going to risk getting you knocked out in the first round," Huebner had said.

"I'm sorry to have to disobey you, sir," Rudder had replied, "but if I don't take it, it may not go."

Now the two younger Frenchmen moved forward quickly between us and, as the boat scraped down, they were in the water. They had on black knee boots and together they pulled the launch another couple of feet up onto the stones. Then they motioned, laughing, and one took the boy on his shoulders and the other took the father, and that is the way Rudder went in the second time, his topcoat open, his hat knocked back on his head and the Frenchman staggering a little under the weight of the 230 pounds.

"This is what we hoped to land in," Rudder said, looking down at the stony beach where the Frenchman had deposited him, "but what we got was bomb holes and muck."

The heavy bombers and the mediums had plastered the cliff, and the near misses had torn the beach open. Most of the Rangers debarked up to their shoulders in mud and water. The DUKWs with the ladders foundered and were useless. Most of the rocket-propelled ropes were so heavy from the wetting that the grapnels failed to carry to the cliff top.

"Right here," Rudder said, "is where Trevor touched down next to me. He was a British commando colonel, Travis H. Trevor, who volunteered to give us a hand and he just stepped out, right here,

The cliffs rise as high as a nine-story office building and on the tableland above them the Germans had observation on the whole Channel area. (Remy Villiers, 1981.)

when a bullet hit his helmet and drove him to his knees. I helped him up and the blood was starting to trickle down his forehead, but he was a great big, black-haired son of a gun—one of those staunch Britishers—and he just looked up at the top of the cliff and he said, 'The dirty ——.'"

Fifteen men were lost on the narrow strip of stones. Some of the wounded crawled from the water line to the base of the cliff.

"Hey, Daddy!" the boy called. "Come here."

Between two large boulders against the base of the cliff the boy had found a hollow shaft of rusted metal protruding from among the smaller stones. He had started to scoop the stones away with his hands, and now one of the Frenchmen got down on his knees and we watched him dig until, smiling, he got up and handed it to us.

"A grapnel," Rudder said, taking it. "One of the grapnels."

There was the hollow shaft, about six inches long and an inch and a half in diameter, and then, at the head of it, the six bent prongs, petal-like, the whole about the size and shape of a small boat anchor. As Rudder held it and turned it over, the rust flaked into his hands.

"This is amazing," he said shaking his head. "After ten years you can walk back here and find one of the grapnels on the ground."

"Can we take it home?" the boy said.

"Certainly we'll take it home," Rudder said. "This must be the last of those grapnels."

He handed it to the Frenchman and pointed to the boat. The Frenchman nodded and ran to the boat and put it in, and now the boy was gone again and the father stood looking up at the top of the cliff, and the jagged dark line against the sky.

"Will you tell me how we did this?" he said. "Anybody would be a fool to try this. It was crazy then, and it's crazy now."

When the naval fire had lifted from the cliff top the Germans had come out of their holes and trenches and concrete emplacements and, in addition to using small arms, they had dropped grenades on the heads of the Americans. In less than five minutes, however, the first Ranger had scaled the cliff, and within thirty minutes the whole force, minus casualties, climbing the ropes attached to the grapnels that had been rocket-launched, had reached the top.

"*M'sieur!*" It was one of the two younger Frenchmen, who had walked ahead of us, west along the small beach. He was standing now, calling and waving to us, close to where the nose of the point knifes into the Channel. *"Regardez, M'sieur!"*

"A rope," Rudder said. "There's still a rope here."

It was a whole length of three-quarter-inch single rope. It had taken on the mustard color of the clay that had washed down around it, and it hung there on the serpentine curve of the slope, still fastened to the iron pickets driven every ten feet into the cliff, its end flapping loose about six feet from the ground.

"Lapres' boat put it there," Rudder said.

Lieutenant Theodore E. Lapres, Jr., was from Philadelphia, and, about three weeks later, he lost a foot outside of Beaumont, just west of Cherbourg. Twice the rope had been cut that first day, and two men were hit getting it up there.

"M'sieur?" the Frenchman said. He was pulling at the loose end and waving it as if to detach it, laughing at Rudder.

"No," Rudder said, shaking his head.

"Can we climb it, Daddy?" asked the boy, who had run up to us now.

"No," Rudder said, shaking his head.

"Why?"

"Because," Rudder said, "we're not going to get you hurt, son, on this cliff . . ."

On the way back to Grandcamp the sea was running with us, so it took us less than a half hour. Once, Rudder noticed the rusted grapnel lying on the floor of the launch and he picked it up and looked at it closely again and shook his head. Then he put it carefully back on the floor of the boat.

"Grappin!" the same young Frenchman said, nodding, and then he laughed and, with his hands and by shaking his body, he made the motions of climbing a rope. "A good souvenir."

When we got back to the quay there was a small group waiting for us, a half-dozen fishermen and a thin, dark-haired, middle-aged man from the Information Bureau of the town. With him was a younger man, in his mid-thirties, and they wanted to know if they could show us the ground where the fighting had taken place at the top of the cliff.

"They can show us if they want to," Rudder said, smiling, "but I know it better than I know the palm of my hand."

The Rangers, fighting until relief could come up from Omaha, had been isolated on the cliff top for two days and two nights. About a half mile of flat, pastured tableland had spread back from the V edge of the cliff to the road that runs east and west between Vierville and Grandcamp, but when the Rangers had reached the top they found it an erupted wasteland of dirt and mud, made unrecognizable by the heavy preparatory bombing from the air and the heavy shelling from the sea.

"Now you stay close to us, Bud," Rudder said. "Don't go running off."

"I just want to see," the boy said.

Rudder had parked the Peugeot on a small patch of level grass at the end of the hedgerowed lane that runs from the blacktop out toward the point of the cliff. We had started along a path between the shoulder-high growth of dark-green thorn bushes with the stalks of small, tight yellow flowers that the French call *ajonc* and the British call gorse.

"There wasn't this growth here then," Rudder said. "It was all just ripped-open dirt."

The bomb and shell holes, one opening into another and some of them thirty feet across and ten feet deep, were grown with grass now, and Rudder picked a path between them. Then he came upon the concrete blockhouse, standing dome-roofed about eight feet above the ground, open toward the Channel, and its floor stewn with concrete rubble. He looked at it a moment, then called the boy.

"Bud," he said, "come back here. I want you to see this."

He walked down the two steps among the pieces of broken concrete, and the boy followed him. Then Rudder turned around.

"This is where the shell hit," he said, pointing up just above his head to a broken section of the corner where two rusted reinforcing rods protruded. "They say it wasn't from one of our ships, but when you look at the direction, it had to be.

"The artillery captain," he said, "a nice-looking, black-haired boy —I wish I could remember his name—was killed right here. The Navy lieutenant, who was spotting with us, fell right here." He pointed. "It knocked me over right here."

He pulled back the right sleeve of his topcoat, unbuttoned his shirt cuff, and exposed his forearm and the small red welt on it.

"This is where the shell hit." (Jean Goron.)

"Right under that," Rudder said, "is a piece of the concrete from right here."

"The colonel was wounded here?" the older of the two Frenchmen said.

"You carry it around in you for ten years," Rudder said, "and you bring it right back where it came from."

"I thought you had two pieces in there," the boy said, looking at his father's arm.

"I've thought about this a lot," Rudder said. "I mean, you wonder how close it really was, if it was as close as it seemed and how a man could live. The way I pictured it, you could just about reach up and touch the place where the shell hit, and you just about can."

The boy had found an old red-handled American toothbrush in the dust and broken concrete on the floor. He handed it to his father and his father looked at it and tossed it on the ground.

"Come around here with me," he said to the boy.

They walked around to the east of the blockhouse. The shelling had ripped half the concrete off the side, exposing horizontal rows of reinforcing rods. Rudder climbed up onto the second one and

73

the boy climbed up beside him, where they could both look toward the lane.

"Earlier that morning we were right here," the father said. "The Navy lieutenant was on my right, where you are, the artillery captain was on my left and we were trying to direct fire over there when I got shot in the leg."

"Where was the German?" the boy said, turning.

"I don't know," Rudder said.

The first time the boy had ever seen the bullet wound had been in the little house on South Bridge Street, sitting one night in the parlor. His grandmother was there and his uncle and his aunt and his sister and his two cousins. Someone had asked about the wound and his father had rolled up the left pant leg and there, just above the knee, was the pink scar where the bullet had gone in and, on the other side, the pink scar where it had come out. It had been a clean penetration, and so it had not looked like much of a wound to the boy.

"This way, Bud," Rudder said now, calling again to the boy.

The boy had run ahead, running along the ridges between the bomb craters. There would be times when he would disappear completely in the growth, and then you would see his red corduroy jacket.

"I just want to see the CP," the boy said, coming back out of breath.

"You'll see it," Rudder said. "Just be patient."

"I think it's over there," the boy said, pointing over the rough ground and the green growth.

"You stick with me, son," Rudder said, "and you won't have to worry about where things are."

"But I can find it," the boy said.

"I'll find it," Rudder said. "I've been here before."

He walked as directly to it as you could, considering the turbulence of the ground. It had been his first command post in France, a hollow scooped out of the edge of the cliff by a bomb, and it was from here that he had sent out his first message: "Praise the Lord," the code meaning: "Rangers up cliff."

"Need ammunition and reinforcements," he had sent out later. "Many casualties."

"No reinforcements available," was the answer that had come back.

Now he stood in the middle of it, and the boy was at the edge, peering down where his father had once rope-climbed, down the sheer drop of about ninety feet, with the narrow stony beach below.

"Bud!"

"Yes?"

"Look, son. I want you to keep away from that edge."

"I'm just looking."

"You could fall off there, and I'd have to go home and face your mother."

"Is that where our flag was?" the boy said.

"No," Rudder said, pointing. "It was right over here."

They had anchored the American flag to the cliff with rocks. When the relief had come on D plus two the tankers had presumed that the Rangers had been annihilated, and so they had started to fire onto the point. He had waved the flag on a stick and the firing had stopped, and now the flag is in the wooden box in the den of the white limestone house in Brady. Along with the flag are the two German revolvers, the two German chrome-plated 20-mm shells, the two German knives, the French beret and the D.S.C., the Silver Star, the Bronze Star with cluster, the Purple Heart with cluster, the Croix de Guerre, and the Légion d'Honneur.

"Mommy finally got a box with a glass in front and put the medals in it and hung it on the wall," the boy had said one night. "Then it fell off the wall and broke to pieces, and after Mommy went to all that trouble Daddy just laughed."

Rudder climbed up now on one side of the scooped earth. He walked around to the side of the buried blockhouse.

"We got our first German prisoner right here," he said. "He was a little freckle-faced kid who looked like an American, and we were so proud of him, because when you're trying to get your first prisoner, it's like diving for pearls.

"Then I had a feeling there were more of them, and I told the Rangers to lead this kid ahead of them. They just started him around this corner when the Germans opened up out of the entrance and he fell dead, right here, face down with his hands still clasped on the top of his head."

It was his first command post in France, and from here he sent out his first message: "Praise the Lord," the code meaning: "Rangers up cliff." (U.S. Signal Corps.)

"How many were in there?" the boy said.

"We killed one and got seven or eight out," Rudder said. "It was right here, too, that we left the artillery captain, lying right here on a litter when we took off on D plus two."

"We can go down in here," the boy said, calling up from down inside the entrance. "It's open and we might find something in here."

"He was only about twenty-five years old," Rudder said. "I'm sorry I've forgotten his name."

We walked back to the car and drove out the lane that leads off the point and then down another lane where Leonard G. Lomell, of Toms River, New Jersey, then a sergeant and later commissioned in the field, and Staff Sergeant Jack E. Kuhn, of Altoona, Pennsylvania, had found the big guns, hidden behind a hedgerow and set up to fire onto Utah Beach. The Americans had bashed in the sights and had blown the recoil mechanisms and the barrels with thermite grenades.

Now you could still see the gun pits dug into the drainage ditch along the hedgerow, almost covered with creeping vines. We walked down the green lane and then walked left along another hedgerow and then down across a hundred yards of field that, in season, would be a field of wheat.

"I want you to picture this, son," Rudder said.

The field was covered with a lush green, ankle-high growth of winter rye and clover. At the foot of the field was a mortared stone wall, about eighteen inches thick and four feet high.

"This is where Sergeant Petty had his squad, Bud," Rudder said, stopping where a rough opening still gaped in the top of the wall. "From here they could look right down into this valley."

"Was there any fighting here?" the boy said.

"There was a lot of fighting here, son," Rudder said. "That first night the Germans attacked right through that orchard there, and got around behind Petty, who was way out here."

Sergeant William Petty had come from Cohutta, Georgia. He was a pale-faced, unimposing kid with slick blond hair and no upper teeth, and he kept coming to Rudder during the heat of that summer of '43 in Tennessee. Rudder had turned him down twice and then, when he had gone over to screen the 80th Division volunteers, Petty was in the front line.

"I thought I discouraged you, Petty," Rudder had said.

"Please, sir," Petty had said. "I'll look better when I get my teeth."

"All right," Rudder had said. "If you want the Rangers that bad, I'll take you."

Petty was made a Browning automatic rifleman. When he got up to platoon sergeant he asked Rudder if he could still carry the heavy BAR. He carried it up the cliff and killed, they figured afterward, about thirty Germans with it, and there are many among the Rangers who today still say that Petty saved their lives.

"These were brave men, here," Rudder said now to the boy.

The boy had thrown his leg over the wall and was looking at the hole that Petty and his men had knocked into the top of the wall to give them a better field of fire for the BAR. He nodded his head.

"You have to remember, son, that it was pitch dark and they didn't know how many Germans there were or where they were."

"Yes, sir."

"You remember how you used to feel when you had to go to the hen house at night at the ranch?"

"Yes, sir."

Rudder turned around and looked back up the slope of the green field. With the toe of his right shoe he made a pass at the rye and clover.

"If I had this kind of cover at home," he said, "I'd sure put some sheep on it."

He had finished with his piece of ground. It was late afternoon and we drove back, through that crossroad outside Formigny and east to Bayeux. That night we sat in the small linoleumed lobby of the Lion d'Or waiting for the BBC news on the small radio standing on the radiator cover. The boy had gone up to bed.

"You wonder so long," Rudder said, "what it would be like to come back. Then you come back and it's hard to know what you feel."

We were alone in the lobby except for the woman in the black dress leaning on the desk with her elbows and watching us and then turning her eyes down when we happened to look at her.

"It was hard to believe when it was going on," Rudder said. "It's even harder to believe now."

When Rudder had come back from the war he had lost himself in his family and his work. There were the two children before he went to war—the boy and Margaret Ann, who is now twelve—and three after the war—Linda, who is seven, Jane, five, and Robert, born last April. There is the office at the Brady Aviation Plant of the Intercontinental Manufacturing Company, Inc., where he is vice-president. He is on the State Democratic Committee and the State Board of Welfare, and for six years was mayor of Brady.

"You think of the wonderful kids you had with you," he said. "You think that if you could have men like that around you in a peacetime world, men as devoted as that, there wouldn't be anything you couldn't accomplish."

"What about Bud?" I said, after a while. "What do you suppose he thinks of all this?"

"It's hard to say," Rudder said. "I kinda hope he'll think a lot about it in years to come."

I thought of the younger of the two Frenchmen from Grandcamp, watching the boy on the top of the point. The Frenchman had been unable to understand what the boy or his father was saying, but he was able to comprehend it, nevertheless.

"The father, he tries to explain to the boy," the Frenchman had said, "but the boy, he looks for souvenirs."

"Yes," I had said. "He was four years old at the time of the war."

"It is like it was with me," the Frenchman had said. "When I was young my father would tell me about his war, the war of '14. I could not understand. Then came the war of '40 and '44. After that I understood war. I understood my war, and I understood the war of my father."

The next morning we had breakfast in the new hotel in Carentan, where, right next to the bar, there is a frosted wall light with the Screaming Eagle patch of the 101st Airborne painted on it. We had lunch in Saint-Lô, that was dust ten years ago and against which, ten years ago, we measured all destruction from then on.

That afternoon we drove south and then, finally, east toward Paris through the winding, climbing country of the Falaise gap, where the Americans and the British had slaughtered most of what was left of the German Army that had tried to hold Normandy. It was about midafternoon, and we had just passed through Argentan, when the boy spoke up from the back seat.

"What did we do with the grapnel, Daddy?" he asked.

"I'm afraid," his father said, "that we forgot it. We left it in the boat."

"But we were going to take it home," the boy said, "for a souvenir."

"I'm sorry, son," his father said, "but we just forgot it."

I thought about the grapnel, lying in the bottom of the boat. We had paid the old man well for his boat and so, I supposed, he would leave it there for a while, thinking that we might still come back. Then one day, I imagined, he would be hurrying forward to check his lines or to catch the engine before it coughed out, and his foot or his pant leg would become entangled in the grapnel. Then he would stop and pick it up and look at it and think of us. Finally he would shrug his shoulders and then, taking a last look at it, he would drop it overboard. The sun would be shining, as I imagined it, and the grapnel would sink through the blue waters to the bottom of the English Channel.

It was the last of the grapnels and it had taken ten years for it to find its place, so that would be the end of it all.

As it turned out, that was not quite the end of it all. Even as I had found Earl Rudder in General Omar Bradley's autobiography, Texas found him in the cover story in *Collier's*. The following year, Allan Shivers, campaigning for his second term as Governor, asked James Earl Rudder to introduce him at political rallies around the state, and the next year, when the Texas Land Office was hit by scandal, he appointed him interim Land Commissioner. In 1957, Rudder was elected to the office, and two years later, he was made President of Texas A&M and, in 1965, of the entire Texas A&M system. When he retired from the Army Reserve in 1967, he was a major general, and had made, at the Army's invitation, two more visits back to "Pointe du Hoe."

The top of the cliff has changed. In 1954, Robert Ravelet, head of the Local Information Bureau, had told us that he had been attempting for years to persuade the proper authorities in Paris to appropriate the land as a memorial to the Americans who had captured it. In 1960, at an obelisk of native stone erected at the cliff edge, the thirty-one acres were dedicated, and in 1978, the preserve was turned over to the American Battle Monuments Commission.

As Major General and President of Texas A&M. (Texas A&M University.)

The access road has been named *Allée du Colonel Rudder,* and now, each year, thousands of tourists, Germans among them, visit the site.

On March 23, 1970, Major General James Earl Rudder died at the age of fifty-nine in St. Luke's Hospital, in Houston, of circulatory collapse. In 1973, the $10 million J. Earl Rudder Conference Center, an auditorium complex surmounted by a twelve-story tower, was dedicated on the Texas A&M campus. Each year, on the anniversary of his death, a memorial service is held by the French in Criqueville, near Grandcamp. His elder son, James Earl Rudder, Jr., whom I knew as the fourteen-year-old Bud, is now forty-two years of age, and an automobile dealer in Dallas.

The monument was dedicated in August 1960, and today the cliff is a tourist attraction. (Robert Ravelet.)

6

Punching Out a Living

It was three weeks and one day away from the fight when Billy Graham drove out to Long Pond Inn to go into camp. When you are a prizefighter and thirty years old and married and have two small kids, you can't get into shape any more living at home.

"You have too many distractions," Billy was saying, driving out. "My wife understands, but take like this morning. At seven-thirty the kids wake me. They wake me at eight-thirty. At nine-thirty, they wake me again. I said to Lorraine, 'Look, can't you keep these kids away from me? I gotta get my sleep.' She said, 'You slept enough, didn't you?'"

So he got up and drove Lorraine down to the supermarket to load her up with groceries for the three weeks. Then they drove over to Sunrise Highway to buy a red wagon for young Billy's third birthday, two days away, and at three o'clock, he left Long Island and drove to Manhattan and then across town and into the Lincoln Tunnel.

When you're a young fighter and make your first big paynight you buy a big yellow convertible. By the time you go into camp for your 118th fight in twelve years, you know it's a hard dollar and you're paying off the house in Springfield Gardens and you have the kids to think of, and so you drive a small sedan.

"With me it's a case of winning every fight now," he was saying, driving. "If you don't have the big punch—you know, the glamour— you have to win for your bargaining power. All you have is your record."

Billy's record, on pages 399 and 400 of Nat Fleischer's *Ring Record Book* with a picture taken 10 years ago, shows 99 wins going into this one, but only 25 by kayo, 8 draws, 10 losses, 8 of them of split decisions.

"A punch is something you're born with," he was saying. "Either you have it or you don't. I gave it a try. I thought punching the heavy bag would do it. In 1946 I knocked out Pat Scanlon in five. I knocked out Frankie Carto in nine and sent him to the hospital. When I fought Tony Pellone he just managed to keep his balance, and I had Ruby Kessler on the deck. The papers were starting to write I was becoming a puncher."

It was a gray afternoon and he was driving out Route 3. It is a wide, flat concrete highway with here and there a gas station or a roadside restaurant or a place that sells outdoor furniture and pottery.

"Then I boxed Tippy Larkin in the Garden, and I was looking to kayo him, too," Billy said. "He won it big. After that, I forgot about the big punch."

After the Larkin fight they talked about it one day in Stillman's— Billy and Irving Cohen who manages him with Jack Reilly. Jack is the one who discovered him in the boys' clubs about fifteen years ago, and Irving does the front work.

"Billy," Irving said, in that soft way of his, "you're trying to put everybody away with two punches. When you try that, you tighten up, so let's get back to boxing. That's what you do best. You'll make money that way."

How much money do you make? In 1949, and always rated in the first half-dozen welterweights, you clear about $7,500. In 1950, you split two fights with Kid Gavilan and clear a little better than $10,000. In 1951, you make about the same, and in 1952 you have your best year and your end comes to about $20,000.

"Every once in a while," he was saying, "Lorraine talks about me

85

giving it up. It's tough on a wife. At first there's some glamour to it. You go out and you're recognized, but you're keeping in shape so you can't go out a lot. She's alone—like now, for three weeks—and it's rough. So I tell her, 'Sure, I'll quit, but what else am I gonna do? Do you want to live on sixty a week? Let me work something out.'"

Greenwood Lake extends north across the line from New Jersey into New York State. The camp is on the highway that runs along the west shore of the lake, a long, low concrete building painted white with green trim, built between the highway and the lake where the shore drops down to the water. At the south end, the steps lead down from the parking space to the bar and dining room and kitchen under the gym and the dressing rooms and the rooms where the fighters sleep.

"Johnny Dee," Billy said to the bartender.

"Billy Graham," Johnny said. "How's Billy Graham?"

Johnny was behind the bar, leaning on it and talking to a customer. In the back of the dining room, Rollie LaStarza was sitting at the end of the table, eating with Nick Florio, who trains him, and with James J. Parker, the heavyweight out of Canada. Eddie McDonald, who owns the place with his wife, Catherine, and Ollie Cromwell, was standing there, a cigarette hanging out of his mouth, watching them eat their steaks and talk.

"How's Billy Graham?" LaStarza said.

"Good," Billy said, shaking hands all the way around. "How are you?"

"He's in great shape," Eddie McDonald said. "He'll lick this guy, take it from me. Rollie will put lumps on Mr. Rex Layne. He'll play football with him."

"How long you been here?" Billy said, sitting down at the other end of the table.

"Five weeks," LaStarza said.

"When you leavin'?"

"Tomorrow morning. When's your fight?"

"Three weeks," Billy said.

There are always fighters coming and going through Long Pond Inn. On the next morning Rollie LaStarza would go into New York to beat Rex Layne in Madison Square Garden, and James J. Parker would knock out Jack Nelson in the semifinal. The following Friday, Paddy DeMarco, who trained here before leaving to finish up in Brooklyn, would lose to George Araujo in the Garden. Two weeks after that, Billy Graham would check out to go into the Garden against Joe Giardello, who held two decisions over him.

"And I'll tell you something else," Eddie McDonald said, still standing, the cigarette still hanging from his lips, the ash on it long now. "Mr. Bill Graham will give Mr. Giardello a real good lickin' this time. He'll win."

"Yeah, I'll win," Billy said, giving a short laugh, "but will I get it?"

The question is what made this fight important. On December 19th, Billy Graham had boxed Joey Giardello, a middleweight out of Philadelphia, in the Garden, and when Johnny Addie had announced the decision there had been a near riot. The referee and one of the judges had given it to Giardello, and there was Billy walking up and down in the ring holding out his hands in appeal and the crowd booing and hollering.

A few minutes later Robert K. Christenberry, chairman of the New York State Athletic Commission, and Dr. Clilan B. Powell, one of the two other commissioners, had changed the card of one of the judges, Joe Agnello, to give Billy the fight. The switch in decision had made headlines, and a week after Billy got into camp it was to make headlines again when a Supreme Court justice named Bernard Botein reversed Christenberry and Powell.

"You'll get it," Eddie McDonald said. "You'll get into great shape up here. Skipper will help you. Skipper!"

Skipper is a brown and white dog, part beagle. Whenever Eddie cannot think of anything else to do he calls the dog and he keeps at him until the dog yawns and makes a guttural sound in his throat that Eddie says is talking.

"Here, Skipper!" Eddie said. "Say hello to Billy. Say 'Mama.'"

The dog was sitting at Eddie's feet. He was just sitting there, looking up at Eddie and not doing a thing.

"This is a real smart dog," Eddie said. "He likes Billy."

Billy put away a steak and some vegetables and a green salad and a cup of tea. Eddie told him to take the back room, and he went up and lugged in his bag and then his road shoes and the black footlocker with his boxing things—gloves, headgear, white terry-cloth robe, long underwear, sweat shirts, windbreaker, and the gray-green Marine toursers he wears on the road. Then he went to the movies.

"You get older," he was saying the next morning, "and you find it takes about three weeks to get ready. The first couple of days I just like to rest—sleep long and eat good and walk."

On Saturday, two days after Billy got there, Irving Cohen and Jack Reilly sent up Frank Percoco, the trainer. Billy went on the road for the first time that morning with Walter Cartier, the middleweight who came up to train for a bout with Randy Turpin in England. In the afternoon Billy went into the gym for the first time.

The gym is a nice, clean place with knotty-pine planking on the walls and the ring set over by the windows that look down and out into the lake. The first dressing room off the showers is for the sparring partners, and the room beyond that is for the fighters; inside is a rubbing table with clean sheets always on it.

The first four days Billy just loosened up. He shadowboxed and did sit-ups on the mat and rolled on the medicine ball to get the weight off his middle. Then he would skip rope and punch the light bag. Frank Percoco left after the fourth day and Whitey Bimstein came up to take over, bringing Johnny Noel, a sparring partner, with him. That afternoon Billy boxed.

At first you go three rounds. After a while, you work it up to six. Irving Cohen earned an edge for Billy by arranging to have the fight go twelve rounds. Cohen figured Giardello is just a twenty-two-year-old kid who never went more than ten and Billy went fifteen twice with Gavilan and knows how to pace himself. Still, you never box more than six in the gym, and you build up your wind and your legs on the road.

Every morning at eight-thirty, Whitey would get Billy up, and Billy would wake Walter Cartier, and they'd go out on the road. Different fighters do it in different ways, but Billy and Walter would just start out from the camp, running easy along the left side of the concrete highway north and into the town of Greenwood Lake, then off to the right along the shore of the lake by the white cottages with the rowboats turned bottoms up on the lawns. Then they'd make the circuit back through the town again and down the highway to the camp, a full distance of 3.3 miles.

When they'd come off the road they'd go to Billy's room. Whitey would bring up hot tea and lemon and they'd sit there with towels around their necks, sipping the tea and sweating and talking. Then Walter would go into his room to lie down and listen to some disc jockey on the radio, and Billy would lie down on his bed and cool out and hear the radio through the wall.

"I used to think a training camp was wonderful," he said, lying there one morning. "The first time I ever went to one I was boxing Pat Scanlon and they sent me out to Ehsan's at Summit as a sparring partner for Dorsey Lay. It cost me nothing, and I thought it was great. It was new. I liked it, you know? It was like I used to read about as a kid, getting up and doing road work, eating with the other fighters."

Whitey came in while Billy was talking. Billy got up and started to undress, taking off the layers of sweat shirts and long underwear so Whitey could rub him down with alcohol.

"Gus Lesnevich was there," he said, "training for a fight in England. Bernie Reynolds was there, but you're not in a camp for pleasure. You got to drive yourself. People say you eat steak every day, but after a while it's not gonna taste so good. A camp is a place for work. A camp costs money."

The camp costs about seven hundred dollars to get ready for a main-event fight. It's ten dollars a day each for you and Whitey and the sparring partner, and you pay the sparring partner five dollars a round. All in all, with publicity, you've paid out about a thousand dollars by the time you climb into the ring.

"At first I'm glad to get here," Billy said. "I got quiet. I can sleep. The food is good. Then you start missing the wife and kids."

One of Billy's brothers, Jackie or Robbie, would drive up with Lorraine and the kids—little Billy and Ellen, who is two—on Sundays. They'd be there a couple of hours, watching Billy work in the gym. Then they'd leave and the rest of the time it would just be the running on the road every morning and the work, sweating, in the gym in the afternoon. Once, some of Billy's pals drove out—Ray O'Connell and Joe De Chara and George Papageorge and a couple of others—and they sat around and amused Billy, but the rest of the time he would just shoot a few games of pool with Ollie Cromwell or listen to Eddie McDonald argue fights or talk to the dog.

"Watch this, Billy," McDonald would say. "Watch Skipper. Skipper is a real smart dog."

There would be the same songs, time and again, on the jukebox, too. A guy and a gal would drop in for a drink at the bar, and the guy would plunk a coin into the jukebox, and out would come "Don't Let the Stars Get in Your Eyes" or "Blues in the Night" or "Glow Worm," over and over.

"Billy can go with any style," Whitey was saying one evening while the jukebox was going and Billy was out taking his walk with Walter Cartier. "Billy don't have to train a certain way for a certain style."

"That's right," Eddie McDonald said, sitting down next to Whitey.

"This fight depends on condition," Whitey said. "Billy's got to set the pace with more infighting. The other guy don't fight inside, and Billy is one of the best infighters in boxing today. The last couple of years he picked up them inside punches."

"Billy can take a punch," Eddie said.

"Nobody in boxing takes a punch like Billy Graham," Whitey said. "All the fights he's been in, and he's never even been staggered. All the tough fights he's in, and I never seen him blow his top."

"Billy will lick this guy," Eddie said. "Billy will lick him, but good. He will make mincemeat of Mr. Giardello."

Billy licked Kid Gavilan for the title, in the Garden on August 29, 1951, but he didn't get it. All the newspapers said he won it, and the writers called him "the uncrowned welterweight champion of the world." But the only title that counts, the only one you can make any money with, is the one you get in the ring.

In the gym, Whitey would stand on the ring apron while Billy was boxing, leaning on the ropes and never taking his eyes off Billy. Every now and then he'd holler at Billy, getting him to throw his punches in combinations and making him move in under Johnny Noel's leads to punch more to the body.

"Stick!" Whitey would call, just loud enough for Billy to hear. "Now inside. Under and over."

It all started when Billy was a kid, growing up around Second Avenue and Thirty-sixth Street, on New York's East Side. There

"Billy licked Kid Gavilan for the title, in the Garden on August 29, 1951, but he didn't get it." (UPI Photo.)

was Robbie, a year and a half older than Billy, and then Billy and then Jackie, five years younger, and then Jimmy, who was three years younger than that.

Billy's old man ran a candy store between Thirty-fifth and Thirty-sixth on Second, where he sold school notebooks and pencils and pens and a little sporting goods, too. At this time, Billy's old man was crazy about Jimmy McLarnin, and he gave Robbie and Billy boxing gloves and they used to square off in the room in the back of the store. When prohibition went out, the candy store became a bar, and then it moved up to the corner of Thirty-sixth and Second, but Billy still calls it "the store."

When Billy was ten, his old man took him up to the Catholic Boys' Club on Thirty-seventh Street between First and Second. It was in an old tenement, and they'd ripped out the walls to make one big room on each floor. The top floor was the gym, with a mat for a ring and a big sandbag.

Every night Billy would go up there from 7:00 P.M. until 9:00 P.M. and Ed Tirnan—a nicely built guy with reddish hair and a little bit of a fighter's nose—would line the kids up and show them how to box. He was the one who taught Billy how to jab—straight out all the way from the shoulder, turning your fist down.

Billy weighed sixty-five pounds and he started to box for the Catholic Boys' Club and later for the Madison Square Boys' Club. He got so good that the other clubs were trying to steer their best kids out of Billy's weight class. In about eighty of those fights Billy won all but two or three.

"School was murder," Billy was saying once. "I went two years to high school, but I couldn't get over that Latin. I didn't study at all. I had my mind set on being a fighter."

Popeye Woods was fighting out of Billy's neighborhood then. This was in the late thirties, and if Popeye had worked at it and lived right he might have been the middleweight champion of the world.

"I'd see him hanging around on the corner or at the Boys' Club," Billy was saying. "I'd say, 'What round you gonna knock him out in?' When he fought at one of the clubs in town I'd save up. A seat was 75 cents upstairs, and to get there I'd sneak on the subway or hitch on a bus or a taxi or any car that stopped for a light."

Billy was walking on the road, walking his breakfast down one morning. There is a place near the camp where a little trickle of a stream comes down the hillside to the highway, and Billy would never walk by it without bending down to get a drink. He'd say it was the best water he ever tasted.

"Popeye used to bust guys up just with his jab," Billy said. "He once told me, 'You can watch a bum, and he may do one thing you can use.'"

Any fighter has a little bit of every fighter he ever saw and admired. Even now, Billy still loops a right hand once in a while instead of shooting it straight because when Billy was a small kid Max Baer had a looping right hand and it made Max the heavyweight champion of the world.

Four times Billy tried to get into the Golden Gloves and each time they turned him down for what they called a heart murmur. It got to be a joke around the neighborhood.

"What's your old man doin'?" the guys would say. "Payin' the doctors so you won't get your brains knocked out?"

Billy went to work as a stock boy, six days a week, at the Lord & Taylor department store in Manhattan. He worked at it for three months. It's the only job he ever had, because one Sunday Jack Reilly came to the family bar and made a suggestion. The way he had it figured, Billy could take out an application for the pros and, if he passed the physical, he could have five or six fights to see how he liked it.

Billy passed. That was early in 1941. Then Jack took him to meet Irving Cohen. They went to a luncheonette and soda fountain at Twenty-ninth Street and Second Avenue.

"Irving came in and he was sitting there," Billy was saying, "and he had a pencil and a piece of paper. He wrote on the paper, and then he said, 'Willie Graham, William Graham, Bill Graham, Billy Graham. I like Billy Graham best. It'll look better in an ad.'"

You do a lot of talking in camp. There isn't much else to do, just working and sleeping and eating and talking, but the one thing Billy never talked about unless somebody else brought it up in a question was Giardello and the coming fight.

"Joey's a good fighter," he'd say. "I have nothing against him. It was the officials who couldn't see it."

For the last day of work, two days before the fight, they brought Jimmy Herring, the middleweight, up from New York to sneak right hands over Billy's left, like Giardello. Just a year before, Billy had outboxed Herring in the Garden and he could handle him again, but that afternoon Billy didn't look good and Herring was dropping that right hand in there almost every time he let it go.

"Don't worry about it," Billy said later. "It'll be all right."

Billy's brother Jackie came up for the last workout and to take Billy's car back. That same day Paddy Young came in to get in shape for Ernie Durando in the Garden. The last night, Paddy drove Billy to a movie in Warwick and by ten o'clock Billy was in bed.

The morning of the fight, he got up at nine forty-five, and he was shaving when Whitey went in at ten to wake him. Whitey helped him pack, and then Whitey and Johnny Dee loaded the stuff into the trunk of Johnny Dee's car.

Johnny drove, with Billy in the front on the outside and Whitey in the back along with Eddie McDonald and his wife. On the way down Whitey fell asleep, and when they got into town they dropped Eddie and his wife off at Eighth Avenue and Forty-eighth Street. Then Johnny drove around to the Athletic Commission offices on West Forty-seventh Street. By the time Billy got upstairs there was a crowd in the big room, with Giardello there in a light-gray suit and sitting on a bench talking with Tony Ferrante, one of his managers, and a couple of others.

"Inside, Billy," somebody said.

In the back room Dr. Alexander Schiff was examining a preliminary boy and he nodded to Billy, who walked over to where Dr. Vincent Nardiello, the ringside physician for most Garden fights, was waiting for him. Billy stripped to the waist and the doctor took his blood pressure and put the stethoscope on him and then examined his eyes and mouth.

"Very good," Nardiello said, finally. "Good luck to you."

For his first pro fight, four rounds with Connie Savoie in St. Nick's Arena on April 14, 1941, Billy personally sold $160 worth of tickets around the neighborhood. When Dr. Schiff had started to examine him that day, Billy was so nervous the doctor made him sit down for a while to relax. This day Billy was completely calm.

On the scales Giardello weighed 155½ and Billy 149¼; when Irving made the match he gave Giardello all the weight he wanted just to get the two extra rounds. Irving figured the weight wouldn't help Giardello much and the distance would help Billy.

Whitey got Billy to try on the gloves and then put on the black trunks with white stripes. Then the newspaper photographers asked Billy to take a fighting pose with Giardello; the two of them stood on a bench with the photographers shooting up from below.

"You watch them take that picture?" Billy said to Jack while Jack was helping him dress.

"Yeah," Jack said.

"Did you see his right hand?" Billy said. He made a fist and shook it to show Jack how nervous Giardello was, and that was the way he himself had been, weighing in twelve years ago for that first fight.

"Are you sure I can handle him?" he had asked Jack after looking at Savoie. "Look how tough he looks."

"He's the walk-in type," Jack told him. "You'll jab his head off."

Billy was so nervous he didn't wait to find out. He walked right out and started throwing punches and flattened Savoie in the first round.

Now, after the weigh-in with Giardello, Johnny Dee drove Billy and Whitey up to the Shelton Hotel on Lexington Avenue and they checked into a room there. Then they went into the dining room, and Billy had his breakfast. It was one-thirty.

"Take good care of Mr. Graham," the headwaiter was telling the waiter. "He fights tonight."

"Orange juice," Billy said, "two soft-boiled eggs, tea, and toast."

While Billy was eating, his mother came in, and he got up and kissed her, and she sat down. She is a little woman—four feet ten— with wide blue eyes, and she didn't say much; she just sat there and watched Billy until he finished eating and got up to go upstairs.

"Good luck, chicken," she said when he bent down to kiss her again, and then she turned to Whitey and said, "I hate to think of it. I don't even watch TV."

Billy bought the papers at the newsstand in the lobby, and then went up to lie down on the bed. He went through the papers quickly, just reading the stories on the fight, spotting the odds. They all had him 8½ to 5.

"They all pick me," he said finally, putting the papers down. "I guess it proves I won the last one. If I didn't, why would they be picking me now?"

"You're right," Whitey said.

At three o'clock they walked to the Scribes Restaurant, not far from the hotel, where Billy knows the bartender. He put in his order—steak and green vegetable and tea—and then he and Whitey went for a long walk.

For that first fight, twelve years ago, he had the steak at home. Then after he took his walk he was thirsty. Jack and Irving had told him not to drink much water, so he had two glasses of milk instead. When he started throwing punches he almost lost everything he'd eaten.

"That shows you how much I knew," Billy said, telling it once. "I was a real green kid."

They walked back toward the hotel and then up fourteen blocks and across one block and then back. All the way along, people kept popping out of the crowd to wish him luck, and at one place a guy came out of a bar and dragged him in to meet a couple of others.

"Its television," Billy said when he came out. "The last couple of years everybody recognizes you."

"Excuse me," a man said, on the sidewalk. "I been thinking of you for three months."

He was a little man, in a camel's hair coat and wearing a gray fedora. He had a small blond mustache, the ends pulled to points.

"I was gonna write you," he said, holding the lapel of Billy's camel's hair. "When you throw that right hand, step in with the right foot. You gotta do that. You see, I used to fight. I fought Young Corbett, Frankie Neil. I fought champions. I was no good, but I had Young Corbett on the deck and not many did that. Like I said, when you throw the right, step in with it. I'd have written you, but you might never have read it. All right?"

"All right," Billy said, nodding.

"So good luck," the man said.

The guy was right, but what they don't understand is that if it's not part of you after all these years it never will be. Try to step in and you're in trouble, because it's against your style and there's no way for you to get out.

When they got back to the hotel it was six o'clock. Whitey went down to the lobby and left Billy alone, lying in the bed with his clothes off for an hour, and at seven he went up again and Billy got up. They were packing the ring clothes into Billy's bag when Robbie came in with another bag, and in it was the blue satin robe with the white trim and the name on the back in white. For his first four or five fights, Billy wore an old flannel, Indian-design bathrobe he used to wear around the house. Then Robbie and Jackie and Jimmy chipped in and they bought him this one. It meant a lot to Billy and he has had it ever since.

"I just spoke to Lorraine," Robbie said. "She's fine."

"I know," Billy said. "I was just talking with her on the phone. She's gonna stay with her mother."

They were married on October 2, 1948, in the rectory of St. Patrick's Cathedral. It was a beautiful day, warm and with the sun shining so that you didn't even need a topcoat. He had seen her the first time a year before when his brother Jackie and Pete Cassidy took him up to her folks' place across the street from the bar. She has blue eyes and long wavy brown hair, and that time she had on a pair of black lounging pajamas with gold on the jacket, and Billy tried to make a date.

"I've made plans to go to the hockey game in the Garden tonight," she said.

"What do you want to watch that nonsense for?" he said.

They used to go to dinner and to dance at the Century Room of the Commodore and the Cafe Rouge at the Statler. At first she couldn't understand how you can go into a ring and punch someone. A few times she watched it, and then she gave up.

It was eight o'clock when they got to the Garden and went into the Fiftieth Street entrance. They had the big dressing room on that side. After a while Jack and Irving came in, and they stood around Billy, who was sitting on the bench against the wall, talking the fight.

"There are three things you got to remember," Jack was telling Billy, and Irving was nodding. "On the break you have to get off fast, because he likes to sneak you there. Second, he's gonna look to throw the right hand over your jab, so after you jab you gotta weave. Third, you must go to his body, and slow him down. He don't like it in the body. Will you remember that?"

"Sure," Billy said. "Don't worry, Jack." Billy was the coolest of them all.

He always bandages and tapes his own hands. When Ferrante and one of Giardello's other seconds came in to watch it and got into an argument with the boxing inspector working Billy's room, Billy just went on taping.

"What's this, a new rule that two of us can't watch?" Ferrante said.

"Yeah," the other guy said, nodding toward the inspector, "and this guy just made it."

"Never mind," the inspector said. "One of you get out."

"If this okay?" Billy said, showing Ferrante the left hand.

"Okay," Ferrante said.

He was as cool as that going out. "The Star-Spangled Banner" caught him just starting down the aisle, and he stood there at ease.

"You're a little nervous," he had explained once at Stillman's gym, sitting on one of the benches behind the ring, "but not afraid. You know you can smother the other guy's leads and handle anything he can do. You're just a little nervous about fighting your best fight."

It was the best house in the Garden in a year, and you could feel it when Billy got into the ring. The wrangle over the last fight made it a natural rematch, and then Giardello said in the papers he was going to knock Billy out.

Joey started out like he meant it. Billy stuck out the left, and Giardello dropped the right over it, and a shout went up. He did it again, and then Billy tried to weave under as they planned and his nose banged into Giardello's head, and when he came up, there was the cut, right across the bridge, and the blood coming out of it and smearing on his nose and cheeks.

Blood always looks bad to the crowd, and when Billy lost the first two rounds they probably thought he was in for it. In the corner, Whitey did a real good job, closing the cut, while Irving and Freddie Brown, who was the other corner man, kept talking.

"Stop fighting this guy and box him," they kept telling Billy. "Get your jab moving and back him up with it and then move inside."

From the third round on, Billy started forcing it. He'd jab real stiff, turn in behind it to make Giardello miss the right, and then he'd bang to the body. By the middle of the fight it was a pro working on a kid.

"Young fighters don't hold their class," Billy said once, "because you have to build up to it. Over the years you build up your stamina, and you go ten rounds over and over and you learn pace."

Sure, Giardello made a fight of it. He's a strong kid and he'd land. In the fourth round he shifted to his left and caught Billy with a right-hand uppercut, and when he came on to take the tenth it was still close.

"Now forget the first ten rounds," Irving said to Billy in the corner. "You must win these next two."

"Sure, Irving," Billy said, looking at him. "Don't worry about it."

Billy just turned it on in the last two. Giardello was swinging instead of punching now, his arms pulling his body after them. And all the time Billy was fighting well, still on a straight line, making Giardello miss and hitting him inside and then rocking his head back. Now he could do the things they had worked on in camp because the pace and the distance were too much for Giardello, a kid who was just in there now on heart.

"And the winner by unanimous decision," Johnny Addie, the announcer, said, "Billy Graham!"

"Don't let anybody tell you otherwise," Billy said in the dressing room. "The kid's a real good fighter."

Dr. Nardiello put five stitches across his nose. Billy just lay down on the rubbing table with a couple of towels doubled under his head and the doctor trimmed the edges of the cut and put in the thread and Billy never moved.

"You don't need an anesthetic," Billy was explaining to them later. "You're still worked up from the fight, and you don't even feel it. You didn't see me move, did you? I'd move if it hurt."

"How Billy came down that stretch," one of the sportswriters said, as Billy was lying there and the doctor was stitching him, "like a thoroughbred."

With the newspapermen asking questions and the guys coming in to shake his hand, it was an hour before he got out of the Garden. Then Robbie drove him down to his dad's place, where there was a big mob and some of them had overflowed to the street.

He was standing there on the sidewalk. They were shaking his

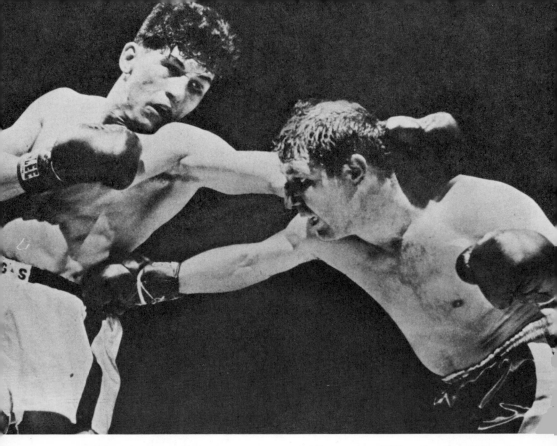

With Joey Giardello, Madison Square Garden, 1953. "When I was a fighter I wanted to give them their money's worth." (Wide World Photo.)

hand and clapping him on the back when Lorraine came out. He threw his arms around her and kissed her and together they walked into the crowded, smoky bar. When he came in, they let out a cheer.

"These," his brother Robbie said, "are his fans. These are the guys who bought the tickets for the four-rounders and the six-rounders and the eight rounds at the Broadway and the Ridgewood and the St. Nick's, and they've been with him ever since. These are the most important guys in the world."

He and Lorraine didn't get back to the hotel until five-thirty that morning, and around noon he and Irving went over to the Garden and picked up the check for $9,400. You take out the dough for the training camp and pay Whitey and take out the third for Irving and Jack and it leaves you about half. Three weeks later, if the nose heals all right and Irving can make another match, you take off again for camp.

After fourteen years of it, and 126 fights in which he was never once off his feet, Billy Graham retired. His skills had waned, and as he put it, he had become bored and disenchanted. A diminishing number, who still remember him, think of him as "The Uncrowned Champ," but I will always remember him as the professional, the honest workman who, more than the champions with their great gifts, represented the rest of us. That was why I wrote about him.

Now, their four children grown into adulthood, he and his wife Lorraine live in West Islip, on Long Island. For twenty-five years he has been a distiller's representative, with the same approach to this calling as he had to the old.

"When I was a fighter," he said, "I wanted to give them their

With restaurateur Uwe Paulsen, twenty-seven years later. "Today, when I get an order for a case, it makes me feel good." (Andrew McKeever.)

money's worth, whether they were for me or against me, and today they don't put the effort in. No matter what I did, I put the effort in, or I wouldn't feel right about it. Today, when I get an order for a case, it makes me feel good. It spurs me, because I'm earning my way."

"But don't you ever miss it," I said, meaning the boxing, "ever wish you were young and back in it again?"

"It's a feeling you can't reproduce in any other field," he said. "Not a lot, but two or three times a year, I'll find myself driving into the city, and what comes to my mind are not the big fights, but those smaller fights in that scramble to get to a main event. That's where it's all at."

7

The Rocky Road of Pistol Pete

"Down in Los Angeles," says Garry Schumacher, who was a New York baseball writer for thirty years and is now assistant to Horace Stoneham, president of the San Francisco Giants, "they think Duke Snider is the best center fielder the Dodgers ever had. They forget Pete Reiser. The Yankees think Mickey Mantle is something new. They forget Reiser, too."

Maybe Pete Reiser was the purest ballplayer of all time. I don't know. There is no exact way of measuring such a thing, but when a man of incomparable skills, with full knowledge of what he is doing, destroys those skills and puts his life on the line in the pursuit of his endeavor as no other man in his game ever has, perhaps he is the truest of them all.

"Is Pete Reiser there?" I said on the phone.

This was last season, in Kokomo. Kokomo has a population of about 50,000 and a ball club, now affiliated with Los Angeles and called the Dodgers, in the Class D Midwest League. Class D is the bottom of the barrel of organized baseball, and this was the second season that Pete Reiser had managed Kokomo.

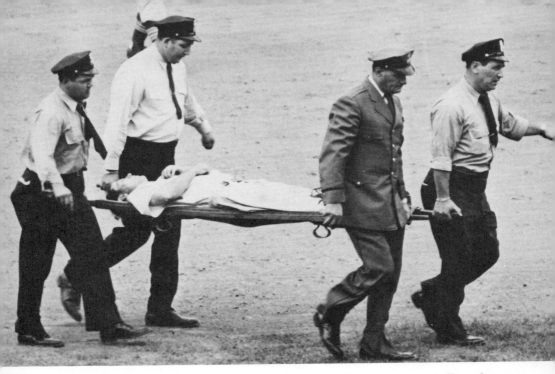

In two and a half years in the minors, three seasons of Army ball, and ten years in the majors, Pete Reiser was carried off the field eleven times. (UPI Photo.)

"He's not here right now," the woman's voice on the phone said. "The team played a double-header yesterday in Dubuque, and they didn't get in on the bus until four-thirty this morning. Pete just got up a few minutes ago and he had to go to the doctor's."

"Oh?" I said. "What has he done now?"

In two and a half years in the minors, three seasons of Army ball, and ten years in the majors, Pete Reiser was carried off the field eleven times. Nine times he regained consciousness either in the clubhouse or in the hospitals. He broke a bone in his right elbow, throwing. He broke both ankles, tore a cartilage in his left knee, ripped the muscles in his left leg, sliding. Seven times he crashed into outfield walls, dislocating his left shoulder, breaking his right collar bone and, five times, ending up in an unconscious heap on the ground. Twice he was beaned, and the few who remember still wonder today how great he might have been.

"I didn't see the old-timers," Bob Cooke, who is sports editor of the New York *Herald Tribune,* was saying recently, "but Pete Reiser was the best ballplayer I ever saw."

"We don't know what's wrong with him," the woman's voice on the phone said now. "He has a pain in his chest and he feels tired all the time, so we sent him to the doctor. There's a game tonight, so he'll be at the ball park about five o'clock."

Pete Reiser is thirty-nine years old now. The Cardinals signed him out of the St. Louis Municipal League when he was fifteen. For two years, because he was so young, he chauffeured for Charley Barrett, who was scouting the Midwest. They had a Cardinal uniform in the car for Pete, and he used to work out with the Class C and D clubs, and one day Branch Rickey, who was general manager of the Cardinals then, called Pete into his office in Sportsman's Park.

"Young man," he said, "you're the greatest young ballplayer I've ever seen, but there is one thing you must remember. Now that you're a professional ballplayer you're in show business. You will perform on the biggest stage in the world, the baseball diamond. Like the actors on Broadway, you'll be expected to put on a great performance every day, no matter how you feel, no matter whether it's too hot or too cold. Never forget that."

Rickey didn't know it at the time, but this was like telling Horatius that, as a professional soldier, he'd be expected someday to stand his ground. Three times Pete sneaked out of hospitals to play. Once he went back into the lineup after doctors warned him that any blow on the head would kill him. For four years he swung the bat and made the throws when it was painful for him just to shave and to comb his hair. In the 1947 World Series he stood on a broken ankle to pinch hit, and it ended with Rickey, then president of the Dodgers, begging him not to play and guaranteeing Pete his 1948 salary if he would just sit that season out.

"That might be the one mistake I made," Pete says now. "Maybe I should have rested that year."

"Pete Reiser?" Leo Durocher, who managed Pete at Brooklyn, was saying recently. "What's he doing now?"

"He's managing Kokomo," Lindsey Nelson, the TV sportscaster, said.

"Kokomo?" Leo said.

"That's right," Lindsey said. "He's riding the buses to places like Lafayette and Michigan City and Mattoon."

"On the buses," Leo said, shaking his head and then smiling at the thought of Pete.

"And some people say," Lindsey said, "that he was the greatest young ballplayer they ever saw."

"No doubt about it," Leo said. "He was the best I ever had, with the possible exception of Mays. At that, he was even faster than Willie." He paused. "So now he's on the buses."

The first time that Leo ever saw Pete on a ball field was in Clearwater that spring of '39. Pete had played one year of Class D in the Cardinal chain and one season of Class D for Brooklyn. Judge Kenesaw Mountain Landis, who was then baseball commissioner, had sprung Pete and seventy-two others from what they called the "Cardinal Chain Gang," and Pete had signed with Brooklyn for a hundred dollars.

"I didn't care about money then," Pete says, "I just wanted to play."

Pete had never been in a major league camp before, and he didn't know that at batting practice you hit in rotation. At Clearwater he was grabbing any bat that was handy and cutting in ahead of Ernie Koy or Dolph Camilli or one of the others, and Leo liked that.

One day Leo had a chest cold, so he told Pete to start at shortstop. His first time up he hit a homer off the Cards' Ken Raffensberger, and that was the beginning. He was on base his first twelve times at bat that spring, with three homers, five singles, and four walks. His first time against Detroit he homered off Tommy Bridges. His first time against the Yankees he put one over the fence off Lefty Gomez.

Durocher played Pete at shortstop in thirty-three games that spring. The Dodgers barnstormed North with the Yankees, and one night Joe McCarthy, who was managing the Yankees, sat down next to Pete on the train.

"Reiser," he said, "you're going to play for me."

"How can I play for you?" Pete said. "I'm with the Dodgers."

"We'll get you," McCarthy said. "I'll tell Ed Barrow, and you'll be a Yankee."

The Yankees offered $100,000 and five ballplayers for Pete. The Dodgers turned it down, and the day the season opened at Ebbets Field, Larry MacPhail, who was running things in Brooklyn, called Pete on the clubhouse phone and told him to report to Elmira.

"It was an hour before game time," Pete says, "and I started to take off my uniform and I was shaking all over. Leo came in and said, 'What's the matter? You scared?' I said, 'No. MacPhail is sending me to Elmira.' Leo got on the phone and they had a hell of a fight. Leo said he'd quit, and MacPhail said he'd fire him—and I went to Elmira.

"One day I'm making a throw and I heard something pop. Every day my arm got weaker and they sent me to Johns Hopkins and took X rays. Dr. George Bennett told me, 'Your arm's broken.' When I came to after the operation, my throat was sore and there was an ice pack on it. I said, 'What happened? Your knife slip?' They said, 'We took your tonsils out while we were operating on your arm.'"

Pete's arm was in a cast from the first of May until the end of July. His first two weeks out of the cast he still couldn't straighten the arm, but a month later he played ten games as a left-handed outfielder until Dr. Bennett stopped him.

"But I can't straighten my right arm," Pete said.

"Take up bowling," the doctor said.

When he bowled, though, Pete used first one arm and then the other. Every day that the weather allowed he went out into the back yard and practiced throwing a rubber ball left-handed against a wall. Then he went to Fairgrounds Park and worked on the long throw, left-handed, with a baseball.

"At Clearwater that next spring," he said, "Leo saw me in the outfield throwing left-handed, and he said, 'What do you think you're doin'?' I said, 'Hell, I had to be ready. Now I can throw as good with my left arm as I could with my right.' He said, 'You can do more things as a right-handed ballplayer. I can bring you into the infield. Go out there and cut loose with that right arm.' I did and it was okay, but I had that insurance."

So at five o'clock I took a cab from the hotel in Kokomo to the ball park on the edge of town. It seats about 2,200—1,500 in the white-painted fairgrounds grandstand along the first base line, and the rest in chairs behind the screen and in bleachers along the other line.

I watched them take batting practice: trim, strong young kids with their dreams, I knew, of someday getting up there where Pete once was, and I listened to their kidding. I watched the grounds-keeper open the concession booth and clean out the electric pop-corn machine. I read the signs on the outfield walls, advertising the Mid-West Towel and Linen Service, Basil's Nite Club, The Hoosier Iron Works, UAW Local 292, and the Around the Clock Pizza Cafe. I watched the Dubuque kids climbing out of their bus, carrying their uniforms on wire coat hangers.

"Here comes Pete now," I heard the old guy setting up the ticket box at the gate say.

When Pete came through the gate he was walking like an old man. In 1941, the Dodgers trained in Havana, and one day they clocked him, in his baseball uniform and regular spikes, at 9.8 for 100 yards. Five years later the Cleveland Indians were bragging about George Case and the Washington Senators had Gil Coan. The Dodgers offered to bet a thousand dollars that Reiser was the fastest man in baseball, and now it was taking him forever to walk to me, his shoulders stooped, his whole body heavier now, and Pete just slowly moving one foot ahead of the other.

"Hello," he said, shaking hands but his face solemn. "How are you?"

"Fine," I said, "but what's the matter with you?"

"I guess it's my heart," he said.

"When did you first notice this?"

"About eleven days ago. I guess I was working out too hard. All of a sudden I felt this pain in my chest and I got weak. I went into the clubhouse and lay down on the bench, but I've had the same pain and I'm weak ever since."

"What did the doctor say?"

"He says it's lucky I stopped that day when I did. He says I should be in a hospital right now, because if I exert myself or even make a quick motion I might go—just like that."

He snapped his fingers. "He scared me," he said. "I'll admit it. I'm scared."

"What are you planning to do?"

"I'm going home to St. Louis. My wife works for a doctor there, and he'll know a good heart specialist."

"When will you leave?"

"Well, I can't just leave the ball club. I called Brooklyn, and they're sending a replacement for me, but he won't be here until tomorrow."

"How will you get to St. Louis?"

"It's about three hundred miles," Pete says. "The doctor says I shouldn't fly or go by train, because if anything happens to me they can't stop and help me. I guess I'll have to drive."

"I'll drive you," I said.

Trying to get to sleep in the hotel that night I was thinking that maybe, standing there in that little ball park, Pete Reiser had admitted out loud for the first time in his life that he was scared. I was thinking of 1941, his first full year with the Dodgers. He was beaned twice and crashed his first wall and still hit .343 to be the first rookie and the youngest ballplayer to win the National League batting title. He tied Johnny Mize with thirty-nine doubles, led in triples, runs scored, total bases, and slugging average, and they were writing on the sports pages that he might be the new Ty Cobb.

"Dodgers Win On Reiser HR," the headlines used to say. "Reiser Stars As Brooklyn Lengthens Lead."

"Any manager in the National League," Arthur Patterson wrote one day in the New York *Herald Tribune*, "would give up his best man to obtain Pete Reiser. On every bench they're talking about him. Rival players watch him take his cuts during batting practice, announce when he's going to make a throw to the plate or third base during outfield drill. They just whistle their amazement when he scoots down the first base line on an infield dribbler or a well-placed bunt."

He was beaned the first time at Ebbets Field five days after the season started. A sidearm fastball got away from Ike Pearson of the Phillies, and Pete came to at eleven-thirty that night in Peck Memorial Hospital.

"I was lying in bed with my uniform on," he told me once, "and I couldn't figure it out. The room was dark, with just a little night light, and then I saw a mirror and I walked over to it and lit the light and I had a black eye and a black streak down the side of my nose. I said to myself, 'What happened to me?' Then I remembered.

109

"I took a shower and walked around the room, and the next morning the doctor came in. He looked me over, and he said, 'We'll keep you here for five or six more days under observation.' I said, 'Why?' He said, 'You've had a serious head injury. If you tried to get out of bed right now, you'd fall down.' I said, 'If I can get up and walk around this room, can I get out?' The doc said, 'All right, but you won't be able to do it.'"

Pete got out of bed, the doctor standing ready to catch him. He walked around the room. "I've been walkin' the floor all night," Pete said.

The doctor made Pete promise that he wouldn't play ball for a week, but Pete went right to the ball park. He got a seat behind the Brooklyn dugout, and Durocher spotted him.

"How do you feel?" Leo said.

"Not bad," Pete said.

"Get your uniform on," Leo said.

"I'm not supposed to play," Pete said.

"I'm not gonna play you," Leo said. "Just sit on the bench. It'll make our guys feel better to see that you're not hurt."

Pete suited up and went out and sat on the bench. In the eighth inning it was tied 7–7. The Dodgers had the bases loaded, and there was Ike Pearson again, coming in to relieve.

"Pistol," Leo said to Pete, "get the bat."

In the press box the baseball writers watched Pete. They wanted to see if he'd stand right in there. After a beaning they are all entitled to shy, and many of them do. Pete hit the first pitch into the center field stands, and Brooklyn won, 11–7.

"I could just barely trot around the bases," Pete said when I asked him about it. "I was sure dizzy."

Two weeks later they were playing the Cardinals, and Enos Slaughter hit one and Pete turned in center field and started to run. He made the catch, but he hit his head and his tailbone on that corner near the exit gate.

His head was cut, and when he came back to the bench they also saw blood coming through the seat of his pants. They took him into the clubhouse and pulled his pants down and the doctor put a metal clamp on the cut.

"Just don't slide," he told Pete. "You can get it sewed up after the game."

In August of that year big Paul Erickson was pitching for the Cubs and Pete took another one. Again he woke up in a hospital. The Dodgers were having some pretty good beanball contests with the Cubs that season, and Judge Landis came to see Pete the next day.

"Do you think that man tried to bean you?" he asked Pete.

"No sir," Pete said. "I lost the pitch."

"I was there," Landis said, "and I heard them holler, 'Stick it in his ear!'"

"That was just bench talk," Pete said. "I lost the pitch."

He left the hospital the next morning. The Dodgers were going to St. Louis after the game, and Pete didn't want to be left in Chicago.

Pete always says that the next year, 1942, was the year of his downfall, and the worst of it happened on one play. It was early July and Pete and the Dodgers were tearing the league apart. Starting in Cincinnati he got 19 for 21. In a Sunday double-header in Chicago he went 5 for 5 in the first game, walked three times in the second game, and got a hit the one time they pitched to him. He was hitting .391, and they were writing in the papers that he might end up hitting .400.

When they came into St. Louis the Dodgers were leading by ten and a half games. When they took off for Pittsburgh they left three games of that lead and Pete Reiser behind them.

"We were in the twelfth inning, no score, two outs, and Slaughter hit it off Whit Wyatt," Pete says. "It was over my head and I took off. I caught it and missed that flagpole by two inches and hit the wall and dropped the ball. I had the instinct to throw it to Peewee Reese, and we just missed gettin' Slaughter at the plate, and they won, 1–0.

"I made one step to start off the field and I woke up the next morning in St. John's Hospital. My head was bandaged, and I had an awful headache."

Dr. Robert Hyland, who was Pete's personal physician, announced to the newspapers that Pete would be out for the rest of the season. "Look, Pete," Hyland told him. "I'm your personal friend. I'm advising you not to play any more baseball this year."

"I don't like hospitals, though," Pete was telling me once, "so after two days I took the bandage off and got up. The room started to spin, but I got dressed and I took off. I snuck out, and I took a train to Pittsburgh and I went to the park.

"Leo saw me and he said, 'Go get your uniform on, Pistol.' I said, 'Not tonight, Skipper.' Leo said, 'Aw, I'm not gonna let you hit. I want these guys to see you. It'll give 'em that little spark they need. Besides, it'll change the pitching plans on that other bench when they see you sittin' here in uniform.'"

In the fourteenth inning the Dodgers had a runner on second and Ken Heintzelman, the left-hander, came in for the Pirates. He walked Johnny Rizzo, and Durocher had run out of pinch hitters.

"Damn," Leo was saying, walking up and down. "I want to win this one. Who can I use? Anybody here who can hit?"

Pete walked up to the bat rack. He pulled out his stick. "You got yourself a hitter," he said to Leo.

He walked up there and hit a line drive over the second baseman's head that was good for three bases. The two runs scored, and Pete rounded first base and collapsed.

"When I woke up I was in a hospital again," he says. "I could just make out that somebody was standin' there and then I saw it was Leo. He said, 'You awake?' I said, 'Yep.' He said, 'By God, we beat 'em! How do you feel?' I said, 'How do you think I feel?' He said, 'Aw, you're better with one leg and one eye than anybody else I've got.' I said, 'Yeah, and that's the way I'll end up—on one leg and with one eye.'

"I'd say I lost the pennant for us that year," Pete says now, although he still hit .310 for the season. "I was dizzy most of the time and I couldn't see fly balls. I mean balls I could have put in my pocket, I couldn't get near. Once in Brooklyn when Mort Cooper was pitching for the Cards I was seeing two baseballs coming up there. Babe Pinelli was umpiring behind the plate, and a couple of times he stopped the game and asked me if I was all right. So the Cards beat us out the last two days of the season."

The business office of the Kokomo ball club is the dining room of a man named Jim Deets, who sells insurance and is also the business manager of the club. His wife, in addition to keeping house, mothering six small kids, boarding Pete, an outfielder from Venezuela, and a shortstop from the Dominican Republic, is also the club secretary.

The Rocky Road of Pistol Pete

"How do you feel this morning?" I asked Pete. He was sitting at the dining room table, in a sweat shirt and a pair of light-brown slacks, typing the game report of the night before to send it to Brooklyn.

"A little better," he said.

Pete has a worn, green, seven-year-old Chevy, and it took us eight and a half hours to get to St. Louis. I'd ask him how the pain in his chest was and he'd say that it wasn't bad or it wasn't so good, and I'd get him to talking again about Durocher or about his time in the Army. Pete played under five managers at Brooklyn, Boston, Pittsburgh, and Cleveland, and Durocher is his favorite.

"He has a great mind, and not just for baseball," Pete said. "Once he sat down to play gin with Jack Benny, and after they'd played four cards Leo read Benny's whole hand to him. Benny said, 'How can you do that?' Leo said, 'If you're playin' your cards right, and I give you credit for that, you have to be holding those others.' Benny said, 'I don't want to play with this guy.'

"One spring at Clearwater there was a pool table in a room off the lobby. One night Hugh Casey and a couple of other guys and I were talking with Leo. We said, 'Gee, there's a guy in there and we've been playin' pool with him for a couple of nights, but last night he had a real hot streak.' Leo said, 'How much he take you for?' We figured it out and it was two thousand dollars. Leo said, 'Point him out to me.'

"We went in and pointed the guy out and Leo walked up to him and said, 'Put all your money on the table. We're gonna shoot for it.' The guy said, 'I never play like that.' Leo said, 'You will tonight. Pick your own game.' Leo took him for four thousand dollars, and then he threw him out. Then he paid us back what we'd gone for, and he said, 'Now, let that be a lesson. That guy is a hustler from New York. The next time it happens I won't bail you out.' Leo hadn't had a cue in his hands for years."

It was amazing that they took Pete into the Army. He had wanted to enlist in the Navy, but the doctors looked him over and told him none of the services could accept him. Then his draft board sent him to Jefferson Barracks in the winter of 1943, and the doctors there turned him down.

"I'm sittin' on a bench with the other guys who've been rejected," he was telling me, "and a captain comes in and says, 'Which one of you is Reiser?' I stood up and I said, 'I am.' In front of everybody he said, 'So you're trying to pull a fast one, are you? At a time like this, with a war going on, you came in here under a false name. What do you mean, giving your name as Harold Patrick Reiser? Your name's Pete Reiser, and you're the ballplayer, aren't you?' I said, 'I'm the ballplayer and they call me Pete, but my right name is Harold Patrick Reiser.' The captain says, 'I apologize. Sergeant, fingerprint him. This man is in.'"

They sent him to Fort Riley, Kansas. It was early April and raining and they were on bivouac, and Pete woke up in a hospital. "What happened?" he said.

"You've got pneumonia," the doctor said. "You've been a pretty sick boy for six days. You'll be all right, but we've been looking you over. How did you ever get into this Army?"

"When I get out of the hospital," Pete was telling me, "I'm on the board for a discharge and I'm waitin' around for about a week, and still nobody there knows who I am. All of a sudden one morning a voice comes over the bitch box in the barracks. It says, 'Private Reiser, report to headquarters immediately.' I think, 'Well, I'm out now.'

"I go over there and the colonel wants to see me. I walk in and give my good salute and he says, 'Sit down, Harold.' I sit down and he says, 'Your name really isn't Harold, is it?' I say, 'Yes it is, sir.' He says, 'But that isn't what they call you when you're well known, is it? You're Pete Reiser the ballplayer, aren't you?' I say, 'Yes, sir.' He says, 'I thought so. Now, I've got your discharge papers right there, but we've got a pretty good ball club and we'd like you on it. We'll make a deal. You say nothing, and you won't have to do anything but play ball. How about it?' I said, 'Suppose I don't want to stay in?' He picked my papers up off his desk, and he tore 'em right up in my face. I can still hear that 'zip' when he tore 'em. He said, 'You see, you have no choice.'

"Then he picked up the phone and said something and in a minute a general came in. I jumped up and the colonel said, 'Don't bother to salute, Pete.' Then he said to the general, 'Major, this is Pete Reiser, the great Dodger ballplayer. He was up for a medical discharge, but he's decided to stay here and play ball for us.'

"So the general says, 'My, what a patriotic thing for you to do, young man. That's wonderful. Wonderful.' I'm sittin' there, and when the general goes out the colonel says, 'That major, he's all right.' I said, 'But he's a general. How come you call him a major?' The colonel says, 'Well, in the regular Army he's a major and I'm a full colonel. The only reason I don't outrank him now is that I've got heart trouble. He knows it, but I never let him forget it. I always call him major.' I thought, 'What kind of an Army am I in?'"

Joe Gantenbein, the Athletics' outfielder and George Scharein, the Phillies' infielder, were on that team with Pete, and they won the state and national semipro titles. By the time the season was over, however, the order came down to hold up all discharges.

The next season there were seventeen major league ballplayers on the Fort Riley club, and they played four nights a week for the war workers in Wichita. Pete hit a couple of walls, and the team made such a joke of the national semipro tournament that an order came down from Washington to break up the club.

"Considering what a lot of guys did in the war," Pete says, "I had no complaints, but five times I was up for discharge, and each time something happened. From Riley they sent me to Camp Livingston. From there they sent me to New York Special Services for twelve hours and I end up in Camp Lee, Virginia, in May 1945.

"The first one I meet there is the general. He says, 'Reiser, I saw you on the list and I just couldn't pass you up.' I said, 'What about my discharge?' He says, 'That will have to wait. I have a lot of celebrities down here, but I want a good baseball team.'"

Johnny Lindell, of the Yankees, and Dave Philley, of the White Sox, were on the club and Pete played left field. Near the end of the season he went after a foul fly for the third out of the last inning, and he went right through a temporary wooden fence and rolled down a twenty-five-foot embankment.

"I came to in the hospital with a dislocated right shoulder," he says, "and the general came over to see me and he said, 'That was one of the greatest displays of courage I've ever seen, to ignore your future in baseball just to win a ball game for Camp Lee.' I said, 'Thanks.'

"Now it's November and the war is over, but they're still shippin' guys out, and I'm on the list to go. I report to the overseas major, and he looks at my papers and says, 'I can't send you overseas.

With everything that's wrong with you, you shouldn't even be in this Army. I'll have you out in three hours.' In three hours, sure enough, I've got those papers in my hand, stamped, and I'm startin' out the door. Runnin' up to me comes a Red Cross guy. He says, 'I can get you some pretty good pension benefits for the physical and mental injuries you've sustained.' I said, 'You can?' He said, 'Yes, you're entitled to them.' I said, 'Good. You get 'em. You keep 'em. I'm goin' home.'"

When we got to St. Louis that night I drove Pete to his house and the next morning I picked him up and drove him to see the heart specialist. He was in there for two hours, and when he came out he was walking slower than ever.

"No good," he said. "I have to go to the hospital for five days for observation."

"What does he think?"

"He says I'm done puttin' on that uniform, I'll have to get a desk job."

Riding to the hospital I wondered if that heart specialist knew who he was tying to that desk job. In 1946, the year he came out of the Army, Pete led the league when he stole thirty-four bases, thirteen more than the runner-up Johnny Hopp of the Braves. He also set a major league record that still stands, when he stole home seven times.

"Eight times," he said once. "In Chicago I stole home and Magerkurth hollered, 'You're out!' Then he dropped his voice and he said, '. . . ! I missed it.' He'd already had his thumb in the air. I had eight out of eight."

I suppose somebody will beat that someday, but he'll never top the way Pete did it. That was the year he knocked himself out again making a diving catch, dislocated his left shoulder, ripped the muscles in his left leg, and broke his left ankle.

"Whitey Kurowski hit one in the seventh inning at Ebbets Field," he was telling me. "I dove for it and woke up in the clubhouse. I was in Peck Memorial for four days. It really didn't take much to knock me out in those days. I was comin' apart all over. When I dislocated my shoulder they popped it back in, and Leo said, 'Hell, you'll be all right. You don't throw with it anyway.'"

That was the year the Dodgers tied with the Cardinals for the

He set a major league record that still stands when, in 1946, he stole home seven times. (UPI Photo.)

pennant and dropped the play-off. Pete wasn't there for those two games. He was in Peck Memorial again.

"I'd pulled a charley horse in my left leg," Pete was saying. "It's the last two weeks of the season, and I'm out for four days. We've got the winning run on third, two outs in the ninth, and Leo sends me up. He says, 'If you don't hit it good, don't run and hurt your leg.'

"The first pitch was a knockdown and, when I ducked, the ball hit the bat and went down the third base line, as beautiful a bunt as you've ever seen. Well, Ebbets Field is jammed. Leo has said, 'Don't run.' But this is a big game. I take off for first, and we win and I've ripped the muscles from my ankle to my hip. Leo says, 'You shouldn't have done it.'

"Now it's the last three days of the season and we're a game ahead of the Cards and we're playin' the Phillies in Brooklyn. Leo says to me, 'It's now or never. I don't think we can win it without you.' The first two up are outs and I single to right. There's Charley Dressen, coachin' on third, with the steal sign. I start to get my lead, and a pitcher named Charley Schanz is workin' and he throws

117

an ordinary lob over to first. My leg is stiff and I slide and my heel spike catches the bag and I hear it snap.

"Leo comes runnin' out. He says, 'Come on. You're all right.' I said, 'I think it's broken.' He says, 'It ain't stickin' out.' They took me to Peck Memorial, and it was broken."

We went to St. Luke's Hospital in St. Louis. In the main office they told Pete to go over to a desk where a gray-haired, semistout woman was sitting at a typewriter. She started to book Pete in, typing his answer on the form. "What is your occupation, Mr. Reiser?" she said.

"Baseball," Pete said.

"Have you ever been hospitalized before?"

"Yes," Pete said.

In 1946, the Dodgers played an exhibition game in Springfield, Missouri. When the players got off the train there was a young radio announcer there, and he was grabbing them one at a time and asking them where they thought they'd finish that year.

"In first place," Reese and Casey and Dixie Walker and the rest were saying. "On top." "We'll win it."

"And here comes Pistol Pete Reiser!" the announcer said. "Where do you think you'll finish this season, Pete?"

"In Peck Memorial Hospital," Pete said.

After the 1946 season Brooklyn changed the walls at Ebbets Field. They added boxes, cutting 40 feet off left field and dropping center field from 420 to 390 feet. Pete had made a real good start that season in center, and on June 5 the Dodgers were leading the Pirates by three runs in the sixth inning when Culley Rikard hit one.

"I made my turn and ran," Pete says, "and, where I thought I still had that thirty feet, I didn't."

"The crowd," Al Laney wrote the next day in the New York *Herald Tribune*, "which watched silently while Reiser was being carried away, did not know that he had held onto the ball . . . Rikard circled the bases, but Butch Henline, the umpire, who ran to Reiser, found the ball still in Reiser's glove. . . . Two outs were posted on the scoreboard after play was resumed. Then the crowd let out a tremendous roar."

In the Brooklyn clubhouse the doctor called for a priest, and the last rites of the Church were administered to Pete. He came to, but lapsed into unconsciousness again and woke up at 3 A.M. in Peck Memorial.

For eight days he couldn't move. After three weeks they let him out, and he made the next western trip with the Dodgers. In Pittsburgh he was working out in the outfield before the game when Clyde King, chasing a fungo, ran into him and Pete woke up in the clubhouse.

"I went back to the Hotel Schenley and lay down," he says. "After the game I got up and had dinner with Peewee. We were sittin' on the porch, and I scratched my head and I felt a lump there about as big as half a golf ball. I told Peewee to feel it and he said, 'Gosh!' I said, 'I don't think that's supposed to be like that.' He said, 'Hell, no.'"

Pete went up to Rickey's room and Rickey called his pilot and had Pete flown to Johns Hopkins in Baltimore. They operated on him for a blood clot.

"You're lucky," the doctor told him. "If it had moved just a little more you'd have been gone."

Pete was unable to hold even a pencil. He had double vision and, when he tried to take a single step, he became dizzy. He stayed for three weeks and then went home for almost a month.

"It was August," he said, "and Brooklyn was fightin' for another pennant. I thought if I could play the last two months it might make the difference, so I went back to Johns Hopkins. The doctor said, 'You've made a remarkable recovery.' I said, 'I want to play.' He said, 'I can't okay that. The slightest blow on the head can kill you.'"

Pete played. He worked out for four days, pinch-hit a couple of times and then, in the Polo Grounds, made a diving catch in left field. They carried him off, and in the clubhouse he was unable to recognize anyone.

Pete was still having dizzy spells when the Dodgers went into the 1947 Series against the Yankees. In the third game he walked in the first inning, got the steal sign and, when he went into second, felt his right ankle snap. At the hospital they found it was broken.

"Just tape it, will you?" Pete said.

"I want to put a cast on it," the doctor said.

"If you do," Pete said, "they'll give me a dollar-a-year contract next season."

The next day he was back on the bench. Bill Bevens was pitching for the Yankees and, with two out in the ninth, it looked like he was going to pitch the first no-hitter in World Series history.

"Aren't you going to volunteer to hit?" Burt Shotton, who was managing Brooklyn, said to Pete.

Al Gionfriddo was on second and Bucky Harris, who was managing the Yankees, ordered Pete walked. Eddie Miksis ran for him, and when Cookie Lavagetto hit that double, the two runs scored and Brooklyn won, 3–2.

"The next day," Pete says, "the sportswriters were second-guessing Harris for putting me on when I represented the winning run. Can you imagine what they'd have said if they knew I had a broken ankle?"

At the end of that season Rickey had the outfield walls at Ebbets Field padded with one-inch foam rubber for Pete, but he never hit them again. He had headaches most of the time and played little. Then he was traded to Boston, and in two seasons there he hit the wall a couple of times. Twice his left shoulder came out while he was making diving catches. Pittsburgh picked Pete up in 1951, and the next year he played into July with Cleveland and that was the end of it.

Between January and September 1953, Pete dropped forty thousand dollars in the used car business in St. Louis, and then he got a job in a lumber mill for a hundred dollars a week. In the winter of 1955, he wrote Brooklyn asking for a part-time job as a scout, and on March 1, Buzzy Bavasi, the Dodger vice-president, called him on the phone.

"How would you like a manager's job?" Buzzy said.

"I'll take it," Pete said.

"I haven't even told you where it is. It's Thomasville, Georgia, in Class D."

"I don't care," Pete said. "I'll take it."

At Vero Beach that spring, Mike Gaven wrote a piece about Pete in the New York *Journal American*.

"Even in the worn gray uniform of the Class D Thomasville, Georgia, club," Mike wrote, "Pete Reiser looks, acts, and talks like a big leaguer. The Dodgers pitied Pete when they saw him starting his comeback effort after not having handled a ball for two and a half years. They lowered their heads when they saw him in a chow line with a lot of other bushers, but the old Pistol held his head high. . . ."

The next spring, Sid Friedlander, of the New York *Post,* saw Pete at Vero and wrote a column about him managing Kokomo. The last thing I saw about him in the New York papers was a small item out of Tipton, Indiana, saying that the bus carrying the Kokomo team had collided with a car and Pete was in a hospital in Kokomo with a back injury.

"Managing," Pete was saying in that St. Louis hospital, "you try to find out how your players are thinking. At Thomasville one night one of my kids made a bad throw. After the game I said to him, 'What were you thinking while that ball was coming to you?' He said, 'I was saying to myself that I hoped I could make a good throw.' I said, 'Sit down.' I tried to explain to him the way you have to think. You know how I used to think?"

"Yes," I said, "but you tell me."

"I was always sayin', 'Hit it to me. Just hit it to me. I'll make the catch. I'll make the throw.' When I was on base I was always lookin' over and sayin', 'Give me the steal sign. Give me the sign. Let me go.' That's the way you have to think."

"Pete," I said, "now that it's all over, do you ever think that if you hadn't played it as hard as you did, there's no telling how great you might have been or how much money you might have made?"

"Never," Pete said. "It was my way of playin'. If I hadn't played that way I wouldn't even have been whatever I was. God gave me those legs and the speed, and when they took me into the walls that's the way it had to be. I couldn't play any other way."

A technician came in with an electrocardiograph. She was a thin, dark-haired woman and she set it up by the bed and attached one of the round metal disks to Pete's left wrist and started to attach another to his left ankle.

"Aren't you kind of young to be having pains in your chest?" she said.

"I've led a fast life," Pete said.

On the way back to New York I kept thinking how right Pete

was. To tell a man who is this true that there is another way for him to do it is to speak a lie. You cannot ask him to change his way of going, because it makes him what he is.

Three days after I got home I had a message to call St. Louis. I heard the phone ring at the other end and Pete answered. "I'm out!" he said.

"Did they let you out, or did you sneak out again?" I said.

"They let me out," he said. "It's just a strained heart muscle, I guess. My heart itself is all right."

"That's wonderful."

"I can manage again. In a couple of days I can go back to Kokomo."

If his voice had been higher he would have sounded like a kid at Christmas.

"What else did they say?" I said.

"Well, they say I have to take it easy."

"Do me a favor," I said.

"What?"

"Take their advice. This time, please take it easy."

Reiser sidelined with broken bones in 1946. (UPI Photo.)

"I will," he said. "I'll take it easy."

If he does it will be the first time.

Twenty years passed before I saw him again, and then I found him in another hospital, St. Anthony's in St. Petersburg, Florida. He had had a heart attack in 1964, but he was with the Chicago Cubs now, working with young ballplayers out of high schools and colleges in an extension of spring training, until two days before, bronchial pneumonia and a heart murmur put him flat on his back once more.

"What," I asked him, "are these kids like who come up today?"

His breathing was clouded and labored, and when he spoke he exhaled the sentences, his voice husky and almost inaudible. I had suggested that I stop by again when he would be feeling better, but he had said that he would rather talk than just stare at the walls.

"You get all kinds," he said.

"You don't think the world is going down the drain because of the younger generation?"

"Hell, no," he said, stopping for breath. "I see too many good ones. It's so much easier to write about kids doing bad things, than about kids doing good things for others."

"When I wrote about you managing in Kokomo," I said, "I told about the time one of your kids had made a bad throw. You asked him what he was thinking while the ball was coming to him, and he said, 'I was saying to myself that I hoped I could make a good throw.'"

"That's right," he said.

"Then you told him how, when you were playing, you used to be saying, 'Hit it to me. Just hit it to me. I'll make the catch. I'll make the throw. Give me the steal sign. I'll go!'"

"That's right," he said. "You have to think positive. I try to tell them that."

"So after the story ran," I said, "I got a letter from a father. He said that he had sat his own kid down and he'd read that to him, and he thanked me. I wrote him back, saying that I appreciated his letter but that he shouldn't thank me. He should thank Pete Reiser."

Scouting for the Chicago Cubs thirty-five years later.
(John Emig.)

"You try to tell these kids," he said, breathing it again, "and one of them said to me, 'I didn't know you played major league ball.'"

Two days later he left the hospital and flew to Thousand Palms, California, to where he and his wife had recently moved. When, over the years since, we would talk on the phone, I would find him having his good days and his bad and in and out of the hospital. He was still with the Cubs, scouting high schools, junior colleges and colleges, and covering the professionals in the Pacific Coast League and the California State League, and always looking, I suppose, for we all do, for an extension of himself.

"So how are you doing?" I asked him the last time we talked. "Have you found a real good one?"

"There's one I've got my eye on," he said, "but other people have their eye on him too. Who knows? It's the luck of the draw."

It would have been some luck and some draw if he had found another Pete Reiser, but it was not to be. He was sixty-two when, on October 25, 1981, that respiratory illness put him down for the last time.

8

Brownsville Bum

It's a funny thing about people. People will hate a guy all his life for what he is, but the minute he dies for it they make him out a hero and they go around saying that maybe he wasn't such a bad guy after all because he sure was willing to go the distance for whatever he believed or whatever he was.

That's the way it was with Bummy Davis. The night Bummy fought Fritzie Zivic in the Garden and Zivic started giving him the business and Bummy hit Zivic low maybe thirty times and kicked the referee, they wanted to hang him for it. The night those four guys came into Dudy's bar and tried the same thing, only with rods, Bummy went nuts again. He flattened the first one and then they shot him, and when everybody read about it, and how Bummy fought guns with only his left hook and died lying in the rain in front of the place, they all said that was really something and you sure had to give him credit at that.

"So you're Al Davis?" one of the hoods said. "Why, you punch-drunk bum."

What did they expect Bummy to do? What did they expect him to do the night Zivic gave him the thumbs and the laces and walked around the referee and belted Bummy? Bummy could hook too good ever to learn how to hold himself in, if you want the truth of it.

That was really the trouble with Bummy. Bummy blew school too early, and he didn't know enough words. A lot of guys who

126

fought Zivic used to take it or maybe beef to the referee, but Bummy didn't know how to do that. A lot of guys looking at four guns would have taken the talk and been thinking about getting the number off the car when it pulled away, but all Bummy ever had was his hook.

Bummy came out of Brownsville. In the sports pages they are always referring to Brownsville as the fistic incubator of Brooklyn, because they probably mean that a lot of fighters come out of there. Murder, Inc., came out of there, too, and if you don't believe it ask Bill O'Dwyer. If it wasn't for Brownsville maybe Bill O'Dwyer wouldn't have become the mayor of New York.

The peculiar thing about Brownsville is that it doesn't look so tough. There are trees around there and some vacant lots, and the houses don't look as bad as they do over on Second Avenue or Ninth Avenue or up in Harlem. Don't tell Charley Beecher, though, that you don't think it's so tough.

"What's the matter you sold the place?" Froike said to Charley the other day. "It ain't the same, now you sold it."

Charley Beecher used to run the poolroom with the gym behind it on the corner of Georgia and Livonia where Bummy used to train. It was a good little gym with a little dressing room and a shower, and Charley was a pretty good featherweight in the twenties, and his brother, Willie, who was even a better fighter, fought Abe Attell and Johnny Dundee and Jack Britton and Leach Cross and Knockout Brown.

"For seventeen years I was in business," Charley said. "Seventeen times they stuck me up."

He looked at Froike, and then he pointed with his two hands at his mouth and his ears and his eyes.

"I had guns here and here and here," he said. "All I ever saw was guns."

The worst part was that Charley knew all the guys. A week after they'd heist him they'd be back for a little contribution, maybe a C-note. They'd be getting up bail for one of the boys, and they just wanted Charley to know there were no hard feelings about the heist, and that as long as he kept his dues up they'd still consider him friendly to the club. That's how tough Brownsville was.

Bummy had two brothers, and they were a big help. They were a lot older than Bummy, and the one they called Little Gangy and the other they called Duff. Right now Gangy is doing twenty to forty, just to give you an idea, and Bummy took a lot of raps for them too because there were some people who couldn't get back at Gangy and Duff so they took it out on the kid.

When Bummy was about seven his father used to run a candy and cigar store and did a little speaking on the side. In other words, he always had a bottle in the place, and he had Bummy hanging around in case anybody should say cop. When the signal would go up Bummy would run behind the counter and grab the bottle, and he was so small nobody could see him over the counter and he'd go out the back.

One day Bummy was going it down the street with the bottle under his coat and some real smart guy stuck out his foot. Bummy tripped and the bottle broke, and Bummy looked at the bottle and the whiskey running on the sidewalk and at the guy and his eyes got big and he started to scream. The guy just laughed and Bummy was lying right on the sidewalk in the whiskey and broken glass, hitting his head on the sidewalk and banging his fists down and screaming. A crowd came around and they watched Bummy, with the guy laughing at him, and they shook their heads and they said this youngest Davidoff kid must be crazy at that.

Davidoff was his straight name. Abraham Davidoff. In Yiddish they made Abraham into Ahvron and then Ahvron they sometimes make Boomy. All his family called him Boomy, so you can see they didn't mean it as a knock. The one who changed it to Bummy was Johnny Attell.

Johnny Attell used to run the fights at the Ridgewood Grove, a fight club in Brooklyn where some good fighters like Sid Terris and Ruby Goldstein and Tony Canzoneri learned to fight, and Johnny and a nice guy named Lew Burston managed Bummy. When Bummy turned pro and Johnny made up the show card for the fight with Frankie Reese he put the name on it as Al (Bummy) Davis, and when Bummy saw it he went right up to Johnny's office.

"What are you doing that for?" he hollered at Johnny. "I don't want to be called Bummy."

"Take it easy," Johnny said. "You want to make money fighting, don't you? People like to come to fights to see guys they think are tough."

They sure liked to come to see Bummy all right. They sure liked to come to see him get his brains knocked out.

The first time Johnny Attell ever heard of Bummy was one day when Johnny was coming out of the Grove and Froike stopped him. Froike used to run the gym at Beecher's and handle kids in the amateurs, and he was standing there talking to Johnny under the Myrtle Avenue El.

"Also I got a real good ticket seller for you," he said to Johnny after a while.

"I could use one," Johnny said.

"Only I have to have a special for him," Froike said. "No eliminations."

"What's his name?" Johnny said.

"Giovanni Pasconi," Froike said.

"Bring him around," Johnny said.

The next week Johnny put the kid in with a tough colored boy named Johnny Williams. The kid got the hell punched out of him, but he sold two hundred dollars' worth of tickets.

"He didn't do too bad," Johnny said to Froike after the fight. "I'll put him back next week."

"Only this time get him an easier opponent," Froike said.

"You get him your own opponent," Johnny said. "As long as he can sell that many tickets I don't care who he fights."

The next week Johnny put him back and he licked the guy. After the fight Johnny was walking out and he saw the kid and Froike with about twenty people around them, all of them talking Yiddish.

"Come here, Froike," Johnny said.

"What's the matter?" Froike said.

"What is this guy," Johnny said, "a Wop or a Jew?"

"He's a Jew," Froike said. "His right name's Davidoff. He's only fifteen, so we borrowed Pasconi's card."

"He can sure sell tickets," Johnny said.

Bummy could sell anything. That's the way Bummy learned to fight, selling. He used to sell off a pushcart on Blake Avenue. He used to sell berries in the spring and tomatoes and watermelons in the summer and apples in the fall and potatoes and onions and beans in the winter, and there are a lot of pushcarts on Blake Avenue and Bummy used to have to fight to hold his spot.

"I was the best tomato salesman in the world," Bummy was bragging once.

It was right after he knocked out Bob Montgomery in the Garden. He stiffened him in sixty-three seconds and he was getting fifteen thousand dollars, and when the sportswriters came into his dressing room all he wanted to talk about was how good he could sell tomatoes.

"You go over to Jersey and get them yourself," he was telling the sportswriters. "Then you don't have to pay the middle guy. You don't put them in boxes, because when you put them in boxes it looks like you're getting ready to lam. When you only got a few around it looks like you can't get rid of them, so what you gotta do is pile them all up and holler, 'I gotta get rid of these. I'm gonna give 'em away!'"

The sportswriters couldn't get over that. There was a lot they couldn't get over about Bummy.

When Johnny turned Bummy pro he wasn't impressed by his fighting, only his following. Every time Bummy fought for Johnny in the Grove he'd bring a couple of hundred guys with him and they'd holler for Bummy. Everybody else would holler for the other guy, because now they knew Bummy was Jewish and the Grove is in a German section of Ridgewood, and this was when Hitler was starting to go good and there was even one of those German beer halls right in the place where the waiters walked around in those short leather pants and wearing fancy vests and funny felt hats.

The fight that started Bummy was the Friedkin fight. Bummy was just beginning to bang guys out at the Grove and Friedkin was already a hot fighter at the Broadway Arena and they lived only blocks apart. Friedkin was a nice kid, about three years older than Bummy, kind of a studious guy they called Schoolboy Friedkin, and there was nothing between him and Bummy except that they were both coming up and the neighborhood made the match.

Like one day Bummy was standing in the candy store and a couple of guys told him Friedkin was saying he could stiffen Bummy in two heats. Then they went to Friedkin and said Bummy said Friedkin was afraid to fight. At first this didn't take, but they kept it up and one day Bummy was standing with a dame on the corner of Blake and Alabama and Friedkin came along.

"So why don't you two fight?" the dame said.

"Sure, I'll fight," Bummy said, spreading his feet.

"Right here?" Friedkin said. "Right now?"

"Sure," Bummy said.

"I'll fight whenever my manager makes the match," Friedkin said, and he walked away.

Bummy couldn't understand that, because he liked to fight just to fight. He got right in the subway and went over to see Lew Burston in Lew's office on Broadway.

"Never mind making that Friedkin match," he said to Lew.

"Why not?" Lew said.

"Because when I leave here," Bummy said, "I'm going right around to Friedkin's house and I'm gonna wait for him to come out, and we're gonna find out right away if I can lick him or he can lick me."

"Are you crazy?" Lew said.

By the time Johnny Attell made the fight outdoors for Dexter Park there was really a fire under it. They had show cards advertising it on the pushcarts on Blake Avenue and Friedkin's old man and Bummy's old man got into an argument on the street, and everybody was talking about it and betting it big. Then it was rained out five nights and Johnny sold the fight to Mike Jacobs and Mike put it into Madison Square Garden.

When Bummy started working for the fight Lew Burston came over to Beecher's to train him. When Bummy got into his ring clothes they chased everybody out of the gym, and Lew told Bummy to hit the big bag. Bummy walked up to the bag and spread his feet and pulled back his left to start his hook and Lew stopped him.

"Throw that hook away," Lew said.

"Why?" Bummy said. "What's wrong with it?"

"Nothing's wrong with it," Lew said, "only for this fight you'll have to lose that hook."

Before that Bummy was nothing but a hooker, but for weeks Lew kept him banging the big bag with rights. Then the night of the fight, after Bummy was all taped and ready, Lew took him into the shower off the dressing room and he talked to Bummy.

"Now remember one thing," he said to Bummy. "I can tell you exactly how that other corner is thinking. They've got that other guy eating and sleeping with your hook for weeks. I want you to go out there and I don't want you to throw one right hand until I tell you. If you throw one right before I say so I'll walk right out on you. Do you understand?"

Bummy understood all right. He was like a kid with a new toy. He was a kid with a secret that only Bummy and Lew knew, and he went out there and did what Lew told him. Friedkin came out

with his right glued along the side of his head, and for three rounds
Bummy just hooked and hooked and Friedkin blocked, and a lot of
people thought Friedkin was winning the fight.

"All right," Lew said, after the third round. "Now this time go
right out and feint with the left, but throw the right and put everything on it."

"Don't worry," Bummy said.

Bummy walked out and they moved around for almost a minute
and then Bummy feinted his hook. When he did Friedkin moved
over and Bummy threw the right and Friedkin's head went back
and down he went with his legs in the air in his own corner. That
was all the fighting there was that night.

Now Bummy was the biggest thing in Brownsville. Al Buck and
Hype Igoe and Ed Van Every and Lester Bromberg were writing
about him in the New York papers, saying he was the best hooker
since Charley White and could also hit with his right, and he had
dough for the first time in his life.

He got fourteen hundred dollars for the Friedkin fight. When he
walked down the street the kids followed him, and he bought them
leather jackets and baseball gloves and sodas, just to show you
what money meant and how he was already looking back at his
own life.

When Bummy was a kid nobody bought him anything and he
belonged to a gang called the Cowboys. They used to pull small
jobs, and the cops could never find them until one night. One night
the cops broke into the flat where the kids used to live with some
dames, and they got them all except Bummy, who was with his
mother that night.

Sure, Bummy was what most people call tough, but if he felt
sorry for you and figured you needed him he couldn't do enough.
That was the way Bummy met Barbara and fell in love.

Bummy was nineteen then and one day he and Shorty were driving around and Shorty said he wanted to go to Kings County Hospital and visit a friend of his who was sick, and there was this girl,
about sixteen years old. They sat around for a while and Shorty did
all the talking, and then the next time they went to see the girl
Shorty was carrying some flowers and he gave them to her.

"From him," Shorty said, meaning Bummy.

When the girl left the hospital Shorty and Bummy drove her

home, and then every day for a couple of weeks they used to take
her for a ride and to stop off for sodas. One day the three of them
were riding together in the front seat and Bummy wasn't saying
anything.

"Say, Bobby," Shorty said all of a sudden, "Would you like to get
married?"

The girl didn't know what to say. She just looked at Shorty.

"Not to me," Shorty said. "To him."

That was the way Bummy got married. That was Bummy's big
romance.

After the Friedkin fight Bummy won about three fights quick,
and then they made him with Mickey Farber in the St. Nick's.
Farber was out of the East Side and had a good record, and one
day when Bummy finished his training at Beecher's he was sitting
in the locker room soaking his left hand in a pail of ice and talking
with Charley.

That was an interesting thing about Bummy's left hand. He used
to bang so hard with it that after every fight and after every day he
boxed in the gym it used to swell up.

"I think I'll quit fighting," Bummy said to Charley.

"You think you'll quit?" Charley said. "You're just starting to
make dough."

"They're making me out a tough guy," Bummy said. "All the
newspapers make me a tough guy and I don't like it and I think I'll
quit."

"Forget it," Charley said.

When Charley walked out Murder, Inc., walked in. They were
all there—Happy and Buggsy and Abie and Harry and the Dasher—
and they were looking at Bummy soaking his hand in the ice.

"You hurt your hand?" Buggsy said.

"No," Bummy said. "It's all right."

They walked out again, and they must have gone with a bundle
on Farber because the day after Bummy licked Farber he was
standing under the El in front of the gym and the mob drove up.
They stopped the car right in front of him and they piled out.

"What are you, some wise guy?" Buggsy said.

"What's wrong with you?" Bummy said.

"What's all this you gave us about you had a bad hand?" Buggsy
said.

"I didn't say I had a bad hand," Bummy said.

"You did," Buggsy said.

"Listen," Bummy said, spreading his feet the way he used to do it, "if you guys want a fight let's start it."

Buggsy looked at the others and they looked at him. Then they all got in the car and drove off, and if you could have been there and seen that you would have gone for Bummy for it.

That was the bad part about Bummy's rap. Not enough people knew that part of Bummy until it was too late. The people who go to fights don't just go to see some guy win, but they go to see some guy get licked, too. All they knew about Bummy was some of the things they read, and he was the guy they always went to see get licked.

Even the mob that followed Bummy when he was a big name didn't mean anything to him, because he could see through that. He could see they were always grabbing at him for what they could get, and that was the thing he never got over about the time he was training at Billy West's place up in Woodstock, New York.

Bummy went up there after he came out of the Army, just to take off weight, and there are a lot of artists around there. Artists are different people, because they don't care what anybody says about a guy and they either like him or they don't like him for what they think he is. They all liked him up there, and Billy used to say that Bummy could have been mayor of Woodstock.

Billy had a dog that Bummy never forgot, either. Bummy used to run on the roads in the mornings and Billy's dog used to run with him. Every morning they'd go out together, and one day another dog came out of a yard and went for Bummy and Billy's dog turned and went after the other dog and chased it off.

"Gee, this dog really likes me," Bummy said, when he got back to the house, and he said it like he couldn't believe it. "He's really my friend."

The fight that really started everybody hating Bummy, though, was the Canzoneri fight in the Garden. It was a bad match and never should have been made, but they made it and all Bummy did was fight it.

Canzoneri was over the hill, but he had been the featherweight champion and the lightweight champion and he had fought the best of his time and they loved him. When Bummy knocked him out it was the only time Tony was knocked out in a hundred eighty fights, and so they booed Bummy for it and they waited for him to get licked.

They didn't have to wait too long. After he knocked out Tippy Larkin in five they made him with Lou Ambers. Just after he started training for Ambers he was in the candy store one day when an argument started between Bummy and a guy named Mersky. Nobody is going to say who started the argument but somebody called Bummy a lousy fighter and it wasn't Bummy. Somebody flipped a piece of hard candy in Bummy's face, too, and that wasn't Bummy either, and after Bummy got done bouncing Mersky up and down Mersky went to the hospital and had some pictures taken and called the cops.

The first Johnny Attell heard about it was the night after it happened. He was walking down Broadway and he met a dick he knew.

"That's too bad about your fighter," the cop said.

"What's the matter with him?" Johnny said.

"What's the matter with him?" the cop said. "There's an eight-state alarm out for him. The newspapers are full of it. He damn near killed a guy in a candy store."

The cops couldn't find Bummy but Johnny found him. He dug up Gangy, and Gangy drove him around awhile to shake off any cops, and finally Gangy stopped the car in front of an old wooden house and they got out and went in and there was Bummy.

Bummy was sitting in a pair of pajama pants, and that was all he had on. There were four or five other guys there, and they were playing cards.

"Are you crazy?" Johnny said.

"Why?" Bummy said, playing his cards, but looking up.

"If the cops find you here they'll kill you," Johnny said. "You better come with me."

After Johnny talked awhile Bummy got dressed and he went with Johnny. Johnny took him back to New York and got him a haircut and a shave and he called Mike Jacobs. Jacobs told Johnny to take Bummy down to Police Headquarters, and when Johnny did that Sol Strauss, Mike's lawyer, showed up and he got an adjournment in night court for Bummy until after the Ambers fight.

The night Bummy fought Ambers there was Mersky right at

ringside. He had on dark glasses and the photographers were all taking his picture and when Ambers beat the hell out of Bummy the crowd loved it.

The crowd, more than Ambers, hurt Bummy that night. He didn't like the licking Ambers gave him, but the hardest part was listening to the crowd and the way they enjoyed it and the things they shouted at him when he came down out of the ring.

"I quit," he said to Johnny in the dressing room. "You know what you can do with fighting?"

Johnny didn't believe him. Johnny was making matches for Jacobs in the Garden then and he matched Bummy with Tony Marteliano, but Bummy wouldn't train.

Only Johnny and Gangy knew this, and one day Johnny came out to Bummy's house and talked with Bummy. When that didn't do any good Lew Burston came out and he talked for four hours, and when he finished Bummy said the same thing.

"I don't want to be a fighter," Bummy said. "I like to fight. I'll fight Marteliano on the street right now, just for fun, but when I'm a fighter everybody picks on me. I want them to leave me alone. All I wanted was a home for my family and I got that, and now I just want to hang around my mob on the street."

Johnny still didn't believe it. They put out the show cards, advertising the fight, and one day Bummy saw one of the cards in the window of a bar and he phoned Johnny in Jacobs' office.

"What are you advertising the fight for?" he said, and he was mad. "I told you I'm not gonna fight."

Before Johnny could say anything Jacobs took the phone. Johnny hadn't told him Bummy didn't want to fight.

"How are you, kid?" Jacobs said. "This is Mike."

"Listen, you toothless ——," Bummy said. "What are you advertising me for? I'm not gonna fight."

He hung up. Mike put the phone back and turned around, and when he did Bummy was suspended and Johnny was out of the Garden and back in the Ridgewood Grove.

When Bummy heard what had happened to Johnny he went over to the Grove to see him. All the time Johnny was in the Garden, Bummy was a little suspicious of him, like he was a capitalist, but now he was different.

136

"I came over to tell you something," he said to Johnny. "I'm gonna fight."

"Forget it," Johnny said. "You can't fight."

"Who says I can't fight?" Bummy said.

"The New York Boxing Commission," Johnny said. "You're suspended."

"Let's fight out of town," Bummy said. "We'll fight where I'm not suspended."

Johnny did it better. He took Bummy back to Mike and Bummy apologized and Bummy fought Marteliano. For nine rounds they were even, and with ten seconds to go in the last round Bummy landed the hook. Marteliano went down and the referee counted nine and the bell rang and it was another big one for Bummy and he was going again.

It was Johnny's idea to get Marteliano back, but Bummy saw Fritzie Zivic lick Henri Armstrong for the welterweight title and he wanted Zivic. If you knew the two guys you knew this was a bad match for Bummy, because he just didn't know how to fight like Zivic.

There were a lot of people, you see, who called Bummy a dirty fighter, but the Zivic fight made them wrong. The Zivic fight proved that Bummy didn't know how to do it.

When they came out of the first clinch Bummy's eyes were red and he was rubbing them and the crowd started to boo Zivic. In the second clinch it was the same thing, and at the end of the round Bummy was roaring.

"He's trying to blind me," he kept saying in the corner. "He's trying to blind me."

When it started again in the second round Bummy blew. He pushed Zivic off and he dropped his hands and that crazy look came on that wide face of his and they could hear him in the crowd.

"All right, you ——," he said, "if you want to fight dirty, okay."

He walked right into Zivic and he started belting low. There was no trying to hide anything, and the crowd started to roar and before it was over people were on their chairs throwing things and the cops were in the ring and Bummy was fined $2,500 and suspended for life.

Before the United States Army decided it had enough trouble without Bummy. (UPI Photo.)

They meant it to be for life—which wouldn't have been very long at that, when you figure Bummy lived to be all of twenty-six—but it didn't work out that way. About three weeks after the fight Bummy walked into Johnny's office with Shorty and Mousie, and they sat around for a time and Johnny could see Bummy was lost.

"You know what you ought to do?" Johnny said. "You ought to join the Army for a while until this blows over."

This was in December 1940, before we got into the war. For a while Bummy sat there thinking, not saying anything.

"Could my buddies go with me?" he said.

"Sure," Johnny said.

So Johnny called up the recruiting officer and Bummy and Shorty and Mousie showed up and there were photographers there and it was a big show. Everybody was for it, and Ed Van Every wrote a story in the New York *Sun* in which he said this was a great move because the Army would teach Bummy discipline and get him in good physical shape.

That was a laugh. The first thing the Army did was split Bummy and Shorty and Mousie out and send them to different camps. They sent Bummy to Camp Hulen, Texas, and their idea of discipline was to have Bummy cleaning latrines with a toothbrush.

"You got me into this," Bummy used to write Johnny. "I'm going crazy, so before I slug one of these officers you better get me out."

Johnny didn't get him out, but he got Mike Jacobs to get Bummy a leave to fight Zivic in the Polo Grounds for Army Emergency Relief. Bummy used to fight best at about a hundred forty-seven pounds, and when he came back from Texas he weighed close to two hundred.

"You look sharp in that uniform, Al," Zivic said to him when they signed for the bout.

"I'm glad you like it," Bummy said. "You put me in it."

You can imagine how Bummy was looking to get back at Zivic, but he couldn't do it. He hadn't fought for eight months, and Zivic was a real good fighter and he put lumps all over Bummy and in the tenth round the referee stopped it. They had to find Bummy to take him back to camp. They found him with his wife and they shipped him back, but then the Japanese bombed Pearl Harbor and the Army decided it had enough trouble without Bummy and they turned him loose.

Bummy fought some of his best fights after that. He couldn't get his license back in New York but he fought in places like Holyoke and Bridgeport and Washington and Philadelphia and Elizabeth, New Jersey, and Boston. He didn't like it in those places, but he had to live and so no matter where he fought he would always drive back to Brownsville after the fight and sometimes it would be four o'clock in the morning before he and Johnny would get in.

It's something when you think about Bummy and Brownsville, when you think of the money he made, almost a quarter of a mil-

The referee, restraining Fritzie, stops the second Zivic-Davis fight. (UPI Photo.)

lion dollars, and the things he had thrown at him and the elegant places he could have gone. It was like what Lew Burston said, though, when he said the Supreme was Bummy's Opera, and the Supreme is a movie house on Livonia Avenue.

You have to remember, too, that Brownsville is only a subway ride from Broadway, but Bummy had never seen a real Broadway show until Chicky Bogad sent Bummy and Barbara to see *Hellzapoppin* the night before the second Farber fight.

"How long has this been going on?" Bummy said when they came out.

"How long has what been going on?" Chicky said.

"People like that on a stage," Bummy said.

"People on a stage?" Chicky said. "For years and years. For long before they had movies."

"Is that right? I'll have to see more of that," Bummy said, but he never did.

All of those fights Bummy had out of town were murders, too, because Bummy wasn't hard to hit, but the people liked to see him get hit and when the Republicans got back in power in New York, Fritzie Zivic put in a word for Bummy, saying he guessed he had egged the kid on, and Bummy got his license back. That's when they matched him with Montgomery.

"What you have to do in this one," they kept telling Bummy, "is walk right out, throw your right, and miss with it. Montgomery will grab your right arm, and that will turn you around southpaw and then you hit him with the hook."

They knew that was the only chance Bummy had, because if Montgomery got by the first round he figured to move around Bummy and cut him up. They drilled Bummy on it over and over, and they kept talking about it in the dressing room that night.

"Now what are you going to do?" Johnny Attell said to Bummy.

"I'm gonna walk right out and miss with my right," Bummy said. "He'll grab my arm and that'll turn me around southpaw and I'll throw my hook."

"Okay," Johnny said. "I guess you know it."

Bummy sat down then on one of the benches. He had his gloves on and his robe over him and he was ready to go when there was a knock on the door.

"Don't come out yet, Davis," one of the commission guys said through the door. "They're selling some War Bonds first."

When Bummy heard that he looked up from where he was sitting and you could see he was sweating, and then he keeled right over on the floor on his face. Johnny and Freddie Brown rushed over and picked him up and they stretched him on the rubbing table and Freddie brought him to, and now they weren't worried about whether Bummy would do what they told him. All they were worried about was whether they could get him in the ring.

They got him in the ring and Burston had him repeat what he was supposed to do. When the bell rang he walked right out and threw his right and missed around the head. Montgomery grabbed the arm and turned Bummy around, and when he did Bummy threw the hook and Montgomery went down. When he got up Bummy hit him again and that's all there was to it.

Montgomery was ten to one over Bummy that night and they couldn't believe it. Bummy got fifteen thousand dollars for that fight and he had borrowed fifteen hundred from Jacobs and the next day when Mike paid him off he told Bummy to forget the grand and a half.

"Take it out," Bummy said, throwing the dough on the desk. "You know damn well if he kayoed me like you thought he would you were gonna take it out."

Bummy thought he'd never be broke again. He got thirty-four thousand dollars the night Beau Jack beat him and fifteen thousand when Armstrong stopped him. Then somebody sold him the idea of buying that bar and grill and somebody else sold him a couple of racehorses and even after Dudy bought the bar and grill from him Bummy was broke.

He should have been in training for Morris Reif the night he was shot. Johnny wanted him to fight Reif, just for the dough and to go as far as he could, but Bummy said that a lot of his friends would bet him and he didn't think he could beat Reif, so instead he was sitting in the back of Dudy's drinking beer and singing.

Bummy used to think he could sing like a Jewish cantor. He couldn't sing, but he was trying that night, sitting with some other guys and a cop who was off duty, when he looked through that latticework at the bar and he saw the four guys with the guns.

"What the hell is this?" he said.

He got up and walked out and you know what happened. When Bummy stiffened the first guy one of the others fired and the bullet went into Bummy's neck. Then the three picked up the guy

143

It was a big funeral Bummy had. . . . It looked like everybody in Browns-ville was there. (UPI Photo.)

Bummy hit and they ran for the car. One of the guys with Bummy stuffed his handkerchief in the collar of Bummy's shirt to stop the blood, and Bummy got up and ran for the car. When he did they opened up from the car, and Bummy went flat on his face in the mud.

When the car started to pull away the cop who had been in the back ran out and fired. He hit one guy in the spine, and that guy died in Texas, and he hit another in the shoulder. The guy with the slug in his shoulder walked around with it for weeks, afraid to go to a doctor, and then one night a cop in plain clothes heard a couple of guys talking in a bar.

"You know that jerk is still walking around with the bullet in his shoulder?" the one said.

"What bullet?" the other said.

"The Bummy Davis bullet," the first said.

The cop followed them out, and when they split up he followed the first guy and got it out of him. Then the cops picked up the guy with the bullet and he sang. They picked up the other two in Kansas City and they're doing twenty to life. They were just punks, and they called themselves the Cowboys, the same as Bummy's old gang did.

It was a big funeral Bummy had. Johnny and Lew Burston paid for it. The papers had made Bummy a hero, and the newsreels took pictures outside the funeral parlor and at the cemetery. It looked like everybody in Brownsville was there.

When I wrote about Bummy Davis I was writing history, for I never met the young man. I saw him in only one fight, and once as he left the offices of the New York State Athletic Commission after a failed attempt to have his boxing license restored. If the piece proves anything, it is that if you are fortunate enough to find the right people who are perceptive enough and sensitive enough, you can still come to know a man.

9

Death of
a Racehorse

They were going to the post for the sixth race at Jamaica, two year olds, some making their first starts, to go five and a half furlongs for a purse of four thousand dollars. They were moving slowly down the backstretch toward the gate, some of them cantering, others walking, and in the press box they had stopped their working or their kidding to watch, most of them interested in one horse.

"Air Lift," Jim Roach said. "Full brother of Assault."

Assault, who won the triple crown . . . making this one too, by Bold Venture, himself a Derby winner, out of Igual, herself by the great Equipoise. . . . Great names in the breeding line . . . and now the little guy making his first start, perhaps the start of another great career.

They were off well, although Air Lift was fifth. They were moving toward the first turn, and now Air Lift was fourth. They were going into the turn, and now Air Lift was starting to go, third perhaps, when suddenly he slowed, a horse stopping, and below in the stands you could hear a sudden cry, as the rest left him, still trying to run but limping, his jockey—Dave Gorman—half falling, half sliding off.

"He broke a leg!" somebody, holding binoculars to his eyes, shouted in the press box. "He broke a leg!"

Down below they were roaring for the rest, coming down the stretch now, but in the infield men were running toward the turn, running toward the colt and the boy standing beside him, alone. There was a station wagon moving around the track toward them, and then, in a moment, the big green van that they call the horse ambulance.

"Gorman was crying like a baby," one of them, coming out of the jockey room said. "He said he must have stepped in a hole, but you should have seen him crying."

"It's his left front ankle," Dr. J. G. Catlett, the veterinarian, was saying. "It's a compound fracture; and I'm waiting for confirmation from Mr. Hirsch to destroy him."

He was standing outside one of the stables beyond the back-stretch, and he had just put in a call to Kentucky where Max Hirsch, the trainer, and Robert Kleberg, the owner, are attending the yearling sales.

"When will you do it?" one of them said.

"Right as soon as I can," the doctor said. "As soon as I get confirmation. If it was an ordinary horse I'd done it right there."

He walked across the road and around another barn to where they had the horse. The horse was still in the van, about twenty stable hands in dungarees and sweat-stained shirts, bare-headed or wearing old caps, standing around quietly and watching with Dr. M. A. Gilman, the assistant veterinarian.

"We might as well get him out of the van," Catlett said, "before we give him the novocaine. It'll be a little better out in the air."

The boy in the van with the colt led him out then, the colt limping, tossing his head a little, the blood running down and covering his left foreleg. When they saw him, standing there outside the van now, the boy holding him, they started talking softly.

"Full brother of Assault." . . . "It don't make no difference now. He's done." . . . "But damn, what a grand little horse." . . . "Ain't he a horse?"

"It's a funny thing," Catlett said. "All the cripples that go out, they never break a leg. It always happens to a good-legged horse."

A man, gray-haired and rather stout, wearing brown slacks and a blue shirt walked up.

"Then I better not send for the wagon yet?" the man said.

"No," Catlett said. "Of course, you might just as well. Max Hirsch may say no, but I doubt it."

"I don't know," the man said.

"There'd be time in the morning," Catlett said.

"But in this hot weather—" the man said.

They had sponged off the colt, after they had given him the shot to deaden the pain, and now he stood, feeding quietly from some hay they had placed at his feet. In the distance you could hear the roar of the crowd in the grandstand, but beyond it and above it you could hear thunder and see the occasional flash of lightning.

When Catlett came back the next time he was hurrying, nodding his head and waving his hands. Now the thunder was louder, the flashes of lightning brighter, and now rain was starting to fall.

"All right," he said, shouting to Gilman. "Max Hirsch talked to Mr. Kleberg. We've got the confirmation."

They moved the curious back, the rain falling faster now, and they moved the colt over close to a pile of loose bricks. Gilman had the halter and Catlett had the gun, shaped like a bell with the handle at the top. This bell he placed, the crowd silent, on the colt's forehead, just between the eyes. The colt stood still and then Catlett, with the hammer in his other hand, struck the handle of the bell. There was a short, sharp sound and the colt toppled onto his left side, his eyes staring, his legs straight out, the free legs quivering.

"Aw ——" someone said.

That was all they said. They worked quickly, the two vets removing the broken bones as evidence for the insurance company, the crowd silently watching. Then the heavens opened, the rain pouring down, the lightning flashing, and they rushed for the cover of the stables, leaving alone on his side near the pile of bricks, the rain running off his hide, dead an hour and a quarter after his first start, Air Lift, son of Bold Venture, full brother of Assault.

Out of ten years of daily journalism, four of them covering sports, this is the sole piece that, I feel, deserves an afterlife, although I am not sure. Some months after the column ran, the editors of *Cosmopolitan* wrote to inform me that I had been chosen as one of "twelve leading American columnists," each of us invited to grant reprint rights to his "favorite column" as part of a new monthly feature. As the five hundred dollars they were to pay me for work already done was more than four times what my impecunious employers were rewarding me for a whole week's labor, this column went out in the return mail. When the reply came back no check fell out, the column rejected because they doubted "that women would understand it."

10

Young Fighter

It was about an hour before the fight, and we were alone in the dressing room. It was warm in the room, and the fighter had stripped and then put on just his ring socks and shoes, and now he was lying on his back on the rubbing table with just a towel across his middle, staring up at the ceiling.

"You know something?" he said after a while.

His voice startled me. I had been sitting there listening to the sounds and the small talk of the preliminary fighters, and occasionally turning my head to watch them beyond the opening at the end of the black shower curtain with the pink flowers on it that hung between them and us.

"What?" I said.

"I feel different tonight," he said slowly, still looking up at the ceiling. "I don't know why, but I do."

"That's sometimes a good sign," I said. "You may fight your best fight."

It was his youth and his lack of experience talking. After he has fought a lot of fights he won't talk like that anymore.

"I don't know," he said. "I never felt like this before."

Why do they do it? In this country last year there were about three thousand professional prizefighters. By the end of the year two of them had lost their lives in the ring, and only about two dozen had profited by as much as ten thousand dollars. The rest fought in the small clubs or populated the preliminaries in the bigger clubs, and Billy McNeece, now lying on his back in the small, musty dressing room at the Eastern Parkway in Brooklyn, is one of these.

"Just before they go into the ring," I said, "most fighters feel tired."

I had been watching beyond the curtain, a preliminary boy named Andy Viserto. He had been moving around with his robe on, shadowboxing and trying to loosen his shoulders, and while he had been doing this he had been yawning. He must have yawned five or six times in the thirty seconds or so that I watched him.

"I don't feel tired," McNeece said now. "I don't know how I feel."

I came to know McNeece through Jimmy August. We were standing together one day in Stillman's, watching the sparring in the two rings, when Jimmy said, "I've got a kid for you. If you're looking for a kid that's typical of the kind that comes into boxing, I've got one—wild, absolutely fearless, makes every fight a war, but a real nice kid with it all."

I have known Jimmy now for close to ten years and respect him as one of the few capable trainers, teachers, and handlers of fighters still in the business. He is a short, stocky, bald man with brown eyes, who quit studying pharmaceutical chemistry at Columbia University thirty years ago to work with fighters, and he is particularly good with the young ones, since he is patient and painstaking and somewhat of an amateur psychologist.

"This kid was sent to me about six years ago," Jimmy said, "by a fighter I used to have, Dennis Deegan, who was a welter, back around 1936–'38. You may remember him. He had about forty pro fights and topped the Ridgewood and the Jamaica Arena."

"Deegan?" I said. "What did he look like?"

"A good left hand," Jimmy said.

"I don't recall him," I said.

"He works as a track foreman on the Independent Subway and he's friendly with the family of this kid," Jimmy said. "One day he come up to me here and told me he had a kid he wanted me to make a fighter of. Then he brings the kid up, and when I got through working with the other kids I started to teach him, believe me, from A to Z."

"Was there anything that impressed you about him from the start?" I said.

"All heart, that's all," Jimmy said. "A big gangling kid, about a hundred forty, like what you call an ostrich, but all fighter."

"I'd like to meet him," I said.

I met him a few days later. It was the middle of the afternoon and raining, and we walked up from Stillman's to The Neutral Corner and sat across from each other in one of the booths in the back room.

The Neutral Corner is a bar and grill on the southwest corner of Eighth Avenue and Fifty-fifth Street, in New York City, half a block north of Stillman's. It is owned and operated by Frankie Jay, Chicky Bogad, and Nick Masuras. Frankie used to manage fighters, including Tony Janiro, a good-looking welterweight of a half-dozen years ago who almost broke Frankie's heart; Chicky grew up with the good Jewish fighters who came out of the Lower East Side about thirty-five years ago, and once, for a few months, he was matchmaker for Madison Square Garden; Nick used to be a fighter himself, a middleweight.

"That scar under your right eye," I said to McNeece, after we had talked a few minutes. "Where did you get it?"

McNeece is twenty-three years old and stands six feet and weighs about one sixty-five. He has pale, freckled skin, red-blond, wavy hair, and pale blue eyes.

"Scar?" he said, feeling with the fingers of his right hand across the scar and then around it. "I haven't got any scar."

"It looks like a scar," I said, and reached across the table and placed my fingers on the little crescent of tightened skin on his right cheekbone. "It's an old one, but it's there."

"I don't think so," he said, puzzled. "I was never cut there."

In the bar and in the back room at The Neutral Corner the walls are hung with black-framed photographs of prizefights and prizefighters, managers and handlers. In each of the half-dozen booths, centered on the wall between the pictures, there is a small, narrow mirror.

"Take a look in that mirror," I said. "You'll see it."

The fighter turned to the mirror, and then he moved his head to get the light right. Then, with his fingers, he went over the small scar twice and turned back with a half-smile on his face.

"You're right," he said. "I didn't even remember it. I got it in a kid fight so long ago I forgot it."

"What about the fight?"

"I don't remember it. I just vaguely remember that I got cut there once in a kid fight. I don't remember anything about the fight, and I didn't even remember that I had the cut."

"The bridge of your nose," I said. "It's starting to broaden. Was it ever broken in a fight?"

"No," he said, feeling his nose. "It's just from my amateur fights and my fights as a pro."

"Does it bother you that your face is getting marked?"

"No."

"When Billy Graham was a kid in school," I said, speaking of the fighter and not the preacher, "he used to box in the boys' clubs. After a fight he'd wear a patch over his eye to school. There wasn't any cut under the patch; he wanted to look like a fighter. Did you ever do that?"

"No," McNeece said. "I never did that, but I was never ashamed of anything for sure. When I get banged, I get banged."

I would say that tells a lot about what makes a fighter right there. I go along with the poet who said my body is the mansion of my soul. I can tell you exactly how I got the scar on my lower lip and the one on the index finger of my left hand and the one on my right knee. That's one of the reasons why I was never a fighter, and why McNeece is.

McNeece grew up in Central Islip, Long Island. There were three kids in the family—his sister Mary, who is a year older than the fighter, and his brother Jimmy, who is a year younger.

"Have you had a hard time around your home?" I said.

"Sure," McNeece said. "My father's a laborer, a construction worker."

"Was he ever out of work?"

"Sure. When the weather is bad or you're sick, you can't work. Ever since we were little kids my mother worked in the state hospital, too. We never had much money."

I will admit that not all fighters are impelled by financial poverty. I have known a few who attended college, but they were less as fighters because of it. There was always the knowledge within them that they could make a living in another way, and so it has always been that most fighters, and the best fighters, are those who know that fighting will give them their only chance to make a real pile.

"I never wanted to be anything else but a fighter," McNeece said.

"Me and my brother—he's in the Navy now—I guess the first thing we ever got was boxing gloves. They threatened to burn the gloves a million times, the fights we used to have."

He was sitting there, friendly and alert to my questions. He had on a pair of gray slacks and a soft yellow sports shirt, open at the neck, and a light-tan wind jacket. He is big-boned and, although considered to be a middleweight, he will probably build up with proper training and with proteins to add about ten pounds of good weight and become a light-heavyweight.

"From a little kid on," he said, "I got all the record books and I know every fighter from away back. My mother used to wake me up at ten o'clock so I could listen to the fights."

I think that's important in this, too. Some fighters have to go against their families to do it, but in the majority of cases the resistance is what the Army used to call sporadic, at best. That is why I decided to drive out to Central Islip to try to find out what forces, outside of himself, impelled this fighter toward the ring, and why, at home, the climate, as they say, was right.

Central Islip is a crossroads town about fifty miles from New York City and in about the geographical center of Long Island. Robert Ripley once ascertained, after what could have been some very pleasant research, that there were more bars per capita in Central Islip than in any other town or city in the United States. Its population has been about 90 percent Irish Catholic, and most of its residents work in the three nearby state mental hospitals and in the Grumman and Republic aircraft plants.

"This is a fighting town," Joe Barlin, the physical education instructor and coach of Central Islip High School, told me. "Kids around here fight more than in any other town I've ever known."

Barlin, McNeece, and I were in the small faculty room off the stage in the gymnasium. Barlin, still a young man, was smoking a pipe.

"I was quite aghast when I first came here," he said, "but I've come to let the kids throw a few punches. You see, it's a hospital town. The parents work around the clock, and the kids are left to shift for themselves more than in most places."

I suppose McNeece was amused by the efforts I was making to reconstruct the background that propelled him into professional fighting. In his own mind it is all very simple. He always wanted to be a fighter.

"If you ask me why he became a fighter," Barlin said, "I'll give you three reasons. One, he's Irish. Two, he's got a younger brother. Three, he was always a fierce competitor."

"My brother and I, we'd be mad at one another about almost everything," McNeece said, smiling. "We fought all the time. When we played on the same teams here they would never put us both into the game at the same time."

While in high school, he had played varsity basketball, soccer, and baseball. He had never failed a subject, but after his third year and at the age of seventeen he quit to enlist in the paratroops.

"Whatever he played here," Barlin said, "he fought like hell all the way. I wish we had more like him. He'd just as soon tell you to go to hell as not, but he'd always tell the truth. He has what I'd call an open personality."

A slim, neatly dressed man in his thirties came in carrying a book and some papers. Barlin introduced him as Ted Jamison, the assistant principal, and after he had shaken hands with me and greeted McNeece warmly, he sat down and I explained my interest in McNeece.

"Would you," I asked him, "say that there is something in the general environment here that Billy has been trying to escape?"

That is, really, the way we regard fighting in our time. We examine the exponents of it, and their origins, as if they were confirmed criminals.

"Definitely," Jamison said. "We have that problem here constantly, and I've even held up Billy, here, as an example of what one individual can do about it. A lot of kids here have a defeatist complex. They say, 'What have I got to look forward to? To work in the hospital or the aircraft plant all my life?'"

"I always said I wouldn't be working in the hospital," McNeece said.

"Exactly," Jamison said. "I just couldn't see Billy doing that. I think he'd go crazy in a factory, too. I think he'd walk out and tell the boss what to do."

"I think I would," McNeece said, smiling.

While the McNeece children were small, the family lived in an aging gray frame house behind a lumberyard near the center of town. Six years ago they moved into a home of their own, a new ranch-type bungalow in a development of small houses on the northeast edge of the town.

155

When we arrived at the house the fighter's older sister Mary was there with her two-year-old son. As I talked with her it was apparent that she sees nothing surprising about the fact that her brother has become a fighter and, as a result, has never attempted to analyze the reasons for his choice of this profession.

"But when you and your brother were small," I said, "I'm sure there were occasions when your parents punished you. Do you recall how your brother reacted to punishment?"

"Oh, yes," she said. "I remember that when my mother would smack him, he'd just stand there. I remember he'd never cry or anything."

The fighter's mother is a small, auburn-haired woman, now forty-four years old, who came to this country alone from Ireland when she was sixteen to live with relatives. On this particular day she got home early from the hospital.

"He wasn't difficult as a child," she said. "I would say he was just adventurous. They used to have the Tarzan movies then, and I'd come home and find rope strung from tree to tree. I did worry a little, but he always seemed to come out all right, and I got over that."

Mrs. McNeice—the fighter changed the spelling of the name when he began to box—said it was much the same when her son started fighting. At first she was nervous, but when she saw that he was not being hurt she ceased to worry deeply, and she has attended each of his fights in and around New York.

"I went to his first one here, at the Eastern Parkway," she said. "He won, and then I felt that I never wanted to change anything, so I still go."

"The chance to make a lot of money draws all fighters to the ring," I said. "Would you say that your son has always been conscious of how difficult it is for many people to make a good living?"

"Often," she said, "he would say to me, 'Someday I want to make a lot of money.'"

"When I was in the Army," the fighter said, "I used to read about guys I boxed in the amateurs moving ahead. I'd tell my mother, 'Wait till I get out of the Army, and then we'll have some of the nice things.'"

"Billy worked after school, too," Mrs. McNeice said.

"Once I worked in the ravioli factory here," the fighter said. "I labeled jars from five in the afternoon to ten. I was about twelve years old, and one day the inspector came in and found me."

When the fighter was thirteen he piled lumber for the Central Islip Lumber Company. When he was fifteen he worked at Camp Upton, Long Island, on a construction job with his father.

"He always brought home the money," Mrs. McNeice said, "and waited for his cut."

Shortly after four o'clock, William McNeice, Sr., came home. He is a thin, ruddy-faced, sandy-haired, blue-eyed man, now fifty years old.

He was born in the Williamsburg section of Brooklyn and left school in the eighth grade at the age of fourteen to work as a truck helper. Then he became a brick handler and finally a construction laborer.

"Coming from the Williamsburg section," he said, when I began to question him about fighting, "I followed fighters since I was a kid. I thought there was nobody like Mike O'Dowd."

This reminded me of the one question I had saved. I wanted to ask it of the mother and father together.

"All of the motion pictures and all of the fiction that are written about boxing," I said, "depict the seamy side. They're concerned with death in the ring or dishonest fights or dishonest managers or gangsters. Were either of you worried about your son getting into a business that is always portrayed in that manner?"

"I never believed that stuff about the cheating managers or the fixed fights," the father said. "I never worry about the boy getting hurt, either. I've seen many fights in my line of work, and I saw many a fight in the Ridgewood or the armories or Ebbets Field. I saw the boy in all his Golden Gloves bouts, and from the way he handled himself I figured he wasn't being hurt."

"But didn't what you had seen in the movies or read about boxing concern you?" I asked the mother.

"Billy used to talk so much about boxing that it never bothered me," Mrs. McNeice said. "I never believed the other things, and I met Jimmy August and Billy's manager and they're nice men."

When McNeece finished his four years in the Army early last year and resumed professional fighting, August turned over the management of him to Irving Cohen. Cohen, a short, semistout, round-faced, blue-eyed, soft-spoken man, manages Billy Graham and managed Rocky Graziano to the middleweight championship. He is completely honest in his dealings with his fighters, and is so cautious that seldom does he put one of them into a ring unless he is reasonably certain that the fighter has better than an even chance to beat the other man.

"Out here," the fighter said now, "I guess the guys that follow boxing were surprised that I got Irving Cohen for a manager."

I did not see the fighter again until the evening of the fight. He had been at Greenwood Lake, New York, for twelve days training to fight Jackie La Bua, another young middleweight, at the Eastern Parkway, and he and August had taken a room at a hotel just off Times Square for the night before the fight.

La Bua had had twenty-five fights and had won twenty-two—McNeece had won ten of twelve—and was working on a winning streak of eleven. Although the New York newspapers had not given much space to the fight, they had been unanimous in the opinion that La Bua was the logical favorite to lick McNeece.

"How is he?" I said to August when I met him in the hotel lobby.

"He's resting," August said. "He'll be down in a few minutes."

"How will he do?"

"Who knows?" August said. "He can lick this guy, but it depends on him. The trouble with him is that he fears nothing."

"I know," I said.

"It's a tough job for a conscientious trainer and manager to put fear and respect in a guy like this," August said. "He takes chances he shouldn't take. He can box like hell, but he gets hit on the chin and then he's a sensational fighter for no reason at all.

"A guy with too much guts is hard to teach. A guy with a little geezer in him is the greatest fighter in the world. You teach him a trick and he'll learn it. This guy, he says, 'Aw, I'll run him out of the ring.'

"So the other trainers," August said, "they say to me, 'Why must he go wild. Why can't you cool him down?' How am I going to cool him down? In one fight he went wild altogether, and he came to me and he said, 'Why can't you control me?'

"He's asking me? I've tried everything. I've conned him and I've abused him, because let's face it. You know what an Irishman or a Jew who can fight can mean at the gate."

"I know," I said.

"Even managers get excited when they think about it," August said. "If I can cool him off and let him use the ability God gave him, good. If I can't, he'll have a short career, and that's what it'll be tonight. If he loses his head, he's gone. If he fights his fight, he'll lick the guy without too much trouble."

The fighter came down and went out and got into his second-hand Dodge convertible. With Jimmy Moulton, a young light-weight who was to box a four-rounder on the card, driving, and with McNeece sitting up front with him, we started for the Arena.

"How are your folks?" I said to McNeece after a while.

"They're fine, thanks," he said. "That is, my mother's fine, but my father's sick. He can't move."

"He can't move?" I said.

"They brought him home from work," McNeece said, "and he couldn't move. He's lying there in the house and he can just move one hand."

"Did he have a stroke?" I said to August, who was riding next to me in the back.

"It must be," August said, shrugging. "They didn't want Billy to know before the fight."

"They tried to keep it from me," the fighter said. "I heard about it and I went out there yesterday."

"The dough you'll get for tonight," August said, "will come in handy."

In the preceding twelve months McNeece had earned nine hundred dollars in purses in five fights. For this one, however, he would clear about a thousand dollars after expenses for his end.

"I'll say," he said. "I'll go out there tomorrow, and we'll take him to the hospital. I'll have the money to put right down."

The Arena's dressing rooms are to the left of the lobby; half of the preliminary fighters are in one room and the men they are going to fight in another, and because McNeece was boxing the ten-round main event, he had a private cubicle, about ten feet by eight, with the shower curtain separating him from the preliminary boys.

In the two and a half hours that we waited there he was more quiet than he had been on the other occasions when I had been with him. If he heard the talk of the preliminary boys he paid no attention to it, resting on his back on the rubbing table and then later he sat up while August bandaged and taped first one hand and then the other, and I thought of what he had told me about his feelings before a fight.

"When you enlisted in the Army," I had asked that afternoon in The Neutral Corner, "why did you pick the paratroops?"

"For the extra pay," he said.

"Had you ever been up in a plane before?"

"Not until I jumped."

"Were you scared?"

"I was as nervous as anybody else, but I think you do it because it's just follow the leader. I always had pride, and if anybody said I couldn't do something I'd do it."

"Did you know any men who wouldn't jump?"

"Sure. They have a heck of a lot of quitters. Maybe almost half the class were quitters, but I never thought about them one way or the other. Some of the guys laughed at them, but at times even I myself felt like saying, 'The hell with this stuff.' That's the reason I wouldn't quit. If the other guy could do it, so could I."

"Did you pray before your jumps?" I said, remembering that he had told me that he and his brother had been altar boys and had attended parochial school.

"I went to church the night before my first jump. I always make a visit to church just before a fight, too."

"For what do you pray?"

"I ask for a real good fight, and that I don't get my eyes busted up."

"Do you pray to win?"

"No. If I ask to win, I still might get beat, and I don't want to be disappointed."

There were about five hundred spectators in the Arena, which will hold four times as many, when McNeece, with August and Cohen and Whitey Bimstein behind him, came down the aisle. When he was introduced from the ring, about half of them set up a noise, and when La Bua, who lives in East Meadow, Long Island, took his bow the effect was about the same.

As the bell rang, McNeece came out fast and he was three quarters of the way across the ring when he and La Bua joined. Immediately it was apparent that La Bua was the calmer of the two, and he met McNeece's rush with two jabs that brought the color to McNeece's face.

"Easy, Irish!" Bimstein hollered up. "Hold it, Irish!"

It was that way through the first minute of the first round, with McNeece's anxiety showing in the punches he was missing and with La Bua pacing himself nicely. Then, suddenly, halfway through the round, McNeece landed a right hand to the body that hurt La Bua and backed him up. The moment he felt La Bua give under the punch, McNeece moved in after it, forcing, and it was apparent now that this, unless La Bua could do something to change it or McNeece lost his head, would be the pattern of the fight.

It was the same in the second round, with McNeece pressing, keeping La Bua from getting set. La Bua's corner must have noticed this, because in the third round La Bua came out and tried to take the lead. He was putting more authority into his jabs, snapping McNeece's head back. For a moment he backed McNeece up, but then McNeece started to drop inside the arcs of La Bua's follow-up punches and hook to La Bua's body, and when he did that it was the same as it had been in the first two rounds.

It would in all probability have been the same for ten rounds except that, in the fifth, a cut opened over La Bua's left eye from one of McNeece's overhand rights. It opened again the sixth, and at the end of the round Dr. Samuel Swetnick, of the New York State Athletic Commission, climbed into the ring. He looked at the eye and then spoke to the referee, and the referee threw his hands out flat to signal the end.

All the way from the ring to the dressing room McNeece, grinning now, his face and hair wet, was accepting the congratulations of his friends. A few minutes later, his green robe over him, he was sitting on the dressing table, holding an ice pack to his left eye, which had purplish welts above and below it.

"You see?" August was saying, bending over McNeece. "When you jabbed and moved under, his right went over your head."

"I know," McNeece said. "It was good."

"You looked very good tonight," Joe Lee, a sportswriter, was saying. He was standing by the table with pencil and paper in hand.

"He was a very tough guy, a very tough guy," McNeece said, and I could see he was starting to unwind now. "He takes a good rap. I'd just wait for him to start, and then I'd shoot inside to the belly."

"Who'd you like to fight now?" Lee said.

"Anybody my manager says," McNeece said.

Billy McNeece (right) in his big win over Garth Panter, before he found that all the money wasn't there. (UPI Photo.)

"You see?" Bimstein said.

"I know," McNeece said.

"You got a little Jew sense in your head tonight," Bimstein said. "Let the Irish out later."

"He means be more deliberate," McNeece said, smiling and explaining the reference to Lee.

"Let me tell you something," Izzy Grove, who had just come in, said. "You got a lot of ability. You can make a lot of money."

"Thank you," McNeece said, smiling and removing the ice pack.

During the middle and late twenties, Izzy Grove was a good middleweight who fought most of the best in and around New York, several champions among them. Now he books dance bands for a living.

"Don't thank me," he said. "Thank yourself. I don't want to tell you how to fight. You got a manager and a trainer to tell you that. Just behave yourself. Don't abuse this body. You got only one."

"I know," McNeece said.

"Have a good time, sure," Grove said, "but not tonight. Wait a couple of days. Don't get drunk."

"Sure," McNeece said.

"Let these words become imbedded in your brain," Grove said, tapping his own forehead. "I know. I been through it. There's no business in the world where you can make more money if you take care of yourself."

"I know," McNeece said.

"Remember this," Grove said. "The whole world loves a winner and the losers are on Strike It Rich."

"Thanks, Mr. Grove," McNeece said.

In the lobby, fifteen minutes later, there were still several dozen men and women waiting near the door to the dressing rooms. They were talking loudly and kidding one another and laughing, and every now and then one of the men would slap another on the back. They were waiting for a young man who, for many reasons, all of them interwoven, always wanted to be a fighter. They were waiting for Billy McNeece.

He is fifty-one years old now, married, with four sons and a daughter, and lives in Oakdale, Long Island, about a dozen miles

At the nuclear power plant where he works the 4 P.M. to midnight shift. (Andrew McKeever.)

from where he grew up. All of that money, of which Izzy Grove spoke, wasn't there for him, and after Billy Kilgore stopped him in five rounds in Miami Beach in 1956, he retired with a record of thirty-seven fights, thirty-one wins, and one draw.

"But I loved it," he said. "It was good to me."

"Was it a tough decision then," I said, "when you decided to give it up?"

"No," he said. "Not really. I had a serious car accident—fifty stitches in the head—and after that I didn't feel the same. You know how it is, too, when you're young. You look at your friends. They're goin' out, and you can't. You want to get married and have kids, and for four years I was going to electrician's school, so I had a trade I could go into."

For a while he had his own electrical firm and, at the same time, he ran a sanitation business. Now he works the 4 P.M. to midnight shift at the Long Island Lighting Company's nuclear power plant on the north shore of the island. Three years ago he underwent open heart surgery in Houston with the Dr. Michael De Bakey team doing a triple bypass.

"So I'm lucky," he said. "I've got my health, and a fine family. We're very close, and three of my boys are fighters."

"So I heard," I said.

"You see," he said, "they grew up around it, with the people talking about it. I love the game, so I guess I encouraged them, even though it's difficult for me to see them fight."

"You don't enjoy watching them fight?"

"I go crazy," he said. "You wouldn't believe it. It's much tougher than being in there. I'm a wreck, but it gives them identity. It separates them from being just a face in the crowd, so if that's the avenue they want to pursue, that's great. If I thought they were taking the chance of getting hurt, though, I wouldn't be for it."

11

The Man with
a Life
in His Hands

"Good morning, Dr. Matthews," the voice of the woman on the phone said. "It is now six forty-five."

He had been lying, there in the gray darkness, half awake, half waiting for the phone to ring.

"At eight o'clock," the woman's voice said, "you're at University Hospital for a lobectomy. At eleven-thirty you're at Mercy for a conference. At one o'clock you have a mitral stenosis there. At four you're at your office to see patients until seven. At eight-thirty you're at the Academy for a meeting of the medical society. That's all."

"Will you be home for dinner?" his wife said after he had hung up.

"About seven-thirty," he said, "but I have a meeting at eight-thirty."

His mother was the one who had started it all. She was a thin, wiry woman with high cheekbones and her black hair drawn back straight, and she was deeply religious. While she was cleaning the house in Colorado or scrubbing the kitchen table until the wood was bleached almost white, she would be casting out her philosophy.

"Be a healer," she would say. "Jesus was a healer, but if you can't be a minister and heal the soul, be a doctor and heal the body."

Now he was walking out through the small lobby of his apartment building, and the doorman gave him the keys to the car. He drove downtown, locked the car, and walked across the street into the hospital.

"Excuse me, Dr. Matthews," the receptionist said, "but your patient's wife and son would like to talk with you."

A woman in her late fifties wearing a green dress and a broad-shouldered man in his thirties were standing there. He was trying to recall the woman when she put out her hand to him.

"We just want to wish you luck, doctor," she said, almost apologetically. She was trying to force a small smile across the fear in her face.

"Look," he said, "please try not to worry. We'll take good care of him."

"I know you will," the man said.

"Now remember," he said to both of them, "I'm not worried, so there's no point in you two worrying."

"Bless you, doctor," the woman said, still trying to smile.

It was the truth. When he was much younger and still insecure, every operation was prefaced by anticipation and tension. He would lie in bed the night before and play it over and over, trying to imagine everything he could possibly run into. Now he was fifty-three and had opened five thousand chests and he had it all so beautifully systematized that each move was almost a reflex. Now, in most of them, all the tension was gone, and so was almost all the exhilaration. Now he just refined and refined and refined.

Walking into the doctors' lounge, he flipped the light button by his name and signed the registry. In the elevator he pushed the button marked O.R., and when he got out he walked down the hall to the doctors' locker room.

"Why!" he said, from the doorway. "Look at all these great surgeons."

"Good morning, Matt," Tomkins said.

"Hello, Tom," he said.

There were a half dozen of them in the room. A couple of them were undressing in front of their lockers. The others were sitting around in the two-piece, washed-green pajamas and the caps, the masks hanging from their necks.

"I've been wanting to ask you about that story in the papers about the Russians," Allerton said.

"What story?" he said, hanging his jacket in the locker.

"You see?" Allerton said, telling it to the room. "The Russians have him beaten and he doesn't want to admit it."

"Beaten?"

"Sure," Allerton said. "The story in the *Times* said they do that operation you do—that pneumonectomy—under a local anesthesia and they do it in twelve minutes. How come it takes you three hours?"

"Look, damn it," he said. "Don't tell me about the Russians. That thing was done nineteen years ago in Toronto with the patient awake but under a spinal, and it was awful even to see. All of a sudden the patient loses his voice and then he turns blue. Don't tell me about that stupid procedure."

"Well, don't get sore at me," Allerton said, still kidding him.

"I'm not sore at you," he said, smiling.

"Didn't you sleep last night?"

"I slept fine," he said, "but how can the Russians sleep?"

He had stripped to his shorts and socks. He took the money out of his wallet and slipped the bills down inside his left sock and flattened them around the ankle. Then he took off his wristwatch and slid it down inside the other sock. He got into the pajamas and put on the green cap. He shook out the mask and tied the bottom strings around his neck and then he put on his half-glasses. Finally he slid his feet into the open-backed, white leather operating shoes.

"Well," he said, shutting the door of the locker and looking around at them, "you successful doctors can sit around and talk about taxes and golf and girls, but I have to work."

Tomkins followed him out into the hall. As they were about to pass the elevator, the door opened and two orderlies pushed a bed out. On it was a gray-haired man.

"Is that our patient?" he said.

"No," Tomkins said. "Ours'll be down in a few minutes. You'll remember him when you see the X rays."

He used to remember them all. At first their faces and the way they handled their fear and their struggles to make a living and their hopes for their families were all a part of it. Then it came to him that he could no longer carry all this, day after day.

One of them had been that white-haired man whose son had brought him from Ireland. The old man had never spent a night away from his wife since they had been married. He had never been out of his own country before and it was the spring of the year. When he had lost him that morning, he had walked the son down to the end of the seventh floor there at Riverside Hospital and they had stood, each with one foot up on that radiator by that low window with the rod across it, and he had tried to explain it. The son had taken it with his face set and nodding, and then they had shaken hands and the son had left. Alone, he had stood there for a long time, looking up the river, alive in the sunlight. Across the avenue the trees were just coming to bud, and he had thought of how green they say Ireland is in the spring and then, perhaps for the last time, he had felt tears in his eyes. Now it is better just to hear what he has to know and not let them tell him about themselves at all.

"Matt," Tomkins said now, "here are the pictures."

They had walked into the operating room and said hello to the anesthetist and the scrub nurse and the floating nurse. He went over to where Tomkins was standing in front of the two X rays clipped to the lighted panels on the side wall. He saw the shadow in the upper lobe of the left lung, almost the size of an orange and partially hidden by the heart shadow.

"Yes," he said. "I remember him now. He's that house painter."

It had been late one day about two weeks before, and he had just finished with a patient when Tomkins had walked in and snapped the films up under the clips. They had looked at them together.

"What's the history?" he had said.

"He's fifty-nine years old," Tomkins had said, looking at the papers in his hand, "and a house painter. About eight months ago he coughed up some blood, and then about two months ago he started again. About a week later he had a pain in the left chest and more blood in the sputum. He says he feels fine now, but his wife says his appetite is poor and he's short of breath. I thought you might come in and talk with him. He's scared."

The man had been standing, with his shirt off, by the table in the examination room. He was about six feet tall, lean, with his hair graying and thin on top.

"Hello, doctor," the man had said, shaking hands.

"Hello," he had said. "What do you think your trouble is?"

"I don't know," the man had said, because very few of them even dare mention it. "I hope nothing much."

"Are you scared?" he had said then, looking right at him.

"No, I'm not scared. But I'm a little nervous."

"A big guy like you? Let me do the worrying. You don't suppose I'd have anything to do with you if I didn't think I could help you, do you?"

"I guess not."

"Of course not. I not only have you but also my reputation to think of. I have to get you well."

It is something you have to do with so many. They come in scared, and you have to get them believing in you so that they don't quit on you when you need them the most.

"I just want to listen to you," he had said then. He had put the stethoscope on him, listening first to the left chest and then to the right.

"You smoke?" he had said.

"Maybe a pack and a half a day."

"How long have you been smoking?"

"Oh, I don't know. Forty years."

"Well, there's nothing wrong with you that we can't fix."

"When must I go to the hospital?"

"In a few days."

They had walked into Tomkins' office then and he had met the wife.

"He's going to be all right," he had said.

"I hope so," she had said. "He's very important to us."

"Why," he had said, trying to brighten her, "his kind are three for a dollar on any corner."

"Maybe," she had said, "but I never found another one."

"You won't have to," he had said.

When they left, Tomkins had followed him back into his office.

"Well?" Tomkins had said.

"It's cancer."

"I'm afraid so."

"Sure. When I put the stethoscope on him I could hear a distinct wheeze right by that lesion."

He had heard it, all right. A healthy lung sounds like leaves rustling in a tree. This one was like a door squeaking or a broken reed on a saxophone, and then there were the symptoms and the history.

Now he walked across the operating room to the tape rack on the wall and tore off a strip of the half inch, about four inches long. One end he stuck high on his forehead, then he ran it across the bridge of his glasses and down onto his nose to hold the glasses firm. He walked out into the hall.

"Good morning," he said.

The patient was lying on the bed outside the door, the sheet tucked up almost to his neck.

"Oh, hello, doctor," he said, turning his head.

"You waiting for someone?"

"Yes," the man said, trying to smile. "I guess I'm waiting for you."

Talking to him he had taken his left wrist and was counting the pulse. Even without a watch you won't be off more than five beats, but more important you can get the regularity and the strength of the pulsation.

"There's something I want to tell you, doctor."

I'd rather not hear it, he thought, but I must. If they want to at this time, you must let them speak.

"I've never been very religious."

"Oh?"

"But I trust in you."

They would be surprised how often you hear this, but maybe that was what you wanted once. You wanted to be somebody. Away back when you were sitting around in the Beta house and the rest of them were going into General Electric or into banks or bond houses and you said you were going to medical school, it separated you immediately. The rest of them looked at you as if you were already a hero.

"I appreciate your trust," he said now, taking the man's right hand in both of his and looking down at him. "Now, in a minute or two they're going to stick your arm with a needle. That's all you'll feel, and the next thing you know you'll be back in your room waiting to kid the nurses."

He put the hand down and picked up the large manila envelope from the foot of the bed. He walked to the window and, taking out the reports, he checked the hemoglobin and urinalysis, the liver test and the electrocardiogram, and saw that all the organs were functioning normally. When he turned back they were pushing the bed into the operating room. He handed the envelope to the nurse who was holding the door open, and he walked to the next door and went in. He peeled the tape from his nose, and pulled the mask up across the lower half of his face. He pressed the tape down over it, knotted the two strings above his cap, and walked to the sink next to Tomkins. He took a brush out of the holder and, with the foot pedal, squirted the Septisol into his hands and started to scrub, first the hands, then the forearms—five minutes in all.

When you have been scrubbing two and three times a day for a quarter of a century, you don't have to set the timer any more. Then, because you scrub so often and for so long, and work always in rubber gloves, your hands become so soft that it is actually embarrassing to shake hands with other men.

When he finished the scrubbing, he rinsed his forearms and hands, pushed the door of the operating room open with his right shoulder, and, his hands up in front of him and palms toward himself, walked across to the table with the sterile gowns and folded towels on it. He picked up a towel and dried his hands and arms. As he did, the scrub nurse came over and shook out a gown. He slipped into it, and the floating nurse tied it in back. Then he opened a towel, ripped open the packet of powder, powdered his hands, and snapped on the gloves.

Once he did not know even how to get into a gown or a pair of gloves. That first day he assisted at the thyroid at Mercy, he couldn't get the hemostats to open and he was shaking all over. It was that short, German surgeon with the silver-rimmed eyeglasses and the fat hands and he was shouting, "Off, off, off!" And then "No, doctor! No, no, no! It's not difficult; hold them like this!"

As he turned back to the room now he saw the patient, the upper half of his body uncovered, thin and pale-skinned on his back on the table under the lights. They already had him under the sodium pentothal. The intratracheal tube was down his windpipe, and the anesthetist was taping it to the left cheek.

"Well, Susie Q," he said to her, "how are you doing?"

"Fine, doctor," she said, looking at him with those big eyes over the mask. "We're doing fine."

"Good morning, doctor," he said to the intern.

"Good morning, sir."

Standing there, his gloved hands folded in front of him, priest-like, he watched Tomkins and the intern while they turned the patient onto his right side with the right arm, the intravenous tubing rising from it, out along the arm board. The left arm was folded across but up high and out of the way. The right leg was bent for stability and the left out straight. He watched them put the pillow under the head, on its side, and the pillow up between the legs. Then Tomkins and the intern anchored the body, pulling the wide adhesive tapes tight across the hip, crossing them there and sticking them to the sides of the table. When the intern started to soap the left chest and back, he walked over and took another look at the pictures, at the shadow lying up there in the lung field and adjacent to the heart.

"Doctor," he said to the intern when he walked back, "you're not trying to scrub my patient away are you? You wouldn't want me to have to go out on the street and find a new one."

"No, sir," the intern said, stopping and looking at him, embarrassed, the swab arrested in mid-air.

"That's fine. I think you can paint him now."

"Yes, sir."

He watched the intern painting. He watched him dip into the pan of disinfectant and swab the whole area with the orange-pink Merthiolate.

"Good," he said, walking up. He saw that the table was at just the right height so that, at the end of the day, he would not feel it across his shoulders. At his left, the scrub nurse had swung the instrument tray across on its stand. He put out his left hand and she pressed the scalpel into it, and he turned it in his hand. With the back of the scalpel he made the scratch, just marking the skin, starting under the left breast and bringing it up in the big C and shifting to his right hand and finishing behind the shoulder blade.

Then he made two small marks, intersecting it, about twelve inches apart.

"So when we put him back together," he said to the intern, "we'll know exactly where the skin edges go."

"Yes, sir," the intern said.

No, he thought, taking the first towel, I wouldn't want to be young like that and starting out over again. He doesn't see it yet, but now that the aging ugliness of this body is about to be draped away, I know that I will find beauty here in the miraculous, clean, functional, always-in-the-same-place orderliness of everything.

He placed the first towel and the three others, as a frame around the scratch. Then, over the whole body, he and Tomkins and the intern spread the green thoracotomy sheet with its white-trimmed opening.

The reason he won't find that beauty, he was thinking, is that he remembers that under this sheet lies a man, and he thinks of pain. Only Tomkins and I really know that we are doing all that can be done for this man.

He and Tomkins clamped the sheet so that one end of it rose above the patient's head, hiding the anesthetist from his view. He leaned over the drape and looked down at her, sitting on her stool next to the respirator and the gas tank.

"Good-by, Susie Q," he said, "I'll see you later."

"Good-by, doctor," she said, looking up at him.

"Is everybody ready?" he said.

"Right, Matt," Tomkins said.

"Yes, sir," the intern said.

"Yes, doctor," the scrub nurse said.

"What time is it?" he said to the floating nurse.

"It's eight twenty-six, doctor," the "float" said.

"Okay, let's go," he said, and he reached across with his right hand. "Knife."

The first knife he had ever used was a bone-handled pocket knife that his father gave him. He was about eight, and for a long time he wore it on a chain and his father showed him how to skin rabbits with it until he became very good at it.

Now he felt the handle of the scalpel press into his hand and he closed on it. With one long, easy, I-have-done-this-5,000-times motion and following the pink-on-pink line of the scratch, he made the

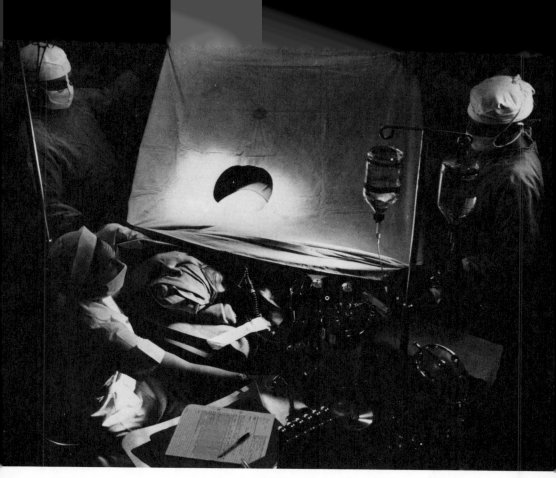

Then, over the whole body, he and Tomkins and the intern spread the green thoracotomy sheet with its white-trimmed opening. (Elliott Erwitt/Magnum Photo Library.)

long curved cut. He saw the pink-painted skin pull back and the yellow of the fat layer follow it, and the tough white tissue, lying there over the muscles.

One day, when he must have been about ten or eleven, he was walking in the canyon east of town with his single-shot .22. It was about three in the afternoon when he saw the cottontail in the shadow of the gray volcanic rocks and he got it with the first shot. When he started to skin it, he found the four young inside, and as he opened each sac there was a gasp. He didn't know then that these were the last breaths of life, so he carried the unborn rabbits back the four miles, carefully wrapped in the skin and cradled in his hands. He put them on the warm asbestos covering on the top of the furnace in the basement where his father found them the next day and explained to him what he had done.

"You see, doctor?" he said to the intern now. "The bigger the incision you make, the more money you can charge. Do you believe that?"

"No, sir."

I'll have to loosen him up, he was thinking. During this early routine you have to keep them loose, these interns and Susie Q and the scrub nurse. You don't want them tired when you get to the critical part of the problem.

"You see," he said, "this patient has been very considerate of us. He has kept himself thin."

On the other side of the table Tomkins was starting to clamp the stockinet onto one edge of the wound. He reached out and the scrub nurse handed him his stockinet. He clamped it to the edge of the cut and folded it back to cover the skin. In the old days they all used linen skin towels, but on Okinawa when they ran out of them, he borrowed the knitted stockinet that the orthopedic boys used. Now, because it is so elastic that it molds itself over the chest wall, a lot of them use it.

"Where did you go to school, doctor?" he said, smoothing down the stockinet.

"At Harvard," the intern said.

"Then you think a good deal of Dr. Churchill."

"Yes, sir."

At Massachusetts General in those early days, when Churchill was going to do a lobe, the word would spread on the grapevine and they would be standing in the halls trying to get a look. Even if he wasn't assisting he'd still be there somewhere, every time he could get free and knew Churchill was going to operate.

"There's a bleeder," he said, spotting the small spurt where the vessel had been severed. "He thinks he can hide, but I recognize him."

After he had sponged, he saw that they had clamped all the bleeders. There would be perhaps a hundred more of these small veins and arteries. He and Tomkins started to tie the first of the three hundred or more knots. Going in, really, is just three cycles of cutting and clamping and tying off—first down to the muscles, then to the ribs, and finally into the chest. He held the first clamp for Tomkins while Tomkins passed the black silk thread behind it, tied it, and knotted it twice more. Then Tomkins held for him.

"No, doctor," he said as the intern cut the thread. "You're holding those scissors like a woman. Here."

You have to learn to pick up scissors all over again. The scrub nurse handed him a pair, and he showed the intern how to hold them, with the thumb and ring finger in the eyes of the scissors, the middle finger to the side, and the index finger down the length of them as a pointer.

"Now you're ready for anything," he said. "Knife."

He started at that triangle where the back and the shoulder muscles join. When he had cut the tough, white tissue there, he turned his left hand palm up, and slid his first two fingers into the opening. Spreading them, he cut the first set of muscles forehanded and saw them snap back cleanly, released by the cut. Then he came back and did the second set of muscles the same way, but backhanded. With each cut, certain of himself, he went all the way through to the periosteum, which is the tissue covering the ribs. This was something that at the start he had lacked the assurance to do and so, like all beginners, he had tended to be a scratcher, making those shallow ineffectual cuts because he was afraid to go deep.

"Sponge," Tomkins said.

"Did you ever play football, doctor?" he said.

"No, sir," the intern said. "But I enjoy watching it."

The trouble with scratching is that you are never quite in full command. You're like a water bug, always hovering on the surface. You don't seem to be able to get down in and run the operation and so it runs you until, with experience, you lick it.

"This is just like football," he said, holding a clamp while Tomkins tied behind it. "Say you're a halfback going wide. You have to have two speeds. That's what we have. These chest openings are automatic, so we just go along one-two-three at top speed."

"I understand," the intern said.

"Then when we get inside and see what the problem is, we slow down," he said, sponging. "But there's one difference. We start fast, but when you're the halfback on that wide play you start out at three-quarter speed. Then when the defensive man commits himself, you go into high. You give him that reserve burst and you're around him. See?"

"Yes, sir."

The metal retractors would be going in now to enlarge the chest opening. The scrub nurse was wringing saline solution out of a hot pack, and Tomkins took it and placed the wet gauze over and around the exposed wall of the cut to protect it from the metal of the retractors. He placed the next one, and Tomkins hooked the curved end of the first retractor over the hot pack and around and under the shoulder blade. The second retractor he placed next to Tomkins and he handed it to the intern. As Tomkins and the intern pulled, the opening began to widen.

"Oh come on, you guys, lift," he said. "You two should go to gym more often. Let's pull that up there."

As they pulled harder, he reached up and under the shoulder blade and felt the muscle attached to the second rib. It is always conspicuous there so that you know at once where you are. Moving his fingers down over the ribs, he counted them slowly.

"Two, three, four, five," he counted and he reached over and pulled the retractor for Tomkins while Tomkins reached up and counted.

"Right," Tomkins said.

"How are you, Susie Q?" he said.

"We're all right, doctor," she said, her voice coming up over the drape. "His pulse is eighty-six, and his pressure is one-thirty over eighty-five."

"Knife."

He made the cut through the periosteum, the tough, adherent covering of the rib. When he dropped the scalpel onto the towel, the scrub nurse handed him the periosteal elevator. It looks like a blunt-ended dinner knife, and it is used to scrape the rib covering out of the way.

"Good girl," he said. "You can scrub on my Olympic team any time."

If you know exactly how to use the elevator, you can do it with just two moves. With the first move he pushed the periosteum back across the upper half of the rib. With the second move he scraped it down across the lower half and, as he did, they saw the clean, almost bloodless, gray-white arch of the rib emerge.

"Very nice, Matt," Tomkins said. "You must have done this before."

"Don't flatter me," he said. "You know it's just as easy as shelling peas. Rib cutter."

With the double-action cutter he severed the rib at one side and then at the other. He handed the cutter back and, with the other hand, gave the severed eight-inch portion of the rib to the intern.

"If you need another rib you can have this," he said. "Our man here will grow a new one in three months."

"No, thank you," the intern said, turning the rib over, looking at it. He handed it to the scrub nurse and she placed it in a sterile towel.

"Sponge count?"

"The sponge count is correct, doctor."

"Now, Susie Q," he said, "you're going to have to work. You're going to have to breathe for this man, because I'm going to open the pleura."

"I'm ready, doctor."

He knew she would be turning on the automatic respirator. He reached in and, with the scissors, severed the inner periosteum and then the pleura, the soft, almost latexlike lining of the chest cavity. When he did, he heard the air rushing in and destroying the chest vacuum, but it was unable to collapse the lung because Susie Q, sitting there below the drape and watching her dials and feeling the pressure in the anesthetic bag with her hand, was maintaining the patient's normal breathing. He could hear the tick-hiss-tick of the respirator.

"Rib spreader."

When he took the rib spreader and started to place it, he had the feeling that something was loose. He turned the spreader over.

"Hey!" he said. "Where's the wing nut? There's no wing nut here."

"Oh," the scrub nurse said. "Oh, it's all right. It's right here."

"I'm glad you're not fixing my car," he said.

She handed him the nut and he put it on. He placed the spreader between the fourth and sixth ribs and set it. Tomkins gave the handle four turns and the opening started to enlarge.

"Fine," he said. "Scissors."

He reached in and, just pushing with the open scissors, he split the muscle between the fourth and what was left of the fifth rib. Now the ribs would not break. Although it doesn't make much difference medically, it is a nice little touch to avoid the break if you can.

"Now you can crank him," he said to Tomkins.

As Tomkins turned the handle, the sides of the spreader moved out and the area opened, five inches by eleven, the rectangle framed by the steel of the spreader. There within it lay the lung, the pink and purple and black marbleized whole of it rising and almost filling the opening, then receding, the ebb and flow controlled by the machine as Susie Q maintained the rhythmic breathing.

"What time is it?" he said.

"It's eight forty-seven, doctor," the float said.

Twenty-one minutes, he thought. Sometimes you can open in twelve minutes, if he's real skinny and everyone is loose and doing his job. Now Susie Q wants to continue normal breathing but that lung is in our way.

"Can you drop your pressure just a little, Susie Q?" he said. "I want you to collapse him a little so we can see what's wrong with him."

"Yes, doctor."

This, now, was the moment. He reached in and, with the rest of them watching in silence and even Susie Q half-standing and looking down over the end of the drape but still reaching down and feeling the pressure bag, he moved his right hand slowly up toward what, until this moment, had been first just a succession of symptoms and then a shadow on an X ray.

He felt the lung, normal and pliable. Then, through the thinness of the gloves, he felt his fingers come to the edges of it, the beginning of the hardness, the spreading patch. Slowly he followed it to the root of the lung, and the root was hard too. From the root he went to the heart and felt the leatherlike spread of the hardness on the pericardium itself, the thin covering over the heart. Then he went down and felt the spleen and the left lobe of the liver through the thinness of the diaphragm and they both felt normal.

It has spread so far now, he was thinking, that if I do anything at all I will have to take the whole lung and the lymph nodes and that hard portion of the pericardium and then denude all the adjacent structures that can't be removed. If I do this he may die right here on this table or in those first few days. If I don't, and if I just close this chest and send him back to that wife and son, the only hope will be in nitrogen mustard and those new chemicals or cobalt or radium. That is the decision, just as plain as that.

Still the only sound in the room was the tick-hiss-tick of the respirator. Manipulating the lung, he turned it enough to expose the yellow-gray waxy growth. When he looked up, Tomkins was looking at him.

"This is a patient," he said, slowly withdrawing his hand, "who was afraid he had cancer of the lung, so for six months he tried to forget it. Now he not only has cancer of the lung but it has extended into his mediastinal structures. Tom?"

He waited, his hand clasped priestlike in front of him again, while Tomkins reached in. So he's not yet sixty, he was thinking. If we take the whole lung, his heart will stand it and, except for the heavy smoking and the normal city smog, his right lung has had only routine abuse. That right lung performs 55 percent of the breathing function anyway, so if we do get away with it, we won't be leaving him a wheelchair cripple.

"Well," he said, when he saw Tomkins waiting for him, "can he stand a pneumonectomy?"

"I say yes," Tomkins said.

At times like this, he had often thought, the only thing to do is to see yourself as the patient. If I'm ever like this, I hope to heaven they don't just sew me up again and send me back. If they lose me, all they have to lose is a little off their reputations, but I lose my life. I want that chance.

"I say yes, too," he said.

He had known he would say it, but you need to think it all out and take that last breather. Besides, if you just do nice, clean cases all the time and never get into the tough ones, you lose not only your touch but your courage. After all these years it's only from the tough ones, anyhow, that you feel any real reward. Now the key to this one is whether we can get that pulmonary artery free of disease.

"If we can get a clean artery," he said, "we can get this out."

So he would leave the bronchus, the tube bringing air into the lung, until later. He would go for the pulmonary artery first and without telling Susie Q, free it and tie it off. Then if she didn't say

181

anything after about five minutes, he would know for sure that the patient hadn't deteriorated and that he could live with only one lung. If it didn't work, he would just have to close him, but until you know where you stand, you don't want to burn that bridge by dividing that artery.

"You haven't got a heavy rubber band," he said to the scrub nurse, "have you?"

"Like this?" she said, holding it out to him on her hand.

"Good girl," he said, taking it. He cut it and put it around the vagus nerve, clamping the other end to the towel drape at Tomkins' side of the opening. This would keep the vagus and laryngeal nerves out of the way.

"So we won't abuse them," he said to the intern.

He started to isolate the pulmonary artery, dissecting the weblike tissue around it. He felt around it and motioned to Tomkins. Tomkins reached in and felt it.

"It looks like we're going to get it," he said to Tomkins.

"Forceps and heavy silk ties," Tomkins said.

"Right-angle," he said.

He put the right-angle under the artery and Tomkins passed the tie to it with the forceps. He brought the end of the suture up and discarded the right-angle. Taking the two ends of the suture and being careful to tie on a straight line so as not to tear, he slid the first knot down around the artery. When he put in the second knot he felt it give and knew that the first had been ineffective, and then he put in a third.

"Good," he said. "What's his heart doing now, Susie Q?"

While you are in there, you are almost one with the patient. You are so much a part of a man who is really a stranger to you that, like the beat of a musician's foot, your head moves a little with the the rhythm of the patient's heart, and he had felt it miss just that once.

"His pulse is one hundred, doctor. His pressure is one-twenty over eighty."

"Good."

Now he could get back to work again. He worked for about five minutes, exposing the veins and preparing them for division. Still he had not heard from Susie Q.

"How are you, Susie Q?" he said finally.

"His pulse is ninety-six, doctor, and his pressure is one-ten over eighty."

Now he knew he could do it. The patient was holding his own. Because he had done so many like this, he knew he could remove this lung and that this patient would live.

"Good," he said. He severed the artery about a half inch beyond the tie and watched the end retract and open. He finished isolating the veins and tied them and divided them.

"Oh, come on," he said. "How about a little light down in here? I suppose I can do this in the dark, but I don't have to. That's better."

"Shall we notify pathology, doctor?" the scrub nurse said.

"Yes," he said, "but it'll be about fifteen minutes."

If this one wasn't so obvious, he was thinking, I'd have waited for pathology, but what I'll really want them to put their microscopes on will be those lymph nodes, when I can get to them.

"A bronchial clamp," he said. "Now, Susie Q, I want this lung to collapse a little."

With Tomkins holding the lung up with the three forceps, he put the first clamp on the bronchus, cutting off the air, and then the second one. He cut through the hard whiteness between the clamps. Then he took the three lung forceps from Tomkins and passed them to the intern.

"Hold these in both hands, doctor," he said. "Now, lift."

The lung came out. The intern stood there holding it, looking at it and then at him.

"You see, doctor?" he said. "You came here wanting to be a surgeon, and you've just performed a pneumonectomy. You've removed a lung."

"Thank you, doctor," the intern said, looser now, passing the lung to the scrub nurse who placed it in a pan. It was ten twenty-nine.

"We lost a little blood there."

"Tonsil sucker," Tomkins said, and the scrub nurse handed him the metal suction tube used in tonsillectomies.

He waited while Tomkins drained the area, then started to remove the first of the chain of lymph nodes. When a cancer spreads through the lymphatic channels, the nodes are the depots at which it stops, but as he took them, almost round and the size of small marbles, he saw that the pigmentation was a normal black and not patched with white.

"We're running into a little luck here," he said. "They look fine."

"Do you want these to go to pathology, doctor?" the scrub nurse said.

"Yes," he said passing her another, "and I want this one marked subaortic node and put in a separate bottle."

"Now look at that," he heard someone say behind him. "I wonder if he knows what he's doing."

"Who's that?" he said recognizing Joe Martin's voice. "Joseph?"

"Yes, sir," Martin said. "I guess he knows what he's doing."

"Listen," he said. "I'd be out of here by now, but I have a patient who didn't want to believe he had carcinoma. How come you always get the easy ones?"

"I've got good contacts," Martin said.

"Call my office, will you, Joe?" he said. "Say I can't get free for that conference at Mercy, but I'll make the heart on time."

He asked for a knife, looking over the top of his half-glasses at the scrub nurse. "Have your fine sutures ready with those long slender forceps. This is a bad bronchus to close because the cartilage of the wall has almost turned to bone. Susie Q?"

"Yes, doctor."

"I'll give you ten breaths and then stop."

"All right."

"Stop."

He cut a half inch off the satin-white toughness of the tubelike bronchus to get beyond where the clamp had crushed the tissue. Then he forced the curved needle and the first suture through the tube and pulled the end partly closed. He drew the stitch up tight, knotted it three times, and let Susie Q take the ten breaths for the patient. Then, the same way, he put in the eight other sutures, spacing them so that each would carry the same load, stopping after each for Susie Q.

"The bronchus is closed," he said finally. "Saline wash, please."

Now he would test it. He would see if he had really closed it so that no contaminated air could possibly get into this chest. He took the pan of saline from the scrub nurse and, tipping the pan, he poured the solution into the open chest until it covered the stub of the severed bronchus.

"Now see if you can make it leak, Susie Q," he said. "I want you to push hard on your bag. You ready?"

"Yes, doctor."

"All right, push. Push hard. Are you pushing, Susie?"

He watched the surface of the saline solution above the stump of the bronchus. There were no bubbles.

"I'm pushing hard, doctor," he heard her say.

"Okay," he said. "You can stop. Good girl."

Now for that patch that had spread onto the heart. With the tonsil suckers Tomkins and the intern drained the saline from the area. When they had finished he took the scissors and, staying at least an inch outside the leathery edge of the gray-yellow lesion on the covering of the heart and working right against the heart itself, he cut away the cancerous area, all of it contained in a severed rectangle about two inches by three and a half. The heart beat bare in the new opening.

He would have to patch this opening. He reached with his index finger between the chest wall and the pleura adhering to it. Freeing the pleura, smooth and more fragile than the heart's own natural covering, he cut a rectangle to match the size of the opening. This patch, translucent and not unlike the latex of his gloves, he spread on the towel to his left.

"A wipe for Dr. Matthews, please," Tomkins said.

He waited, aware for the first time that he was sweating, while the float wiped his brow with the gauze.

"Thank you," he said. "How's he doing, Susie Q?"

"All right, doctor, we're keeping his pressure up. He's one-ten over eighty."

"We'll be about a half hour closing," he said.

He looped a silk thread into each of the four corners of the patch of pleura. Holding up the patch by the top threads, the bottom threads dangling, he laid it over the opening, right against the heart.

"Keep a little tension on," he said, passing Tomkins the two threads. Then he took the bottom threads and adjusted the patch. He sewed the four corners, then stitched the bottom and the other three sides. Any good tailor would be appalled by the crudeness of it, but it would keep the heart from popping out through the opening like that one he lost that way about ten years ago. In ten days the patch would grow right into place.

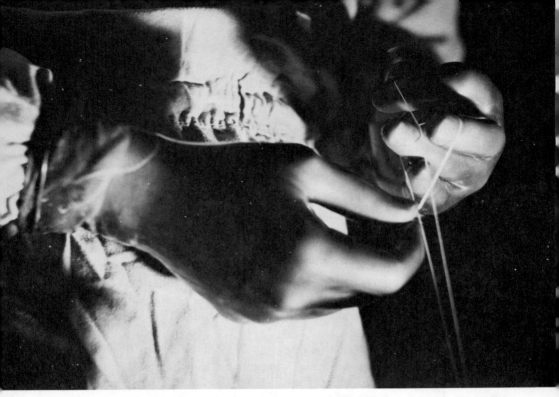

"Keep a little tension on," he said, passing Tomkins the two threads. (Elliott Erwitt/Magnum Photo Library.)

"Matt?" he heard Bradley from pathology saying from the door. "The frozen section shows your patient has carcinoma of the lung."

"Thanks, Brad," he said. "But we couldn't mistake this one."

"Also a couple of the nodes are suspicious, but we'll have to wait for final microscopic examination."

"I got them all anyway," he said. "There's a bleeder, Tom."

"I'll get it," Tomkins said.

"Now, doctor," he said to the intern, but holding the clamp while Tomkins tied, "you're familiar with the symptomology in this case?"

"Yes, sir."

"And you know that cancer of the lung is a great mimic?"

"Yes, sir," the intern said, cutting the tie.

"Then what other diseases cause the symptoms this patient had: pain in the chest, blood in the sputum, and loss of appetite?"

"Well, TB and pneumonia."

"That's right. So you'll remember that in this case the patient was fortunate because his cancer didn't masquerade as bursitis or arthritis or gall bladder or heart disease. But then he abused that good luck by ignoring it for six months."

"Yes, sir."

He syringed the area with saline, then poured in the rest of the saline from the pan. He saw there was no air bubbles, waited for the suckers to empty the chest again, and shook in the antibiotic powder. Next he put in the drainage tube between the second and third ribs.

"Crank him down," he said to Tomkins, and Tomkins turned the handle of the rib spreader and took it out. "Now we can go back to our one-two-three."

"Approximator," Tomkins said.

He waited while Tomkins, setting the fingers of the rib approximator along the slide, pulled the ribs back into position. He restored the muscles to their normal state, and then he sewed through the tough fascia, just catching a piece of each muscle.

"You see how easy it is, doctor?" he said to the intern.

"Well," the intern said, hesitating, "I don't know."

"Now you've scrubbed with a lot of different doctors in this hospital," he said, "so you've seen cancer in a variety of organs."

"That's right, sir."

"In the male over forty, what's the most frequent cancer of any organ?"

"Well," the intern said, "I was going to say cancer of the prostate or of the stomach."

"They're both close," he said, "but the answer is cancer of the lung."

"Yes, sir."

"How are you now, Susie Q?"

"All right, doctor. His pulse is eighty-two. His blood pressure is one-twenty over eighty."

Tomkins took off the skin snaps and discarded the stockinet on one side while he did the other. Then with a straight needle, matching the cross marks he had made across the first scratch, he put in the first stitch and pulled the Merthiolate-painted skin together. Tomkins matched the other marks, then he started from one

end and Tomkins from the other, sewing, tying at half-inch inter-
vals, closing the wound.

"No," he said to the intern, who had reached in and cut the
threads of the first tie close to the knot. "We cut all the ties at once
and about a half inch from the knots so there's no chance of them
coming undone."

When they had finished and the intern had cut the ties, he laid a
doubled strip of gauze over the closed wound. He held it there
while Tomkins stretched the four-inch elastic tape over it and
pressed it down.

"Tom," he said, "you're a gentleman. You've made me look good
all morning."

"Any time, Matt," Tomkins said.

"How about finishing up for me right now?" he said. Looking at
the wall clock he saw it was eleven-forty. "I want to get over to
Mercy."

"Sure, Matt."

"Thank you, all," he said.

"You're welcome, doctor."

The float untied his gown and he slipped out of it and left it in
her hands. He tossed the rubber gloves to her and pushed the door
open. In the hall he slipped his mask down and pulled the tape off
his forehead and his glasses.

The locker room was empty. He stripped out of his pajamas and
threw them with the cap and the mask into the canvas hamper. He
took his money out of his left sock and put it in his wallet and took
his watch out of the other sock and put it on his wrist.

He dressed, aware for the first time of a slight fatigue. When you
really feel the all-over tiredness, though, is not on cases like this
when you've won but when you've worked for three or four hours
and lost. Then it all seems so pointless, and when you get home
your wife knows it the moment you walk through the door.

He walked to the elevator, pressed the button, and rode down. In
the lounge he signed out and flipped off the light button next to his
name. When he walked out of lounge, he saw the broad-shouldered
young man waiting for him right there and looking right at him.

"I'm sorry, doctor," the man said, "but I couldn't wait. I . . ."

"That's all right," he said smiling. "Your father's doing fine."

"God bless you, doctor," the man said, the tears coming into his

*The locker room was empty, and he was aware for the first time of fatigue.
(Elliott Erwitt/Magnum Photo Library.)*

eyes. The man smiled and shook his head. "God bless you always."

"That's all right."

"Will you tell my mother now? It's been a long wait for her."

"Certainly."

The man walked, hurrying, ahead of him to the waiting room. The woman in the green dress was standing there. There were tears in her eyes, too, as she looked into his face.

"The doctor says he's fine, Mom," the man said. "He says he's all right."

"That's right," he said, smiling and taking the woman's hand. "We got it all out, and he's in the recovery room now. Pretty soon they'll be taking him back to his own room."

"May God bless you, doctor," she was saying.

"You'll be able to see him for a few minutes tonight," he said.

"God bless you, again," she said, still holding his hand, the tears still welling out of her eyes.

"That's all right," he said.

Well, he was thinking as he left them, this is what it is all about and what he had wanted to be.

As he drove west on Washington Street he was aware, starting to unwind, that he had had only two cups of coffee at the apartment and that he was hungry. With the heart at Mercy and then the office, he would not get another chance to eat until seven-thirty, so he would stop at the hot dog cart down at the corner by the warehouse. He swung his car across the street and up onto the concrete apron next to the cart. He turned off the motor and waited while another customer was served.

"So what's yours, Mac?" the man said.

His name was not Matthews, his associate was not Tomkins, and the hospital was not University. He was Dr. J. Maxwell Chamberlain, his associate was Dr. Thomas McNeill, and the place was Roosevelt Hospital in New York City. The pseudonymity was imposed for reasons of medical ethics but as much, it seemed to me, because of the politics and petty jealousies that should not, but do, exist in the most professional of our professions.

He was born in Waterville, Kansas, and received his bachelor's and medical degrees from the University of Colorado, where he quarterbacked the football team from 1925 through 1927. During World War II he was a lieutenant colonel in the Army Medical Corps in the Pacific, and later, as a superb technician, he was one of the great thoracic surgeons of all time.

Beyond that, Max Chamberlain was a great teacher whose operative procedures, taught at the O.R. table to interns and medical students, are being practiced and passed on today. I know, for as I

J. Maxwell Chamberlain, M.D. (Fred Ayer, Jr.)

watched over his shoulder while he performed three-dozen opera-
tions for cancer of the lung and then, as he spent countless post-
operative hours answering my questions, he taught me enough to
translate into lay language who a surgeon is and what he does.

Of the hundreds of subjects I have interviewed and tried to come
to know, there has been only one other who has had such clarity of
recall of his beginnings, his development, the origins of his skills,
his aspirations, his fears, his failures, and his successes, and who so
well understood what I was trying to do. Around Max Chamberlain

191

and his life I framed a novel, *The Surgeon,* that, because of what he was and gave to me, was published in twenty-five editions in twelve languages. In that he was pseudonymous, too.

Early in the evening of May 24, 1968, just east of Sturbridge, Massachusetts, at the age of sixty-two, Dr. J. Maxwell Chamberlain died in an automobile accident. Dr. Thomas McNeill now practices in Florida.

12

G.I. Lew

There is a major general named Robert N. Young. He had the 2nd Infantry Division in Korea, and now he is commandant of the Infantry Center and the Infantry School at Fort Benning, Georgia. We were sitting in his office and he was just back from Korea and I think he felt a little out of place with the wall-to-wall carpeting and the air conditioning and the paneled walls.

"I brought two fine combat men back with me," he said. "I had places for a staff, but I didn't have a staff, so I picked two good combat sergeants. I brought back a sergeant named Adams and a sergeant named Jenkins."

"I know the sergeant named Jenkins," I said.

"He's a great combat soldier," the general said. "He's famous up and down the front."

I knew the sergeant named Jenkins, all right. It was one of those blue and pink evenings they were getting in that summer of 1944 off the Channel coast of France. We were tied up with a Coast Guard LST several hundred yards off the beach, and it was quiet and the air was soft and the water was almost flat and had in it those colors of the sky.

The Army had pushed inland and I was coming back from England, trying to get with the Army. I was sitting in my jeep among the other jeeps on the forward deck, reading, when I heard them talking off to the right.

"You want to know something?" the first one said, in the high voice of a kid.

"Sure," the second one said.

"You know who's on this tub tied up with us?"

"Sure," the second said. "Betty Grable."

"Lew Jenkins," the first one said. "He was the lightweight champion of the world."

"Why don't you ——" the second one said.

I think this is the way to start telling you about Lew Jenkins, but I am not sure. Maybe I should tell you about the time he was in the peacetime Army in Japan and this big mess cook picked on him. He stood about six feet two and weighed about two hundred forty pounds and Lew stands five feet seven and goes to about a hundred forty-five now. Lew put his right hand in his back pocket and kept it there. He cut the big guy to ribbons and knocked him down a half-dozen times with left hooks before the big guy quit.

"But he wasn't a bad guy," Lew said. "After that he didn't bother us and he'd give us anything we wanted. He was an all right guy."

Anyway, I don't think anybody who ever became big in sports lived as wildly as this man and I don't know of anybody who ever came off the sports pages and stood up like this man in war. I want to tell you how they used to have to feed him whiskey from the water bottle to keep him from coming off a drunk in the middle of a round and falling on his face on the canvas, and I want to tell you how he won the Silver Star in Korea long after they made him a bum in the newspapers and long after I knew he would do it or die trying, if we ever had another war.

"Lew," I said to him, "how's the Coast Guard?"

All I had to do was step from our ship to his and there we were sitting on the deck in the natural beauty of that early summer of 1944. There was the quiet, with just the water lapping a little between the two ships, and the clean air and, all around us, the pastel colors.

"I guess it's all right," Lew said, in that Texas drawl. "But I don't like it."

"Why?"

"I don't want to knock the Coast Guard, or the Navy, either," he said, "but we don't fight."

There he was sitting on a deck housing with me, and he had on a pair of dirty blue jeans and a faded blue shirt and a dirty white cap stuck on the back of that wild bush of hair. There he was, a skinny little guy with the heavy brows of a fighter and those pale, sunken eyes and that sad face, and he had put the 1st Division ashore at Sicily and the 36th Division ashore at Salerno. He had put the British ashore behind the Japanese lines in Burma and the British ashore here in Normandy on D-Day. He had been up and down many beaches in the small boats, bombed and strafed and shelled, and with them getting killed all around him, and now he was telling me it wasn't fighting.

"Sure, the Coast Guard and the Navy been in there," he said, looking at me in that sad way. "We ain't always had it easy, but we take the Army in there and then we go away and leave 'em. It ain't the same as the Army."

"I know," I said.

"When I say the Army," he said, "I mean the soldier. I mean like the First Division. Before we took them in, I talked with them and when I talked with them I knew this was the greatest army in the world. Then I took them in and I seen them get killed, and you know what I'd do now if I had a house?"

"No," I said.

Of course, he didn't have a house. When he was a guy making $25,000 in one night fighting Henry Armstrong in the Polo Grounds, he had two houses. He had one in Sweetwater, Texas, where he came from, and one in Florida, but while he was running those LCVPs up on the beaches and his only home was a tired old LST, they sold him out of both houses.

"If I had a house," he said, "and a soldier didn't have a house, I'd give it to him. If I didn't, I'd be stealin', because he earned it. There ain't nothin' they shouldn't give a soldier if he's a soldier like in the First Division or the Thirty-sixth or one of them."

"I know what you mean," I said.

"I see sometimes that a landing was easy," he said. "Sometimes they say that a landing was easy, and I remember some soldier I saw get killed. I think about how, back home, some person is goin' to hear that this soldier got killed and that person is goin' to be just as miserable as if our whole Army got killed. I think about that a long time."

"I know," I said. "Many times I've thought the same thing."

"When they told us we were takin' the British in here," he said, "my heart wasn't in it. You know where my heart was?"

"No."

"My heart was with the First Division here. I wanted to be with them I knew. Then I saw the Limeys get killed and then I liked them, too."

"There's no difference between any of them, Lew," I said.

"You know what got to me?" Lew said.

"No."

"When I put the Thirty-sixth Division in at Salerno. That's the Texas Division and it was two or three in the mornin' and I put them on the beach and they were just mowin' them down. Just everybody was gettin' killed, and I'd walk up there to see who wanted to go back and they were just piled up.

"My mind and soul was with the soldiers on the beach, and they'd load me up with wounded and I'd go from ship to ship and the medics would say, 'Take 'em away. We can't handle any more here.' There'd be men with their legs blown off and there'd be men with their sides blown open, and they wouldn't say a word. There wasn't one of them let out a moan, and I hid my head in my hands and I cried.

"I never did go for cryin' as a kid or nothin'," Lew said, "but I wanted to go and fight with them and help them, but I was afraid if I did I'd get courtmartialed. I felt so cheap. My own state's men were dyin', and I felt so ashamed bein' off the beach."

He just looked at me and I looked at him. We didn't say anything.

"I just prayed," Lew said. "I just prayed for another war to start, for me to be a front-line soldier."

I never forgot this. That's why I can give it to you now, word for word. I came back off the war and Lew came back and he was broke and took a few dinky fights up around New England. Then he went back to Texas, and every now and then I used to see in the agate fight results at the bottom of the sports pages that he was fighting out there.

Then one day in the winter of 1946 there were some of us out at Lee Oma's training camp at Teddy Gleason's at Greenwood Lake, New Jersey. Oma was getting ready to fight Gus Lesnevich in the

Garden, and we were standing around there where the ring was set up next to the bar, waiting for Oma to work, when Al Buck came off the phone.

Al writes boxing for the New York *Post*. He had been talking to his office.

"Do you want a laugh?" he said.

"What?" I said.

"My desk just told me," he said. "Lew Jenkins has enlisted in the Army."

"Oh?" I said.

"What is it?" somebody else said. "Is he going for that bonus they get, or is it a gag?"

I didn't try to explain it to them. They all knew Lew and they all liked him, but there were some of them who had written when Lew was champion and Red Cochrane knocked him down five times in the Garden and Lew didn't fight a lick, that he was not only a disgrace to himself and the title he held, but to the whole fight game.

They didn't know that he had three broken vertebrae in his neck after piling his motorcycle into a traffic circle in Jersey, blind drunk at three o'clock one morning less than three weeks before the fight. They knew a lot about Lew and they put it in the papers, but they didn't know the half of it.

"Here were two youngsters," Cas Adams wrote in the New York *Herald Tribune* when Lew fought a hell of a draw in the Garden with Fritzie Zivic, who was the welterweight champ, "in perfect condition and with the sole idea of knocking the other fellow out."

Lew was in perfect condition all right. At 3 A.M. on the day of the fight he was drunk on Broadway with some guys from Texas and he'd been loaded every night for a week.

"You know something, Lew?" I said to him once. "They say in the fight game that Harry Greb was the greatest liver anybody ever saw. Even Greb couldn't have lived like you."

"People who knew Greb," Lew said, "say he was a junior compared to me."

He didn't say it as a boast. He never says anything as a boast, but just as a matter of fact, and always sadly. Lew can be very funny, but even when he comes up with a line that makes you laugh out loud there is only that little weak smile around his mouth and then

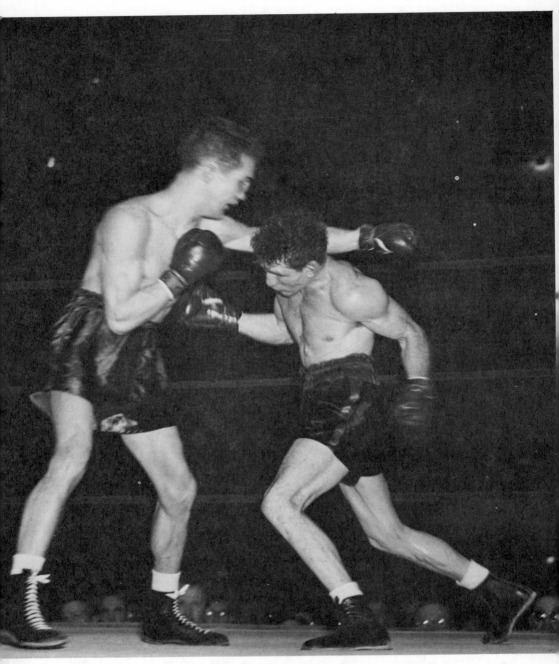

At 3 A.M. on the day of his fight he (left) was drunk on Broadway . . . and he had been loaded every night for a week. (UPI Photo.)

it goes away and there is just that sad, puzzled expression, with those deep eyes trying to find an answer somewhere off in the distance.

Take the night he fought Joey Zodda outdoors in the Meadowbrook Bowl in Newark. In the third round he hit Zodda with that straight right and down went Zodda in his own corner. There he was, stretched out, but one of his seconds was thinking and he reached up with the smelling salts and made a pass with it under Zodda's nose.

Zodda got up, and when he did Lew got mad. He moved at him again, belted him another right hand, and knocked him halfway across the ring. When Zodda went down Lew didn't even look at him, but just turned and walked to his own corner.

"Willie," he said to Willie Ketchum, who trained him when Lew would train. "He can give him all the smellin' salts he wants now. The man's gone."

Well, Willie had to laugh. Lew didn't mean it for a laugh, but the sad way in which he said it made it a laugh. There is so much about people and about life that saddens Lew, because he was born into sadness.

"Nobody," he told me once, "really knows the poor people of Texas in my time."

The way he felt about the poor people of Texas is the way he feels about the poor guys of the infantry, and he came from one and he joined the other. In between he was a champion of the world and he made enough money for you and me to retire on. All of this and his title he threw away because he had no understanding of it and it meant nothing to him. All he understands is trouble.

"The poor old private," he was telling me once. "The only time he's first is when they say, 'Take that objective there.' I stand back with them at shows. I eat with privates. The noncoms eat together in a circle, but I eat with privates. I always wanted to be with the underdog. They hold up."

It was that way with Lew when he was a fighter. He made his greatest fights when nobody believed in him and his worst when he was the favorite. He was four to one underdog the night he won the title, because only then did fighting have some meaning.

I know, you see, that he didn't enlist for Korea to win a war or save a world, but just to be a part of that misery that is the private property of the front-line soldier. He became a great front-line soldier because he came into the world in misery and because, when he was making all that money and had a chance to rise above it, he felt like a stranger and was not at home in success and so he sought his level.

Lew was born on December 4, 1916, in Milburn, Texas. There were seven kids in the family, five of them girls, and Lew was the third born, with two girls ahead of him. His old man was a blacksmith in Brownwood, and for a while he tried running a second-hand clothing store. He could never make a go of anything, and every time he tapped out he would load the family in an old covered wagon and hitch up the two old mules and they'd push off in hope but knowing that nothing would ever be any different.

"I come from a poor, ridiculous family," Lew once said to Jimmy Cannon, the sports columnist, and Jimmy said that tells all of it.

From Brownwood they went to Abilene and then back to Brownwood. They hit Big Spring and then, in 1929, Sweetwater.

"Any little old house," Lew says, "cost five dollars a month rent, so we lived in tents. We used to live in tents on the side of Highway 80."

They would pick cotton, the whole family. They would go out in the fields at sunup and they would be out there at sundown. You could pick two hundred pounds a day and, when you got good at it, maybe three hundred, but in those days they were paying only thirty-five cents a hundred.

"We'd pick fourteen hours," Lew says, "and no ten-minute break or nothin'. We'd get to the end of a row and my Dad would say, 'Come on.' In cold weather your hands would chap and the burrs would prick 'em. That's the way it was with the poor people of Texas in my time."

When Lew was sixteen he started to fight in an alley. He never had an amateur fight in his life because there was a pie shop next to the alley and the wise guys would hang around the alley and match the Mexican kids. Lew would fight the Mexicans and the winner got a pie.

It was amazing the way Lew could punch with that straight right hand. It is one of those things you either have or you don't, and if you have it you were born with it. Lew was born with it, and he had it in the alley in Sweetwater and he had it in the Garden in New York.

"Jenkins looks about as much like a fighter as a Bohemian free-verse writer," Joe Williams wrote once in the New York *World-Telegram*. "A starved cannibal wouldn't take a second look at him. He has a hatchet face, a head of wild, stringy hair, and deep, sunken eyes that seem to be continuously startled. Where he gets his punching power is baffling."

They described him as a floor mop walking on its stick end. They said you had to go back to Willie Jackson and Richie Mitchell and Charley White and Benny Leonard to remember any lightweights who could punch like him, though.

It was that same year, when Lew was sixteen, that his father died and Lew met up with the T. J. Tidwell carnival. As part of the come-on they would pair kids off to box on the ballyhoo platform and Lew went up there and belted a couple of guys out. When the carnival came back to Sweetwater in 1934, Lew joined it.

The carnival moved through Texas and New Mexico and Oklahoma, and Lew would take on all comers. He would get 10 percent of what came in to see him fight and he'd fight three times a night and make, maybe, a buck and a half.

"They weren't fighters," he says, "but neither was I. I only weighed about a hundred and twenty pounds, and some of them were heavyweights."

The carnival folded in January 1936, and Lew went to pick cotton in Mesa, Arizona. He and a couple of buddies cleaned out an old chicken house and were living in that when he read in a newspaper that Jim Braddock, who was heavyweight champion of the world, was going to box Jack McCarthy, his sparring partner, in Phoenix.

"I never seen a champion or been close to one," Lew told his pals. "I'm gonna get me a fight on that card."

One of them went with him. They bummed into Phoenix and the promoter gave Lew one dollar in advance on the five dollars he was to get for boxing four rounds. The fight was a week off and Lew's buddy starved out and caught a freight, but Lew lived on oatmeal and water and fought the guy and licked him. He picked up the four dollars and bummed to Dallas and lived for a week on doughnuts and coffee.

"You could get doughnuts and coffee for a nickel," he says, "and after I licked the guy he told them I won because I had a big steak. I could have killed him, because I had to lay back between rounds because I was exhausted and the referee had to tell me I was winnin', to keep on. Why would that guy lie that I had a steak?"

"I don't know, Lew," I said. "I don't know why."

"But why would he lie?" Lew said.

After the fight in Dallas, Lew caught a freight for El Paso and he enlisted in the cavalry at Fort Bliss. This was in 1936 and he wasn't yet twenty, and he enlisted because he was hungry and tired of sleeping out.

"They think more of a horse in the cavalry," Lew used to say, "than they do of a man. Horses cost a lot of money, and they could get all the men they wanted for twenty-one dollars a month."

While he was in the cavalry, Lew used to fight pro at El Paso and Silver City. He weighed only 136 pounds, but he was the welterweight champion of Bliss, and when he had a sixty-day furlough coming up in 1938, he decided he wanted out.

"You know what I'd like to do?" he said one night.

He was sitting and talking in barracks with a friend of his. His friend's name was Al Humphrey and this was just before Lew's furlough.

"What?" Al said.

"I'd like to get out," Lew said, "and fight Armstrong and Ambers. I'd like to go over to Dallas now and get me some fights."

"I'll give you five bucks," Al said.

Lew never forgot that. He doesn't know what ever became of Al Humphrey, but, even with all the things that have happened to Lew, he never forgot that.

"He was just a private," Lew says, "and he let me have all the money he had."

It cost him four dollars to get to Dallas. The promoter there remembered him from the night two years before when he licked the guy who said Lew had a steak, so he started putting Lew in about every other week. Lew boxed ten fights there, came off pneumonia weighing a hundred thirteen pounds, and got four bucks for two fights with a carnival. He drifted to California, Chicago, and Mexico.

In Mexico City he picked up enough of a stake to get to New York. He got fifty bucks to box a Mexican and seventy-five to blow the duke to him. The next night he got another seventy-five to carry a guy in another town, and when he hit New York in July of 1939, he had eight bucks in his pocket.

When Lew came to New York he was sent to Frank Bachman. Frank is in the printing business now but was managing fighters then, and Frank took him up to Stillman's and introduced him to Willie Ketchum.

Willie looked at Lew and Lew didn't look like anything. He was skinny and undernourished and weighed 129 pounds and looked like he was ready to fall apart. Willie looks at hundreds of fighters, and this looked like just another one to him.

There was one thing Willie saw, though, when he put Lew in the ring. Lew had one good combination. He would paw a left in your face to bring your hands up, and then he'd throw that straight right hand into the body.

"You got the right punch for these fellas around here," Willie told Lew, "but I want you to do something."

"What?" Lew said.

"Forget the right hand," Willie said.

"That's my best punch," Lew said.

"Forget it," Willie said. "Jabs and left hooks. The left is the weapon. The right comes after it."

Willie worked on that with Lew, and Willie got to like him. Lew was a little worried about the big town, and Willie put in a lot of time with him because he felt sorry for him.

Lew must have been in town a couple of weeks when Bachman made him with Baby Breese, eight rounds in the Queensboro Arena. Breese was a tough Scandinavian out of Kansas, and he weighed about 138 to Lew's 129, and in the fourth round he cut Lew over the left eye.

"I'm tired," Lew said, when he came back to the corner. "I got enough."

"Wait a minute," Willie said. "There's nothing wrong with the eye, and I'm the guy who's gonna fix it. You can't do this here. This ain't Texas. They'll suspend you and you won't get paid."

Willie pushed Lew out and he finished good and won. He licked Joey Fontana and Breese again, and then he started to put together the seven straight kayoes that got him the Ambers fight and the title.

Every fight with Lew was a war, because he wasn't what you'd call a stylist and he was hungry and there was a lot of fire in him in those days. When he fought Primo Flores in the Bronx Coliseum, Flores had him down five times before he caught Flores coming in with a right hand. Lew came to in the shower that night, and Lester Bromberg of the New York *World-Telegram* had to tell him he won.

By now Hymie Caplan had moved in on Bachman. Hymie was a pasty-faced, blue-eyed, blond little guy, and he had Ben Jeby and Lou Salica and Solly Krieger, who held titles at one time or another. Hymie knew fighters, but he never knew Lew.

"Left jab!" Hymie was hollering from the corner the night Lew was fighting Mike Belloise in the Coliseum. "Right cross! Uppercut! Underneath!"

Willie took it as long as he could. Lew was getting licked, and finally Willie turned to Hymie.

"Leave him alone, will you, Hymie?" Willie said. "He can't grasp that. He ain't that kind of a fighter."

Hymie didn't say anything and now it was the end of the sixth round and Lew came back to the corner. Willie bent over him and looked at him.

"How do you feel?" he said.

"I'm tired," Lew said.

"Do me a favor," Willie said. "Throw a couple of punches. This guy is out."

Lew went out and threw a right hand under the heart, a right on the chin and another right under the heart. The fight was over.

After that Johnny Attell, who was making matches for the Garden then, went up to the little hotel Lew was living in and signed Lew to fight Billy Marquart in the Garden. When Hymie heard it he blew his top.

Marquart was out of Winnipeg, Canada, and he had just come off stretching Billy Beauhuld in five at the Garden. Jack Hurley had him, and he was one of those hands-down, walk-in hookers like all of Jack's fighters.

"Are you out of your mind?" Hymie screamed at Lew. "This guy is a murderous puncher. He'll kill you."

"I'll kill him," Lew said. "This is goin' to be a short trip. I'll knock this guy out so they'll have to let me fight for the title."

"You're crazy," Hymie said.

Hymie tried to break the match. They wouldn't let him out of it, and the night of the fight Marquart was nine to five over Lew.

"Never mind," Hymie said to Lew in the dressing room. "Don't worry if he knocks you out, because we'll start building you up all over again."

"Ain't this awful?" Lew said, turning to the others. "There ain't anybody here believes in me. I'm the lone man who believes."

Lew was a vicious man that night. The referee was Eddie Joseph, and once he had to pull Lew off Marquart while Marquart was through the ropes and going down. It ended in the third with Joseph holding Lew off with one hand and counting Marquart out with the other.

Then they made Lew in the Garden with Tippy Larkin. Larkin was a real good stand-up boxer with a beautiful left hand, and Angelo Pucci, who had him, figured Larkin could move around Lew and stab him and cut him up and tie him up inside.

"You know what I'm gonna do to that man tonight?" Lew said to Willie in the dressing room.

"What?" Willie said.

"I'm gonna knock him out," Lew said, "and pick him up by his legs and drag him to his corner."

"Listen," Willie said. "Don't get heated up. With this Larkin everything has to go his own smooth way. You go out there and you jab him."

"Jab him?" Lew said. "Why do I want to jab him? I want to knock him out."

"Jab him," Willie said, "because he won't be looking for it. He thinks he's gonna jab you."

"I think that's crazy," Lew said.

He walked out and he jabbed Larkin, though. He hit him three stiff jabs and Larkin didn't know what to do. He backed off and made a lunge at Lew and missed. Lew jabbed him again, and when he did Larkin was so surprised he just stopped to decide what to do. When he stopped, Lew threw that right hand, on a straight line from the shoulder, and it hit Larkin on the chin. Larkin stood still for a second and then he shuddered and, as he started to go, Lew hit him three more—a left, a right, and another left—and Larkin landed on his face underneath the ropes.

When the referee started the count, Willie started up the steps.

All he was afraid of was that Lew would pick Larkin up by the feet and try to drag him to his corner.

"You know something?" Lew said, sitting on the rubbing table in the dressing room. "That man was the most convinced knocked-out man I ever knocked out."

The newspapermen, crowding around him, laughed. That was another of those times when he didn't mean it for a laugh, though, and when he said it as a kind of sad fact and in his sad way.

"Shucks," he said. "That Ambers doesn't figure to be tough for me, either. The fighters up in this country ain't so hot. They were better when I read about them in the Texas newspapers."

The Ambers fight was the last time Lew was ever in shape. Nobody could see him winning it because Ambers had fought all the good men and licked Fritzie Zivic and Tony Canzoneri and Henry Armstrong and, as it was, Lew almost walked out on the fight.

Lew was training at the Long Pond Inn on the New York end of Greenwood Lake. One day they announced he would work twelve rounds, and there were a half-dozen sportswriters from New York up to see him and watching him in that pine gym near the lake. Hymie was there too and when Lew started to work Hymie started to shout.

"Jab!" Hymie was hollering. "Cross! One-two! Turn 'em off!"

Willie could see what would happen, and he was standing across the ring and he was trying to flag Hymie down. Nobody could flag Hymie down, though, and at the end of the fourth round Lew jumped through the ropes, ripped off his headgear and gloves, and headed into the dressing room.

"What's the matter with him?" Hymie said to Willie.

"I told you," Willie said. "He don't like that stuff. With all these newspapermen here he thinks you're trying to show him up."

Hymie took the newspapermen down to the bar and conned them and then he sent them off. In a couple of minutes he ran up to Willie in Willie's room.

"Quick," he said. "He's puttin' his suitcases in his car and he's leavin'!"

When Willie ran out, there was Lew pulling out into the road in his black Ford. Willie ran to Hymie's car and he got in and he chased Lew until he caught him in Suffern, New York, which is about twenty-five miles from camp.

"What are you doing?" he said to Lew after he squeezed him off the road.

"I'm goin' back to Texas," Lew said.

"But you can't," Willie said. "You're fighting for the lightweight championship of the world."

"I don't care," Lew said. "I can knock this man out, so I don't care."

It took Willie a half hour to persuade Lew to come back. He told him about all the money he could make and about how much it would mean not only to Lew but to Willie, too, and finally Lew said he'd turn around if Hymie would stay away from him and if he could train in New York.

Hymie was with Lew, though, the night of the fight. Two hours before Lew climbed into the ring with Ambers for the biggest night he would ever know as a fighter, Hymie was showing him off in the restaurants around Broadway. Two hours before a fight a fighter lies down on a hotel bed somewhere and rests, so the sportswriters never will forget this guy walking around in an old rumpled suit and a flannel shirt, with his hair sticking up and that seamed, drawn, leathery face, shaking hands and smiling that small, sad smile when somebody asked him how he figured he would do with Ambers.

"You would have thought," Frankie Graham wrote in the New York *Journal-American* long afterwards, "he was going to fight some stumblebum in an out-of-the-way fight club, for all the tension he showed."

Ambers never had a chance. He was four to one over Lew, though, because they said Lew was strictly a long puncher and Ambers would fight him in close and Lew would never hit him. Even if he hit him, they said, nothing would happen because men like Jimmy McLarnin, Canzoneri, Armstrong, and Pedro Montanez hadn't been able to stop Ambers.

Ambers was on the floor before the fight was a minute old. In the second round he came back and started to take the lead when Lew dumped him with a left hook. Just as the bell sounded, Lew hit him a right on the chin and then he belted him two more before Billy Cavanaugh, the referee, could pull him off. In the third, Lew was on top of him and knocked him down for seven. Ambers got up

Ambers was on the floor before the fight was a minute old. (*International News Photo, courtesy of* The Ring.)

groggy and Lew piled in and that was the end. Lew was the light-weight champion of the world.

"But how about hitting him after the bell at the end of the second round?" one of the newspapermen asked Lew in the dressing room with everybody milling around and the noise and the photographers taking pictures.

"I didn't hear any bell," Lew said.

When the cops finally cleared everybody out, Lew sat there on the rubbing table for a minute, not saying anything. Then he looked up at Willie.

"Willie," he said, "you know damn well I heard that bell."

"I know," Willie said.

"But when they start to go," Lew said in that sad way, "they got to go."

It was then that Lew started to live. He won the title on May 10, 1940, and two months later they put him into the Polo Grounds with Armstrong, a guy who once held the featherweight, lightweight, and welterweight titles at the same time, and one of the greatest little men who ever climbed into a ring.

Armstrong was still the welterweight champion with no title going in this one and they made him nine to five over Lew. If they knew Lew was up drinking until four o'clock every morning, he'd have been ninety to one and no takers.

Lew was down seven times in six rounds. Armstrong tried to finish him in the fifth and Lew cut him over both eyes and had Henry's legs wobbling when the round ended. In the sixth, Armstrong dropped Lew twice with hooks in the body and when the bell rang Hymie had to lead him back to his stool.

"I want air," Lew was saying.

Arthur Donovan walked over and looked at Lew sitting there, gasping. He took one look and walked out to the center of the ring and threw his hands out, palms down.

"How'm I doin'?" Lew kept asking in the dressing room. "What round did I get him in?"

"You didn't," Hymie said.

"You're crazy," Lew said, his eyes firing up. "I wasn't knocked out. I wasn't hurt."

"Donovan stopped it," Hymie said.

"You mean I couldn't get up?" Lew said, and he started rambling now. "Get me another fight. Get me another shot at him."

All of a sudden he stopped talking. He looked around at those looking at him. "Say, listen," he said to Henry McLemore, the newspaperman. "Where am I?"

On September 16, Lew fought Bob Montgomery over the weight in Shibe Park in Philadelphia. The fight was postponed once when one of Lew's sisters called him from Texas and told him their mother was dying.

Lew was sitting there in the bedroom looking at his mother, who didn't recognize anyone now, when he got a call telling him he had to come back and fight or he'd be suspended and fined.

Lew had a new convertible, with less than three thousand miles on it, and he and Eddie Carroll started back. Eddie was a tall, lean welterweight from Canada, and he and Lew took turns driving right around the clock.

In Sparta, Tennessee, Eddie was driving and Lew was asleep in the back seat when they went off the side of a mountain. The car rolled down the hill and wedged against a tree and Lew was thrown out.

"When I come to," he was telling me, "Eddie was pinned behind the motor and he was bleedin' and moanin'. There was this little old Brownie camera in the car, and I grabbed that and he was moanin' and I said to him, 'Wait a minute. Hold still. This'll make a hell of a picture.'"

If you want to understand Lew Jenkins, listen to this. This is Lew Jenkins.

"But there was something wrong with the camera," Lew said. "The camera wouldn't work, but wouldn't that make a hell of a picture?"

"Yes," I said. "It would."

Lew had a cut on the top of his head and one knee was cut and there was something wrong with his hip. The next day he took a secondhand automobile guy out to look at the car.

"Ain't that a wreck?" Lew said.

"It sure is," the guy said. "I'll give you two-fifty for it."

"Make it three hundred," Lew said, "and you can have the tree, too."

"O.K.," the guy said.

When Lew got to Philly, he ached all over, so he just figured there was no sense in trying to train. He and Willie had a suite in a good hotel where there is one of those businessmen's gyms in the basement, and Lew was supposed to train in the gym.

He tried to go two rounds in the gym, but he couldn't. Herman Taylor was promoting the fight, and he was going crazy. "He's a disgrace," he kept saying to Willie.

"I know," Willie would say. "What can I do?"

Willie was living in the big suite alone. Lew would be gone all night and they got a doctor to give him some treatments on the hip, but they could never find Lew.

The fight was on a Monday and the Friday afternoon before that Lew showed up, stewed. He flopped into bed and he slept until Saturday morning.

"I'll tell you what we'll do," he said to Willie when he woke up. "Let's go on the road."

Willie got a cab and they rode out to Fairmount Park. Lew got out of the cab and disappeared. He was gone for an hour and a half.

"Where is he?" the cab driver kept saying to Willie.

"I don't know," Willie said. "Maybe he fell in the lake."

After a while they saw Lew coming down the road. His arms and his legs were going, and he was flying. He got back in the cab and they went to the hotel. He had a meal, flopped into bed, and that afternoon he worked a couple of rounds in the gym. He had another meal and he slept until Sunday morning.

Sunday morning they went out to the park again, and he disappeared for another hour and a half. He ate, went back to bed, woke up at midnight, ate, and slept until it was almost time to go to the weigh-in.

"Man," he said when he got up and stretched, "I feel good."

"You must," Willie said, looking at him. "How good can you feel?"

With that Hymie came in from New York. He waited until Lew went into the bathroom.

"Willie," he said, "what shape is he in?"

"What shape can he be in?" Willie said. "He's lucky if he can climb up the three steps to the ring."

In the third round Lew was on the floor. He had just belted Montgomery a right in the belly and Montgomery had hit him a long right on the chin and there he was, face down on the canvas.

"Well," Willie said, turning to Hymie in the corner, "that's two in a row."

"But look!" Hymie said. "He's gettin' up."

Lew got up at nine, punching. He happened to hurt Montgomery with a right hand, and Montgomery went into his shell. While he was in the shell he kept walking to Lew, though. If he had just walked away, Lew had to fall on his face, the shape he was in.

"Lew," Willie said after the ninth round, "it's the last round. That guy just about got to his corner."

"I know," Lew said, gasping, "but I can't get off this stool."

Willie pushed him off. Halfway through the round he was bleeding from the mouth and nose, but he kept throwing punches and they wrote in the papers later that this was the most savage fight in Philly since Lew Tendler and Willie Jackson, fifteen years before.

"And at the end," Willie says, "the referee walks over and he lifts Lew's hands and he says, 'The winner, Lew Jenkins!' I just stood there and I said to myself, 'Did I see this thing? Can it be true, with his hip and his knee and the way he's living?'"

"How could I do that?" Lew was asking me. "How could I even stand up for ten rounds in those fights with good men the shape I was in?"

"I don't know, Lew," I said. "Don't ask me."

After the fight, Lew went back to Sweetwater and the day he got there his mother died. He bought a new Caddy in Dallas and he drove back to New York. Then he put the Caddy in a parking lot and took a plane to Miami. He was walking along the streets in Miami when he happened to look in a window and he saw a half-dozen new motorcycles.

"How do you turn one of these things on?" he asked the guy in the store. "And how do you turn it off?"

The guy showed him and Lew asked the price and the guy said five hundred dollars. Lew paid him, and the guy fixed up the license. Lew took the motorcycle out on the street, ran it once around the block and took off for New York.

"Man," he was telling me, "you fall off a motorcycle about ten times goin' sixty miles a hour and it raises hell with your insides. I was near shook to death by the time I got to New York."

They matched Lew to defend his title against Pete Lello in the Garden on November 22, 1940. Lello was out of Gary, Indiana, and they called him "The Gary Gunner." Lew was supposed to be training at Pompton Lakes, New Jersey. He trained there for a number of fights after that, if you want to call it training, and it was always the same deal.

"He'd disappear," Allie Stolz was saying once, "and he'd be gone three or four days. Then he'd call me up and he'd say, 'Where have you been?' I'd say, 'Me? Where have *you* been?' He'd say, 'Don't go away. I'll be right out.' Sometimes he'd come out that day. Sometimes it would be another three or four days."

Allie Stolz was a real good lightweight. He was telling Frankie Graham and a few of us about it one time up in the Garden.

"After a while he had three motorcycles," Allie said. "He had one for straight speeding and one for hill climbing, and one that, so help me, ran in curves and circles. One day he was missing from camp and just about when it was time for him to box we heard a terrific clatter out on the road that runs past the camp, and there he was at the head of about fifty guys on motorcycles, waving to us as they roared past."

Lew also had a guitar and a phonograph and a stack of cowboy records. He'd play them over and over again, and then take the guitar and strum it and sing songs.

"Don't I sound like him?" he'd say.

"No," Allie would say.

Then he'd write a couple of songs a day. No matter what the words were, though, the tune was always the same.

"Listen to this one," he'd say, and he'd start out strumming and singing.

"I heard that one yesterday," Allie would say.

"No you didn't," Lew would say. "I just wrote it. I hear fellas get a lot of money for writing songs. I'm gonna write some more and sell them and make a lot of money."

One night Allie went with Lew to some roadside joint around Pompton. Just before they got to the place, Lew took a wad of bills out of his pocket, and this will show you how much he needed to make more money writing songs.

"He had one for straight speeding and one for hill climbing, and one that, so help me, ran in curves and circles." (*UPI Photo.*)

"I got five hundred," he said to Allie, handing him some bills. "Here. You take this two-fifty and keep it for me. I don't wanta spend it all tonight."

They walked into the joint and there were a lot of people there and everybody knew Lew. Everybody was saying hello to him and calling him "Champ" and he was buying everybody a drink.

"See what those people over there will have," he would say to the waiter, and then guys started to come up to touch him for a sawbuck or two.

"Say, Allie," Lew said after a while. "Give me that money I gave you."

"Nope," Allie said. "You gave it to me to keep for you and that's what I'm gonna do."

"Give me that money," Lew said. "It's mine, and you got no right to keep it."

"Drop dead," Allie said.

Lew kept after him, though. He kept arguing with Allie, and he put on such a hurt that finally Allie gave him the other two-fifty.

The next morning the two of them got up in camp, and Lew went through his pockets. He didn't have a dime.

"Did you give me that money back last night?" he said to Allie.

"Yep," Allie said.

"What did I do with it?" Lew said.

"You spent it."

"You ——," Lew said. "What did you give it to me for?"

At the weigh-in for the Lello fight, Lew did a funny thing. He asked Lello for an autographed picture, and Lello gave him one. This was the first time anybody ever heard of a fighter, especially a champion, asking the other fighter for an autographed picture, but Lew is a lot like a small boy.

The afternoon of the Lello fight the cops picked up Hymie. Hymie was one of five they grabbed and Bill O'Dwyer was King's County DA then, before he became Mayor of New York and Ambassador to Mexico, and he described it as a $4,000,000 marked-card swindle.

There was a real-estate dealer who was taken for $150,000 and a Park Avenue doctor for $18,000. Two manufacturers from Philly had lost $40,000 and $25,000 apiece and some jeweler went for $75,000 and some yarn manufacturer for $100,000. There were thirty-eight other businessmen who said they lost $700,000 in two years, and the cops said Hymie was the godfather and had been putting up the dough for the expensive establishments.

Hymie went to Sing Sing for it, but it was always around town that he took the rap for somebody else. When he was dying of cancer about three years ago, I went over to see him in the hospital in Brooklyn, and I wanted to ask him then about it, but I never did.

"I'll get him off," Lew said, when he heard they had Hymie.

They were holding Hymie in a Brooklyn hotel, and when Lew got on the phone with the dicks he knew he wasn't going to get Hymie off. He pleaded with them just to bring Hymie to the fight, so he could see it, and when they wouldn't do that he asked them to put Hymie on the phone.

"Listen, Hymie," he told him on the phone, "When you hear the building shake, that's Lello hittin' the floor."

He hit the floor, too. In the second round they were coming out of a clinch and Lew threw a hook and Lello started down. Lew was mad about Hymie, and he was right on top of Lello and he chopped a right into him as he was going. Lello rolled over on the canvas and got up at nine. The crowd was roaring now and Arthur Donovan moved in to wipe Lello's gloves, but as he lifted them Lew belted Lello a right and down he went again. Donovan waved Lew back and he picked up Lello to give him a breather, and Lew hit Lello another right and another left and dumped him for eight. When he got up, Lew knocked him down again with another right for nine. He staggered toward Lew and Lew hit him with a straight right and a hook and Lello went to his knees in Lew's corner and Donovan caught him as he was about to pitch forward on his face and stopped it.

"Did you miss Hymie?" one of the newspapermen asked Lew later.

"I missed Hymie," Lew said, with that sad, faraway look in his eyes, "but I didn't miss Lello."

"Against Lello, Jenkins looked like a great champion," Dan Parker wrote in the New York *Daily Mirror*. "Certainly no lightweight within the memory of this present generation of fans could hit like this bag of bones."

Fritzie Zivic had just won the welterweight title from Armstrong, and so they put Lew and Fritzie together in the Garden on December 20. This figured to be a tough fight for Lew, even if he bothered to get in shape, because Fritzie knew everything there was to know about handling himself in a ring, and Sugar Ray Robinson told me once that he learned more fighting Fritzie than he ever learned fighting any other man.

The fight was on a Friday night, and the Saturday before that Lew and Willie were coming out of a movie in Pompton late in the afternoon. Lew had on his old roadwork clothes, and it was cold and there was ice on the ground.

"Willie," he said, "I wanna see somebody in this little bar down here."

"Please," Willie said. "Why do you want to see somebody?"

"I just want to see him," Lew said.

They went into the bar and Lew had a beer. Then the bartender bought him one back. Lew said the guy wasn't there, so they went to another bar. He bought and the bartender bought. They drove over to Paterson to the New York Bar and he had five or six more. At midnight they were in the Top Hat in Jersey City, where somebody loaned Lew a jacket and tie so he could get in, and at 4 A.M. the place closed down so Lew was standing outside gabbing with a ring of guys.

Willie was standing there, too, but he got tired of waiting. He went across the street to get the car and turn it around, and when he got back Lew had gone. He didn't show up again until the next Monday night, and then he decided to finish training in New York.

Every night he was out until 2 or 3 A.M., and Willie could never find him. On the morning of the fight he left him at three o'clock on Broadway, and at ten-thirty Willie was in the lobby of the hotel waiting for Lew to go to the weigh-in, but there wasn't any Lew.

"You waiting for Lew Jenkins?" a bellhop said to Willie finally, about eleven.

"Sure," Willie said.

"He's gone an hour and a half ago," the bellhop said.

"Are you kidding?" Willie said.

"No," the bellhop said. "I saw him go out with a pair of ice skates."

Willie went down to the boxing commission and tried to stall them. Zivic was there waiting and so were the newspapermen, and when Lew finally walked in at one o'clock, General John J. Phelan, who was the boxing commissioner then, was ready to fall out of his shoes.

"I got lost in the subway," Lew said.

Lew was never any good with a lie, though. It seemed like he always had to get it off his chest.

"You know, Willie," he said, when they were alone later, "I didn't get lost in no subway."

"I know," Willie said.

"I went ice skatin'," Lew said.

"Why?" Willie said. "Why on the day of a fight?"

"Well," Lew said, "somebody told me it's good for your legs."

After the weigh-in they went to eat, and they went up to the suite in the Astor. Lew took a cigarette—he always smoked three or four in the dressing room before he got into the ring—and he just sort of fell back on the bed with his hat and his coat and his shoes on, and he went to sleep.

Willie took the cigarette out of his hand, and there must have been twenty guys in the room, smoking cigars and hollering to be heard. Every now and then the phone would ring, but nothing bothered Lew until seven o'clock when Willie woke him.

"Man, I feel good," he said, stretching, and that was the night he and Zivic fought that great draw and Cas Adams wrote about the two finely conditioned young athletes. How would he know?

It was after they made Lew with Ambers again over-the-weight that he and Al Dunbar, a welterweight, were in the auto wreck. Early one morning they hit that bridge going into Paterson on Route 4.

"He's been in an auto accident," Mike Jacobs said, calling Willie on the phone and getting him out of bed. "They think he's dead."

He didn't have a scratch on him, but that same day he was back in New York and riding a cab. The cab hit the back of another car, and Lew pitched forward and came up with a bad knee.

"You see," he said to Willie. "I smash that car to pieces and nobody would think I'd come out of it alive. Now I'm ridin' in a cab and mindin' my own business and I hurt my knee. It don't pay you to mind your own business."

Two weeks before the Ambers fight he got the grippe. For seven days he was running a fever and in bed, but Willie always said it won him the fight.

"This is one guy," Willie said, "that the grippe helped. He rested for seven days."

When they came in from Pompton for the weigh-in it was snowing. About two o'clock in the afternoon they were sitting in Lindy's and Lew had had his big meal.

"Willie," he said, "I got to deliver some tickets."

"Lew, it's bad weather," Willie said. "Let me deliver them."

"No," Lew said, shaking his head. "These are personal friends, and I got to deliver them myself."

Off he went, and Willie went to the suite in the Astor to wait. At eight o'clock they were supposed to be in the Garden, and at eight-fifteen Lew came in.

"Whatta ya know?" he said, with a big smile on his face.

"Oh-oh," Willie said. "You're drunk."

"Willie," Lew said, "I like you. You're a man."

The blizzard had closed down all the cabs, so they walked the eight blocks to the Garden through deep snow. They had to sneak him into the room, and then send out for mouthwash to get rid of the smell of drink in case General Phelan should drop in to see him.

In the first round he had Ambers on the ropes and he had Ambers out. Arthur Donovan broke them and Lew pinned Ambers again and twice more Donovan broke them.

"Man," Lew said, when he came back to the corner, "that man ain't lettin' me knock him out. He's disturbin' me. I'll hit that man."

"Please, Lew," Willie said. "Don't."

It took him four rounds to sweat the drink out, and in the sixth he had Ambers going and in the seventh he finished him. He was a great finisher, and he must have hit Ambers thirty punches, and that was the night Al Weill retired Ambers.

"Willie," Lew said in the dressing room, "how come I didn't knock him out as quick as I did the last time?"

"I don't know," Willie said, looking at him amazed. "I can't imagine."

The story they like to tell about Lew, though, has to do with the second Montgomery fight. After knocking out Ambers again Lew was still a big draw, and when Jacobs made Lew and Montgomery for a return in the Garden there was a pretty good gate involved.

Mike had his office in the Brill Building then, on Broadway just south of 50th Street. It was a couple of days before the fight that

Mike was coming out of the building to have lunch across the street at Lindy's when he heard this motorcycle roaring through the traffic. He was standing on the curb now, and he looked up and there was Lew on his cycle swinging into Broadway from 50th.

"Hey, Mike!" Lew hollered. "Look! No hands!"

Montgomery gave Lew an awful cuffing around, and after it was over they had to put twenty stitches over Lew's eyes and across his nose. A little thing like being stitched up never bothered Lew, though. In September of 1941 he was in Minneapolis to fight Cleo McNeil, and he had an abscess in his throat. He had trouble swallowing and couldn't eat, so Willie took him to a doctor. The doctor lanced the infection and Lew just swallowed.

"That's fine," he said. "I'm hungry."

Lew knocked McNeil out in the third round. He hit him so hard that the punch ripped McNeil's cheek and upper lip open like it had been done with a knife.

"That guy had something in his glove," McNeil said when he came to his corner.

"Sure," one of his seconds said. "His fist was in there."

Lew was to fight Cochrane in the Garden three weeks later, and he had driven his car to Minneapolis. Willie didn't want him bouncing back in the car so he drove the car back and he sent Lew back by train. Willie drove to Pittsburgh to see Harry Bobo fight Bill Poland, and that morning he turned on the radio in his hotel room to listen to the news while he was shaving.

"Lew Jenkins," he heard the man say, "the lightweight champion of the world, is in critical condition in a New Jersey hospital as the result of a motorcycle crash."

At that time Benny Goodman was playing at Frank Daley's Meadowbrook in Jersey, and Peggy Lee was singing with the band. Lew used to ride his cycle out there from Pompton Lakes, and he'd sit in the back with the band after they came off the stand and he'd drink. About three o'clock in the morning he got on his cycle to find an all-night spot, and he hit a traffic circle.

Lew woke up eight hours later in a hospital. He was so bad they had already put down the dough to hold the room for a week, and they had his arms and back and neck taped. Two hours after he came to, he had them carry him back to camp, and he stripped all the bandages off.

"I had to train," he told me, "but I couldn't even wash my own face."

After the Cochrane fight, when Red knocked him down five times and Lew couldn't figure it out, they discovered the broken vertebrae in a clinic in Fort Worth. They put a cast on, and Lew went out the back door while the newspapermen were waiting at the front door because he was matched to defend his title against Sammy Angott in the Garden in a month.

When Lew got out of the place he took the cast off. He never told Willie what was wrong with him, but Willie could see he had nothing and Angott won fourteen out of the fifteen rounds. Nineteen months after he had won the lightweight title, Lew had lost it. Adding the Cochrane and Angott fights, Lew lost nine in a row and eleven out of twelve before he enlisted in the Coast Guard in 1943.

One night he woke up in the waiting room of the railroad station in St. Louis with two cops beating on his skull with billies. He was drunk, and it cost him ten dollars to get out of the can and get to Pittsburgh where Zivic stopped him in ten rounds.

He was in New Orleans on the night of August 17, 1942, to fight Cosby Linson. The fight was in Victory Arena, outdoors, and Lew walked up to the gate and showed his ticket.

"You can't go through here, Mac," the guy on the gate said. "Fighters go around the side."

"But I'm fightin' the main event," Lew said, "and I just saw the guy I'm fightin' go through here."

"I don't know nothin' about that," the guy at the gate said. "All I know is, you gotta go around the side."

What Lew said I won't repeat. He went down the street and into a bar and he started loading up. There couldn't be any fight without him, so in about an hour they came looking for him. Linson licked him, but he made them take him through the front gate.

Ten days later he was in Detroit to fight Carmen Notch. At 4 A.M. on the day of the fight he was blind drunk in the hotel lobby with his bags packed and hollering that he was going home. They had to get him a bottle to keep him in his room, and that was one of the times when they had to give him whiskey between rounds for fear he'd sober up. He got licked, but he made one of his greatest fights that night.

The next month he fought Al Tribuani in Wilmington, Delaware. The week of the fight he was drunk on Broadway, and he got into a bar fight with a couple of sailors. He grabbed a glass and cut his left hand across the palm, and it took thirteen stitches to close it.

"This will heal all right," the doctor told him, "but I've got bad news for you."

"What?" Lew said.

"You'll never be able to close the index finger of that hand."

"Then how can I punch?" Lew said. "How can I make a fist?"

"I don't know," the doctor said. "I'm afraid you can't."

Lew and Willie walked out of the doctor's office together. Lew didn't say anything for a while.

"Don't worry, Willie," he said, suddenly, "I know what we'll do."

"What?" Willie said.

"We'll cut it off, and we'll make it even with the knuckles."

"You're out of your mind, Lew," Willie said. "Don't even talk about it."

"But you have to, Willie," Lew said. "Please, Willie. You got to cut it off."

"All right," Willie told him. "I'll cut it off."

Lew was up at Stillman's and he was training with one hand. They got another doctor to take the stitches out, and the cut reopened. They bandaged it up and Willie sent Lew and a sparring partner to Wilmington with Artie Rose, the second. At midnight Artie called Willie at his apartment in New York.

"You got to come out here quick, Willie," Artie said. "They're drunk and they're breaking up the town."

"I thought you were gonna keep an eye on him," Willie said.

"I did," Artie said, "but they went into the diner on the train and when they came back they were drunk."

"Forget it," Willie said. "There's nothing you can do. Go back to sleep."

Lew and his sparring partner had had a bottle of gin apiece on them when they went in to eat. Lew was still rummed up when Willie got to Wilmington the next day, and he was just starting to come out of it in the dressing room.

"Get me in there," he kept saying. "I'm gonna die."

Willie sent Artie out to get him a bottle of whiskey. Then it came time to bandage Lew's hands.

"Now we got to face it," Willie said. "I can't bandage you, Lew, with this stiff finger."

"Give it to me," Lew said. "I'll fix it."

He walked up to the wall with his finger sticking out straight. He put it against the wall and he pressed it and Willie says he couldn't watch it. Willie says he felt himself getting sick, but Lew pressed until he closed the finger and he's been closing it ever since.

"You see?" he said. "There it is."

Willie bandaged him, and he put a sponge in the left glove to keep the blood from the cut from running down Lew's arm as Lew punched and the cut opened. As they were about to leave the dressing room Lew was good and high with the whiskey, and he hit the door with his right fist and Willie says he split it just like it had been hit with an axe.

"I'm ready," he said.

Of course he wasn't ready. Tribuani didn't discover this, though, until the third round, and from then on he knocked Lew down six times in the next seven rounds. The crowd was booing and calling Lew a bum, and when Lew and Willie got back to the dressing room Willie called it quits.

"Lew, you got to quit," Willie was saying, and the tears were coming into his eyes and starting down his cheeks. "If you don't quit I'm through, anyway. I can't stand it to see a great fighter like you gettin' licked by guys like this. I can't stand it."

Well, that was Lew's fighting career. He had forty fights after that, between wars, but they were little fights and didn't mean anything because he was done. Then I met him that beautiful evening off Normandy. In war he had finally found a meaning in living, and then I lost him again to hear, out at Oma's camp, that he had reenlisted.

"You remember," he was telling me, "how they were all saying in '46 that we were gonna fight the Russians? I read all that in the papers and I went right to Baltimore to enlist and I told them I wanted to be in it."

At the time they were hoping to throw Lew in with Charlie Fusari in Jersey City. Charlie is a Jersey boy and was going good then, and they were talking about giving Lew six thousand dollars, with it being sure that Charlie would belt him out.

"I got a chance to make this six thousand," Lew told the colonel at the enlistment center. "If I sign up now, can I get off to make that fight?"

"No," the colonel said. "I'm afraid you can't. When you're in the

Army, you're in. Why don't you fight that fight and get the six thousand, and then come back and enlist?"

"No," Lew said. "I'm afraid if I wait I might talk myself out of it. You better give me that paper. I'll sign it now."

He signed it, but no war came. At the end of 1948 he was discharged after two years in Japan. He fought around Philly, training by playing the guitar in Big Bill's nightclub and singing songs like "I'm a Plain Old Country Boy" and "Take an Old Cold 'Tater (and Wait)." Then came the invasion of South Korea, and Lew stood up to what he told me about praying for another war.

"There's nobody can know what it's like," he was telling me right after the general brought him back. "There's nobody but the front-line soldier knows, with the shellin' and the woundin' and goin' without food and bein' so tired that you want to die. The poor front-line soldier, he knows, but nobody knows if they ain't been there."

Lew arrived in Pusan on July 2, 1951, when the 2nd Infantry was in reserve. On the 15th they went into the line to relieve the Marines around the reservoir near Bloody Ridge and Heartbreak Ridge, and they held there until August 8th when they attacked Hill 772.

Lew was a platoon sergeant in George Company and they moved out about four miles while it was still dark. Charley Company took over their positions, and at dawn they started up the hill. The hill was mined and they lost twenty-one men to mines. They were getting shelled from beyond the hill and then they began to get small arms and mortars, but by noon they were within fifty yards of the top. By six o'clock that night they had been forced off.

"I ain't so young any more," Lew was telling me, and he'll be thirty-six this December. "And my legs ain't so good. I'd get to the top of a hill and I'd be so tired I'd holler, 'Dig in! Dig in, everybody!' Then I'd just turn around and I'd holler, 'Kill me, you ——! Kill me! I'm so tired I don't care!' I was too tired to dig in, but there was only one fella ever beat me to the top of a hill and he was twenty-two years old and from Philadelphia and a squad sergeant. I just had to do it, and you know why?"

"No," I said.

"I had my pride," he said sadly, in that way of his. "I was Lew Jenkins, and the rest of them were kids and they looked up to me."

225

That is the truth, and they say that the kids used to flock to Lew for courage. He says he was as scared as any of them, but he couldn't let them know it.

"We'd have to take a hill," he told me, "and I'd be scared, but they'd all be watchin' me so I'd make up a rhyme about the hill so rough and tough, we'll get them gooks, sure enough. Then they'd all holler, 'Listen to old Lew, he's singin'! There he goes!' Then they'd all follow me, and we'd take that hill."

On the 17th day of August they set up a roadblock and they held it for ten days against the Chinese Reds. Sixty-eight out of a company of two hundred eventually got out, and Lew said he'd have gone back to battalion with the rest of them but he was too tired to make it.

"They were shootin' them down all around me," he told me. "It was rainin' and I lay in a creek bottom and I didn't care if I got killed, and I could see 'em takin' prisoners and killin' our guys. I remember one kid was nineteen years old and with his leg blown off and when they started to take him out they went by me and he said, 'So long, Lew. I'll see you.'

"I had a kid in my platoon, one of those screw-off kids you give details to. He got it through the leg and the arm when it was man eat man and this kid was about seventeen and he come limpin' out two or three miles in the rain. Then I got a letter from him later from the hospital and it was signed: 'Your Buddy, the Detail Kid.' He wanted to know who got out and who got killed, and that shows you he was a real man.

"When they had us surrounded there was another kid I could see was breakin'. I told an officer about him and he said, 'He's fine. He's bigger and stronger than I am.' The kid wasn't even in my platoon, but he used to come to me. This second day he come to me he started to scream. He was hollerin', 'We'll all get killed! They'll kill us all.' I patted him on the shoulder and I told him tanks were comin' up to get us and they were goin' to give us artillery for support.

"Hell," Lew said, "none of that was goin' to happen, but I had to tell him somethin'. Then I saw him walk over to some trees, and I heard a shot and I walked over to the trees. There was the kid and he had put his rifle under his chin and he pulled the trigger. I looked at him with the blood runnin' all over and his face blown and I got sick and I threw up right there."

226

When Lew was telling me this there wasn't anything I could say. I would say that I knew, but I didn't know.

"We'd have to attack sometimes through the gook dead," he said, "and there'd be so many of them I'd get sick to my stomach there."

In the ten days at the roadblock Lew formed a company of Americans and some remnants of the 36th ROK regiment and they sent another company down to him. That is what he got the Silver Star for, and the citation says that George Company and Fox Company were being withdrawn when Lew went up a draw with the 4th Platoon and that they held there and saved the battalion from being surrounded.

The last I heard of Lew was late in July and he was still at Benning but in the hospital. He had malaria and a fever of 105.6 and he was delirious. They said he was hollering about wanting to go back to Korea, but that wasn't because he was out of his mind. When I was with him and we'd sit and drink two and three glasses of iced tea at a time in the EM canteen, trying to get cool on those hot, muggy Georgia afternoons, he'd tell me the same thing.

"It ain't soldierin' here," he'd tell me. "I got to go back to the front lines. The poor front-line soldier, he's just miserable. They need me there."

You know he means it, too. Here's a guy who's had it good and had it bad. I've known lots of them who have been up and down, but I never before knew one who liked it better down than up. Not like this one.

I keep trying to figure him out. I often think of how much was written about Lew when he was a fighter and the lightweight champion of the world, and of how many people knew his name. I think of how they used to boo him and rip him apart in the newspapers because he gave them plenty of reason. Then I think of how little they really knew about him.

I keep saying I don't understand him, but now that I've seen Lew again and written all this, I can't help wondering if it doesn't all tie in to a kid picking cotton.

I'm not too sure, but I think the way he lived when he was champion shows you he was ashamed of success, as he was ashamed that evening off Normandy when the front-line soldier had less and was giving more.

He was born to misery and it kept drawing him back again like a

After they gave him the Silver Star. (Acme Photo, Courtesy UPI.)

magnet. Once, when he was picking cotton on his own and all he owned was in his burlap sack and the clothes on his back, he gave his sack to another picker so the guy could get a start. To do something like that you have to be what Lew Jenkins calls a guy when he likes him. He calls him a man.

He used to write to me, sometimes on Army requisition forms and sometimes on lined paper torn from a spiral notebook. The letters came from Hawaii and Germany and Fort Ord, California, and he was disillusioned and unhappy.

"It ain't the same, old pal," he wrote once, and ahead of his time.

G.I. *Lew*

"If you could see what's happening to our Army now it would make you sick, but I just mind my own business and I do my job until I can get out."

After he had put in his twenty years he got out, and he and Lupie settled in California. He tried it as a car salesman, but Lupie said that he felt sorry for the poor people who had to trade for the trucks and cars. He worked on a golf course as a greenskeeper, and then drove a laundry truck until a heart attack slowed him.

Five years ago I visited them in their condominium in Concord. He was amazed that he had lived to celebrate, some months before, his sixtieth birthday. He hadn't had a drink in twenty-five years.

"I just had to quit," he said. "I was just bein' crazy. I said to myself, 'I can't go on. I got a son and a wonderful wife, and my wife and son are doin' without.'"

Lew II is now in his mid-thirties, married and the father of three small children. He has an engineering degree and heads his own computer firm, and it was obvious that he and his family were a joy to his parents who had been hurt by what they saw as the disintegration of America around them.

"There's no honesty in anything," Lew said, "and there's no faith in anything anymore."

"I don't know the answer, Lew," I said. "I guess we just have to ride with the punches."

"And it's comin'," he said, "and the Man upstairs better say somethin'."

When I left them I tried to say that, obviously, the problems of peace are more complex than the problems of war. I said that the willingness of man to sacrifice himself for others is still inherent in man, and to be drawn upon if man can find a way in peace. Then, in the parting, I said I just wanted to thank him again for all he had done in two wars.

"Hell, what I did was nothin'," he said, "compared to all them that got killed. They gave their lives, and it's such a goddamn shame."

That which he had found in war, though, he tried to express in peace, and on the corner of Ygnacio Valley Road and Michigan Street in Concord now there is a traffic light. The residents, who know the story that goes with it, call it "The Lew Jenkins Light."

"Kids were gettin' run over on their way to school," Lew was tell-

Lew and Willie, thirty years later. (*Sacramento* Bee.)

ing me one night on the phone. "One got killed and so many almost got killed that I just had to do somethin', and I appointed myself a crossing guard.

"Every day, for five or six years, I went out there from seven A.M. to eight-thirty, and at the beginnin' the cops didn't like it. They wanted me to stop, and I told them, 'Why don't you do it? Then I'll stay home.' After a while, though, they understood and they left me alone.

"Then this last Christmas," he said, "the young ones, they brought me presents—cookies and candies, all wrapped up, and cards. It made you want to cry, the poor little things."

When his heart could no longer make it on its own, a pacemaker was implanted. He lived with that for some months, until Lew II called to tell me that his father, hospitalized again, was slipping away and then, the next night, to let me know that he had just died. On November 6, 1981, Lew Jenkins was buried, among those to whom he had so belonged as to no others, in Arlington National Cemetery.

13

Great Day at

Trickem Fork

There were three dozen or more of the Negroes—men, mostly old men, and women and children—and they were standing under and around these two oak trees that were planted about thirty feet apart in front of the Rolen School, which is just west of the Mount Gillard Baptist Church on the north side of U.S. 80 at Trickem Fork, Alabama. Trickem Fork is about twenty-two miles from Brown's Chapel in Selma and about thirty-two miles from the state capitol in Montgomery. It is in the heart of what they call the Black Belt, and it was four-twenty in the afternoon, with the sun descending in the clear blue sky, but warm still, and with the buds just starting on those two oak trees that were planted there thirty-four years ago and have trunks now that are as big around as a man's waist.

"They oughta be comin' pretty soon now," one of them said, looking west and into the sun where the two-lane highway curves to the right. "They oughta be here any time."

It was a big thing. It was bigger than they knew. They knew that Martin Luther King was going to lead all these whites and Negroes together from Selma right past Trickem Fork to Montgomery, but they did not know that it was a big thing in newspapers all over the

world. They did not know that it was on television not only all over
the United States but in Europe too, and that, the day before, some
people had walked seven miles on the island of Guam, and a thousand had marched in New Rochelle, New York, and two thousand in
Portsmouth, Virginia, and twelve hundred had climbed Mount
Royal in Montreal. All they knew was that Martin Luther King was
going to lead whites and Negroes right past the two oak trees in
front of the Rolen School at Trickem Fork.

"I remember the day," Jesse Favor said, "when we planted those
trees. I was ten years old then, and those trees weren't no bigger
'round than my wrist. The school was in good shape at that particular time."

The school is in bad shape now. It sits up on red bricks, and
there are five wide unpainted wooden steps leading up to the two
front doors. Half of the second step has rotted away and has never
been replaced, and there are holes in the walls where the asphalt
shingles have been broken and have fallen to the ground. Inside
there are three classrooms, for the first through the sixth grades,
and three teachers, and there are broken blackboards and holes in
the floor with Alabama license plates nailed over them. There are
potbellied stoves in the rooms, but in the winter the Negro kids
wear their outdoor clothing, because the wind comes through the
walls and up through the floor, and the latrine is out in back.

"In my day," Jesse Favor says, "there was a sign out here that de-
clared this was a school, and they had four teachers, and the principal's name was Professor Wiley Thomas. One mornin' in January of
'31 he sent seven of us to get two trees, and we went back about a
quarter mile. It was forest then, and it became farmland, and now
it's pasture. I remember we watered them trees two to three days,
and then we had a good rain, and we didn't have to water them no
more."

Jesse Favor would know. Once Jesse Favor rigged up a gallon
water jug over a watermelon. He rigged it so it would drip slowly
onto the roots of the melon, and each day he'd refill the jug, and
the melon grew to eighty pounds. Jesse Favor knows a lot of things.
He was the eleventh of twelve children, and he learned to read
when he was six by following a story about a one-eyed ape that appeared every day in the newspaper. He couldn't go to school regularly because he had to help out in the fields.

"In the fifth grade," he says, "I stayed out of school five years and went back and in five months finished two grades. Then I stayed out two years and finished through the ninth grade."

After Jesse Favor grew up, though, he spent about four hundred dollars on books, and he learned to do electrical work, and he studied veterinary medicine by mail. Then he got what he calls "the tools," and people used to come to him when they wanted their cows vaccinated and their horses shot.

Jesse Favor is forty-four now and five feet nine and a hundred-sixty pounds and all solid, and he and his wife, Zola Mae, live with their six children in a four-room cabin two miles north and west of Trickem Fork. He works for the railroad, in a track gang, but last year they gave him only four months work, and he made only a little over sixteen hundred dollars.

"You know somethin'?" Jesse Favor says, with the pride almost everybody has in the place where he lives, bad as it may be. "If you're in Los Angeles or Dallas, you can go to a bus station and buy a ticket for Trickem. It'll say Trickem on that ticket, and that bus is gonna stop and let you off right by those trees."

"Here they come now!" somebody standing under one of the oak trees said. "Here they come now."

There had been about thirty-two hundred outside Brown's Chapel in Selma the morning before, and there must have been about two hundred inside, milling around in the aisles, and under the balcony that runs around the two sides and back, and up on the stage where there is a white cross with light bulbs in it over the altar. Most of the big people were inside—Dr. Ralph J. Bunche, an undersecretary of the United Nations, Paul Screvane, New York City Council president, and Mrs. Constance Baker Motley, Manhattan Borough president—and by the time the Rev. Dr. Martin Luther King, Jr., got there the bare floorboards were strewn with paper coffee cups and sandwich paper, and smoke from a garbage fire was coming through a window.

"Hey, you stop that!" somebody hollered at the four Negro kids feeding the garbage fire in the back yard. "You put that out!"

Outside on the steps was a lectern covered with a white cloth. The smoke from the garbage fire was coming between the church and the parsonage, and cinders were falling on the crowd when Martin Luther King spoke.

As soon as they had left Brown's Chapel and turned right on Alabama Avenue they had encountered the hostile whites. (Bruce Davidson/Magnum Photo Library.)

"You will be the people that will light a new chapter in the history books of our nation. . . . This is one of the greatest demonstrations for human rights in history. . . . We have waited for freedom. We are tired of waiting. Now is the time. . . . Walk together, children. Don't you get weary, and it will lead us to the promised land. And Alabama will be a new Alabama, and America will be a new America."

As soon as they had left Brown's Chapel and turned right on Alabama Avenue, they had encountered the hostile whites. The women were the worst. The white men watched from the sidelines and, for the most part, smirked and said nothing, but the first two women, in their early fifties, plump, dressed for Sunday and their gray hair professionally set, were standing opposite the Selma Arms Company.

"I ain't seen a nigger I know yet," the one in the brown and white checked coat said to the one in the gray coat.

"We shall overcome," . . . *"We shall overcome, some day."* (*Bruce Davidson/ Magnum Photo Library.*)

"If I see any I know," the one in gray said, "I'll run out and kick 'em."

"Look!" the one in the brown and white checked coat said, liking the idea that had just come to her and shouting it, not at her friend, but at the marchers. "You ever see a white nigger? Look at the white niggers! White niggers!"

"You should hear this," said a thin, middle-aged man in a gray suit, a transistor radio to his right ear. "They're playin' 'Bye, Bye Blackbird'!"

"White niggers! White niggers!" the woman in the brown and white checked coat was shouting.

"We shall overcome," the marchers were singing, their eyes straight ahead. "We shall overcome, some day."

Then they were across the Edmund Pettus Bridge where, two weeks before, the state troopers had tear-gassed them and clubbed them, and at the first crossroad a white woman in her early thirties was standing with a boy of about six and a girl of about four. She was wearing a car coat and corduroy slacks, and when she began to shout, the boy and the girl turned and looked up at their mother.

"You all got your birth control pills?" their mother shouted. "You all got your birth control pills?"

The white nuns took the worst of it. What Sister Patrice, from San Mateo, California, and Sister Mary Leoline, from Kansas City, heard concerning their chastity out of the mouths of the white women of Alabama should not be printed.

"Lordy!" Mrs. Mary Jane Jackson said now, standing under one of the Trickem Fork oak trees with her husband Will, his brother Gulley, and Mrs. Juanita Huggins. "Look at 'em come!"

To see them, they had to look into the sun, so that the marchers came to them almost as silhouettes. There were only three hundred of them now, because a court order cut down their number when the highway narrowed to two lanes, but, walking three abreast and with the vehicles, they stretched back around the curve of the road. First there were the two Alabama Highway Patrol cars, the Confederate flags painted on the front bumpers, the speedometers holding between 2 and 2.5 miles an hour, and then the four unmarked Government cars, an Army Jeep, the big open truck with the TV and newsreel cameramen and the photographers, and then the marchers. Then there were the ambulances, two more Army Jeeps, the communications van, the latrine truck, and then the press cars, and overhead were the helicopters and the light planes.

"Lordy!" Mrs. Mary Jane Jackson said. "I didn't ever thought I'd see anythin' like this!"

Mrs. Mary Jane Jackson is seventy-three, and her husband is two years older, and they have lived here all their lives. Mrs. Mary Jane Jackson says she got into the second grade in school but she never did get out. She and her husband farmed eight acres, until they both got what she calls "the arthrite," and they reared ten children, and now seven of them live in Detroit where, she says, some do housework, and some are in steel work, and some work at the auto place.

"The first time I hear of Martin Luther King," she says, "was when they bomb his house. Then I always love to hear his name called and look at his picture, because I hear nice things about him. I believe God like him, too."

236

The front line of the march was at the two oak trees now. The Reverend Andrew Young, the executive assistant to Dr. Martin Luther King, saw the Rolen School, but he did not recognize it, unmarked and barnlike, as a school, and so he called attention instead to the Mount Gillard Baptist Church.

"Now, look at this!" the Reverend Andrew Young was shouting, turning in the front line of the march, and calling back and pointing. "Look at that church with the shingles off the roof and the broken windows! Look at that! That's why we're marching!"

As he said it, the front row of the marchers stopped, and the rest halted behind them. When they did, the women ran out from under the trees.

"I done kissed him!" Mrs. Juanita Huggins cried. "I done kissed him!"

"Who?" somebody else said. "Who you done kissed?"

"The Martin Luther King!" Mrs. Juanita Huggins said. "I done kissed the Martin Luther King!"

"Who? You?"

"That's right." Mrs. Mary Jane Jackson said, "and me too. I told him that I pray that God would keep His arms around him, and he say, 'Yes. Trust in Him.'"

"You scared?" somebody else said.

"I weren't scared at all," Mrs. Mary Jane Jackson said. "I trust in God, and I'll hug the Martin Luther King anytime I see him. They can't bother me 'bout huggin' the Martin Luther King."

"Now are you people gonna register to vote?" the Reverend Andrew Young asked. "We're not just marching here for fun."

"Yes, sir," they said, nodding. "Yes, sir."

The Reverend Andrew Young had known that this second day was going to be a tough day, with the first flush of enthusiasm gone, and the muscles tightening in the legs, and the blisters forming on the feet, and that is why he had used the Mount Gillard Church to keep them going. He had known it was going to be a tough day when he had looked out of the pink and white communications van in the middle of the campsite at 7:10 A.M. and had seen them standing in the chow line.

It was a long chow line, snaking out and around and back, and it was below freezing, and there was frost on the ground, and they were all cold. They had not washed, and few of them had slept after most of the kerosene space heaters had burned out in the two big tents. There was one young, dark-haired white woman with a dark-blue blanket over her shoulders and wearing blue jeans and black sneakers, and she was standing, trying to warm her feet, in ashes and oatmeal. She said that she was from Portland, Oregon, a writer, and the ashes were warm from a refuse fire of the night before and, as the others came by and tossed the paper plates with the remains of the breakfast on them into the ashes around her feet there was still some warmth in the oatmeal, too.

They came from everywhere. Charles Campbell, a Negro high school teacher, came from Hawaii where, he said, there is proof that the races can live together. An inflamed tendon in his right heel was giving him pain, and he was embarrassed that the lei he was wearing was made of plastic. Charles B. Rangel, a Negro lawyer, came from New York where, he said, he had never before heard from a white woman, or from anyone else, the cry "Niggers! Niggers! Kill the Goddam niggers!"

"I was in Korea," he said, "and I got the Bronze Star and the Purple Heart, but when I woke up at the campsite this morning, under similar surroundings, I had a strange feeling. I mean this was America, but American troops were guarding *me*."

"Actually, on a march like this," Dr. William Lyon, a white clinical psychologist from Los Angeles said, "you need constant stimulation. After we got away from the populous areas, where we got the jeering, things kind of flattened out. You'd think, 'If somebody'd just throw a rock at us. If a guy everybody liked had a heart attack.' You can't kill dragons if there aren't any."

Dr. Lyon is thirty-seven years old and has an actor's good looks, and he is married and has two children. He is studying now at Bloy House Theological School of the Episcopal Diocese of Los Angeles, but both he and his wife are from the South, and he said that they both felt that at least one of them should have a stake in this march.

"I don't mean it's being easy," he said. "Most of us aren't used to having people shout at us: '—— you! Go home!' Most of these ministers haven't heard a cross word in ten or fifteen years, and it's been scary at night. I mean, you look out and see the campfires burning, and the troops standing around them. The troops don't exactly reassure you, either. At night we were trying to get one of our medical vehicles into the campsite, and this National Guard Jeep was partially blocking the entry. We asked them if they'd please back up a little, but they didn't look at us or say a thing, and they didn't move the Jeep. Later another one of them walked by one of our cars and, with his bayonet, he put a scratch from one end to the other.

"The college students here," he said, "they're above average intelligence, and they really care, but they're mostly the disinherited. You rarely see a good-looking one, or an athlete, or a wealthy one. These kids here are mostly the semi-outcasts.

"I'd say that I've talked with about fifteen people," he said, "and seven or eight knew I was talking professionally. On the first day, there was this older man from San Francisco who was disoriented— not sure why he was here—and I convinced him that he'd fulfilled his obligations, and he went back.

"Then there was a college kid who would have done all right, except that he'd gone two or three nights without sleep, and he hadn't eaten regularly. He was agitated physically, with his lips moving, and a priest spotted him and brought him to me.

"On the first night, just as dusk came, a priest came up, and he'd seen a lot of combat in Europe. With the darkness coming on he'd started to panic, so I told him he was showing good judgment in confessing. I said I'd get him back to Selma, and I went looking for transportation. When I got back they were babying him, and he was sitting there crying, with a nurse holding his hand, afraid now to go back to Selma.

"The most extreme," he said, "was this university chaplain. The students had taken up a collection, and they wanted representation, and he'd had to come. Somebody had spotted him early, and we'd noticed at speeches he'd stand up in front with his arms folded across his chest and a kind of defiant look on his face. Then, at about two-thirty in the morning I saw him standing around one of the fires with a group of young Negroes. He had a can of vegetable soup in his hand, and he was using the label for a religious text and delivering a sermon about southern okra.

"I got him out of there, and I wanted to get him to sleep, but he couldn't find his bedroll. So I gave him mine, and I put him down where I could watch him, and a few minutes later I looked for him, and there was my bedroll, with him inside of it, moving across the ground like a caterpillar.

"We got him into a car then, and we took him into St. Jude in

Montgomery. On the way he was ranting, and it turned out he hated Negroes, Catholics, Episcopalians, almost everybody. At St. Jude they had him on the surgical table to give him a shot to quiet him, and there were four of them holding him when he got his arms loose, and he sat right up. There was a nun in white standing at the foot of the table, and he looked right at her and said: '——, ——, Sister!' There was a Negro doctor there who said he'd take care of him and see that eventually he'd get back to his university."

"All right!" The Reverend Andrew Young was saying now. "Let's get moving again. Let's move out!"

So the great Freedom March passed the two oak trees at Trickem Fork, three abreast. The federalized Alabama National Guardsmen, the Confederate flag sewn over their left breast pockets, leapfrogged the column and covered the crossroads and the culverts and the bridges that the Regular Army demolition men had already searched. At the end of the line, as the open, slat-sided truck with the four latrines on it started to pull back onto the highway, the white marshal named Frank Soracco, from Oakland, California, came running back.

"Now listen to me!" he hollered to three Negroes on the truck. "I don't want you ridin' anybody in those toilets!"

"What's that?" one Negro said.

"You heard me," Soracco said. "Some people have been ridin' in those toilets instead of walkin'. If there's anybody in those toilets, you stay there until they get out, and if you're a half mile back, you let 'em run."

A half mile down U.S. 80 from the two oak trees in front of the Rolen School, a Negro named Frank Haralson came walking across the fields on the left. He is sixty-two years old, and he has lived around Trickem Fork all his life, and he walks with a cane because, after he fell off a construction job over in Tyler five years ago, they never did get his left ankle set back quite right. From the porch of the four-room cabin where he lives with his wife and the two youngest of his seven children, he had seen the marchers coming away off to the right, and now he was waiting for them under a stand of pine.

"If I educated," Frank Haralson said, "I don't know—oh, Lordy!— what I woulda been. My Daddy he put two of his girls through school, and he put me to plowin'. Then one year he had bad luck.

"If I educated," Frank Haralson said, "I don't know—oh Lordy!—what I woulda been." (*Bruce Davidson/Magnum Photo Library.*)

He'd paid all his debts, and he had nine bale left, and a bale bring fifty, sixty, maybe seventy dollars, and I coulda gone to school. Then a fella burned him out, the whole nine bale, and it just an old grudge.

"But I never did get on welfare," Frank Haralson said. "I always did have a little piece of a job. The lowest I ever work was a dollar and a half a day for carpentry work, but then I work me up to two dollar. But if I educated, I just don't know. Maybe I coulda been a blueprint man.

"I tell ya," Frank Haralson said. "Around here the average man just make out. The big fish eat the little fish. I'm sixty-two now, and they still call me 'Boy.' There's a man here, and he's ninety, and they call him 'Old Man.' Around here you just go from boy to old man."

"Do you remember," the reporter said to him, "when you first heard of Martin Luther King?"

"Sure," Frank Haralson said. "In '55, when he started the bus boycott. I workin' there in Montgomery in a chair factory at the time. I had transportation, and I picked up many people on the streets. The people practical give up, but they hold out."

So Frank Haralson stood under one of those pine trees and waited for the first row of marchers to reach him. When they did, he walked right out with that cane and stuck out his right hand, and a man in the middle of the front row took it.

"Did you ever see Dr. Martin Luther King?" another man in the front row said to Frank Haralson.

"No, sir," Frank Haralson said.

"Well, you're shaking hands with him now," the man said.

"Oh, Lordy!" Frank Haralson said.

Then Frank Haralson, with his cane, got into the line next to Martin Luther King, and he walked the two and a half miles to the next campsite.

Back near the end of the column the Reverend Sherrill Smith, a Roman Catholic priest from San Antonio, Texas, was marching, his aquiline, almost handsome face burned red by the sun, his black raincoat over his right shoulder, his breviary in his hands, his lips moving with the words: "May He not suffer your foot to slip; may He slumber not who guards you."

At seven o'clock that morning the Reverend Sherrill Smith had been standing outside the men's tent, watching the others in the chow line. The collar of his raincoat was up, and he had his hands deep in the pockets.

"How did you sleep, Father?" a reporter said to him.

"Not at all," he said, smiling. "I was near the tent flap, and it was too cold, so I got up, and I walked around and I stood by the fire."

"Are you the outdoor type?"

"Hardly," he said, smiling. "Once, with a friend, I went fishing up near Eau Claire, Wisconsin, and we caught no fish, and we slept out on the stony ground and got no sleep. I said, 'That's the last time, brother.' I was thirty then, and now I'm forty-three. Unfortunately I'm also rather fastidious, so I'd be wrong if I said this is easy."

"I want you to think about something, Father," the reporter said. "We know why the Negroes are here, and we know why some of the extreme white types are here, but I doubt that you're an extremist. When I see you again, I'd like you to tell me exactly why you're here."

"I know what you mean," he said, "and I'll give it thought."

They next saw each other during a fifteen-minute rest break. The Reverend Sherrill Smith was sitting on his raincoat on a grassy bank on the side of the highway.

"I've been thinking," he said, "and I suppose that each of us is here because of what he is himself, and it isn't always easy to explain ourselves."

He grew up on the north side of Chicago, and was graduated from Northwestern, and in World War II he served four years in the Navy, first on an old World War I destroyer and then flying Curtiss Helldivers. After the war he was in charge of a group of women in the mail-order department of a chain store.

"I was twenty-eight," he said, "and I was sitting up all night reading theology and smoking cigarettes. I was engaged to be married, and it was a difficult decision. It was one or the other, and I broke my engagement.

"From my youth, I was a typical Northerner. I brushed shoulders with Negroes daily, but I never really saw them. While I was in the service, though, we came up through Georgia, and I saw for the first time the terrible gulf between the Negro and the white man. It was like another country.

"Of course," he said, "as a priest I represent the church, and I've felt great anguish about the silence of the church in the South. We've made enough high-sounding statements, and it just seemed to me that the time had come when we should be eyeball to eyeball. As a man I've felt this keenly.

"All I know," he said, looking right at the reporter, "is that I just had to put my feet on this highway, and I just had to walk."

The marshals were blowing their whistles now, and he got back in line. One of the Negro marshals was holding up an olive-green alpaca-lined jacket.

"Whose is this?" he was shouting. "Whose is this?"

"Leave it there," the marshal named Soracco said.

"But it belongs to somebody," the other said.

"If they're stupid enough to leave it there," the marshal named Soracco said, "they don't deserve to get it back. Just leave it there."

"It's mine," a Negro girl said. "Thank you."

The next day there was a light drizzle sifting down, the earth smell coming up out of the ground when they started out again at eight o'clock. Those who did not have raincoats, fashioned coverings out of clear plastic, and where they went through the Big Swamp, U.S. 80 is elevated and the National Guardsmen, in their olive-green ponchos, stood facing away from the marchers and toward the swamp and the tangle of old oaks hung with Spanish moss and the scrub growth and the dwarf palmettos.

At nine fifty-five the rain started, and at ten twenty-five the big rain hit. It hit with drops as big as quarters, pouring down on them with a great clap of sound, and coming back off the blacktop and crushed-gravel highway in a spray as high as their knees. When it hit, a short sigh went up from the marchers, and then their faces changed. Their faces seemed to fill with a joy, and their next strides to lengthen, and then their mouths opened and the cry came out: "Free-dom! Free-dom! Free-dom!"

On the cars of the state troopers and the Army Jeeps and the trucks the headlights were on, and the rain fell on the bedrolls and sleeping bags and blankets and on a maroon flannel blazer with brass buttons, all wedged between the backs of the latrines and the slatted side of the open truck. None of these things ever dried, and the clothes never dried, and the next day, when the sun came out between showers, there were the odors. There was the odor of wet

The next day there was a light drizzle sifting down, the earth smell coming up out of the ground when they started out again at eight o'clock. (Bruce Davidson/Magnum Photo Library.)

clothing and of unwashed bodies and of opened oranges, and there was the sweet smell of the lotion they rubbed onto their burned and even blistered faces. They stepped over a brown dog, killed by a car, and over many a dead yellowhammer, which is the state bird of Alabama.

Where U.S. 80 widens out to four lanes again they became, on that fourth day, a flooding stream. New marchers poured in from the side roads, and some came out from Montgomery in cars and some in buses. They carried flags and banners. Their clothes were clean. The new white faces were unburned by the sun, and the new Negro faces were open with laughter. On the last day there were more than 25,000 marchers and, as they walked through Montgomery six abreast, they were calling to the Negro women on the old wooden porches along Oak Street.

"Come on!" one old Negro marcher was calling, waving to the women. "Come on! We're not afraid!"

At the barricades in front of the state capitol they filled the plaza of Dexter Avenue, up which, 104 years before, had moved the inaugural parade of Jefferson Davis, president of the Confederacy. From his office in the white marble capitol, George Corley Wallace, governor of Alabama, looked down through the venetian blinds at the upturned black and white faces.

"I say to the white citizens of Alabama," the Reverend Ralph Abernathy was saying from the flatbed truck, his voice booming out of the loudspeakers, "how long can you afford the luxury? . . . This march is to give courage to the white citizens of Alabama who, for too long . . . To the Negro citizens of Alabama, you are not an island. . . . Will you march your children to the library? Will you march yourselves to adult education centers? . . . What do we want?"

"Free-dom! Free-dom!"

"When do we want it?"

"Now!"

"We have been drenched by the rain," Martin Luther King was telling them. "Our bodies are tired . . . our feet are somewhat sore. . . . They told us we wouldn't get here. And there are those who said we would get here over dead bodies."

"Speak! Speak!" . . . "Yes, sir!"

"Segregation is on its death bed in Alabama and the only thing uncertain about it is how costly the segregationists and Wallace will make the funeral."

"Speak! Speak!" . . . "Yes, sir!"

One of those listening was Mrs. Viola Liuzzo, thirty-nine, white, a civil rights worker from Detroit and the mother of five. In three hours she would drive a group of marchers back to Selma and then, in the light-blue 1963 car with Michigan license plates, a nineteen-year-old Negro named Leroy Moton riding with her, she would return along U.S. 80 toward Montgomery. As she listened now, she had five hours to live.

About three hundred yards east of the two oak trees in front of the Rolen School at Trickem Fork, a dirt road runs south from the highway. Three miles down the road, in the middle of a field, forty-two-year-old Ella Mae Williams, which is not her name, lives with the youngest of her nine children. A Negro, she lives in a weath-

. . . she lives in a weathered three-room shack with a tin roof and no panes in the windows and no electricity, and the nearest water a mile away. (Bruce Davidson/Magnum Photo Library.)

ered three-room shack with a tin roof and no panes in the windows and no electricity, and the nearest water is a mile away.

"Is she married?" a reporter asked John W. Moorer, who was sitting in front of the fire in Ella Mae Williams's shack. John W. Moorer, also a Negro, is sixty-five, and he lives a quarter mile across the fields, and he was wearing a pink shirt and dark-brown trousers and a brown fedora.

"No, sir," he said, shaking his head. "She ain't never been married."

"How do you support yourself and your children, Miss Williams?" the reporter asked.

She was wearing a faded lavender flannel robe and soiled white sneakers over men's socks. One sock was black and the other blue, and she had her youngest child in her arms.

"Just what I make by the day on the farm," she said, "when they hire me."

"She do hoein'," John W. Moorer said, "and she pick cotton."

"How much cotton can she pick a day?"

"Babe?" John W. Moorer said. "How much you pick?"

"A hunnerd," she said.

"That's a hundred pound," John W. Moorer said. "That get you a dollar twenty-five."

"When you pick cotton, Miss Williams, what time do you start in the morning?"

"Oh, work at six. Stop at eight."

There were two double beds in each of the two main rooms, the bedding—blankets and comforters and pillows—tumbled and faded and gray. The walls and ceilings of the rooms were covered with graying, yellowing pages from magazines, and on one page there was a picture of Ford Frick, the baseball commissioner, and on another, of Charles de Gaulle. One page was titled: "These Recipes Are Money Makers."

"Miss Williams," the reporter said, "what do you and your children eat?"

"Mostly fatback and bread."

"Your children who go to school, do they take their lunch?"

"Dog!" Ella Mae Williams said, raising her voice. "Shut your mouth!"

A brown and white dog had been running around outside the shack. Now he was under it, sniffing up through a hole in the floor, and barking.

"They take their sandwich and carry their water."

"What kind of sandwich?"

"Peanut butter mostly," she said, and then, raising her voice, "Shut up your mouth, dog!"

"Do they always have sandwiches for lunch?"

"No, sir. Sometimes it be a week they don't have anything."

On top of the blankets on one of the beds there was a book. The title was *Neighbors on the Hill,* and the name Belva Ann was printed in it in pencil, and the reporter read the first paragraph: "Far out in the country, away up on a hill, there lived a boy named Dick and a little girl named Nancy. They lived in a big white farmhouse on the hilltop."

"Miss Williams," the reporter asked, "did you ever go to school?"

"Yes, sir. I went three year."

"Did you like it?"

"Yes, sir. I like it very much. Then my mamma took sick, and they couldn't keep me in the school."

"When you were young, what did you want to be?"

"I wanted to be a teacher. My teacher was Miss Mary Frances Owens, and she was just nice to the children and try to teach them everythin', and that's what I wanted to be."

"What do you hope your children will be?"

"I hope they decide to be teachers or nurses or secretaries, or whatever they like to be. I just do my best to keep 'em in the school."

"Have you heard about the Freedom March that went by Trickem Fork last week?"

"Yes, sir. I hear about it."

"Do you know why people from all over the nation came to march here?"

"No, sir," Ella Mae Williams said. "I don't know why they march."

Jesse Favor was sitting in Mary Cosby's general store, a mile north of U.S. 80 where it passes the Trickem Fork oak trees. In Mary Cosby's general store they sell Cabin Home Corn Meal and Goody's Headache Powders and Scotch Snuff and Tampa Nugget cigars and at this time of the year they used to sit around there and talk mostly about the Trickem Eagles. The Trickem Eagles are the New York Yankees of the Lowndes County Baseball League, and Jesse Favor was the Eagles' first manager.

"I'm a guy like this," Jesse Favor was saying now, the half-dozen others sitting, and standing around, and listening to him. "I always have tried to fight for what I thought. Up to now I've just been talkin', but now I got somebody behind me."

"That's right," someone said.

"You know when it come to me?" Jesse Favor was saying. "It come to me that day in February when the Reverend Bevel came out here from Selma."

The Reverend James Bevel is a short, wiry, hard-faced Negro, a Baptist minister out of Dickson, Tennessee. He is the Alabama project director of Dr. Martin Luther King's Southern Christian Leadership Conference.

"He come out here right to this store," Jesse Favor said, "and he said, 'Take me around.' There were eight people here in this store, and most of them just left. That made me mad."

"I remember," one of the others said.

"If just a few of us get registered," Jesse Favor said, "it won't mean much. That's why we got to get as many of the people as we can to go down."

"That's right," someone said.

The county seat of Lowndes County is at Hayneville, seventeen miles to the southeast. In Lowndes County the Negroes outnumber the whites almost four to one, but until the week before the Freedom March not one Negro voter had been registered in Lowndes County in sixty-five years.

"We went down there," one of them said, "more than thirty of us, to register on the first Monday in March, and they told us one of the registrars was sick, and they didn't know where the other was. We went back on the third Monday, but they wouldn't let us in the registrar's office. You know where they had it set up to register us?"

"Where?" one of the reporters said.

"In the old jailhouse. They had the two tables set up in this room with the gallows on the left. While you're fillin' out the paper, one white man is sayin', 'I guess many a guy dropped through there.' Then another is sayin' 'I wonder if the old thing still works.'"

"And the literacy test wasn't easy," Bill Cosby said.

Bill Cosby is thirty-five now, and he does well. He owns eighty-one acres, half in cotton, and runs the general store with his wife. He finished the tenth grade and had three years of vocational training. Starting in 1948, he put in three years, nine months, and twenty-seven days in the Army, thirty-three months and thirteen days of that time in Korea and on Okinawa.

"And still can't vote," Frank Haralson said.

"They gave me hard questions," Bill Cosby said. "The first was: 'What part does the Vice-President play in the Senate and the House?' The second was: 'What legal and legislative steps would the State of Alabama and the State of Mississippi have to take to combine into one state?'"

"In eight hours," Jesse Favor said, "they registered sixteen. They got to do better than that, and we got to get more out. You know, when the march stopped here the people said that for the first time they knew what it's about, and they're gonna participate. I know they mean it, because they had their own children in the march."

"They tell us," Frank Haralson said, "that we better not have the mass meetin' Sunday night."

"I heard that," Jesse Favor said, "but they always pick some weak mind to tell it to."

"I'll be there," Frank Haralson said. "Even if nobody else be there, I'll be there."

There were more than 170 of them, men, women and some children, there at 7 P.M. The day before, Jesse Favor had spent four hours bringing electric cable through the siding of the Mount Gillard Baptist Church, so that the outside of the church would not be shrouded in darkness while they sat inside.

"You know how much longer this church is gonna be here?" a young Negro from the Student Non-violent Coordinating Committee said, standing on the front step. "About two weeks."

"You really think so?"

"A lot of people are gonna get killed. I say, 'Get your soul ready.'"

Inside they filled the worn and scarred oak pews. In the humid air their faces glistened. Up on the platform, with the altar behind him, sat Jesse Favor, as recording secretary of the Lowndes County Christian Association for Human Rights.

"Keep your eyes on the skies. Oh, Lord! Oh, Lord!" they were singing. "Keep your eyes on the skies."

"Now I hope," the first speaker was saying, "that tomorrow morning at eight o'clock we'll have the same number at the Lowndes County jailhouse that we have here tonight."

"I'd like to say something," someone else said. "We must have some means of communication for safety, because you never know at what hour of the night you might need help. I think we should have two-way radios, walkie-talkies, like the people on the other side have. I say this because we've had quite a few accidents along here on lonely roads where cars have been forced off the road, and people have been beaten to death and then put back in the car, and the car run off the road like it's an accident."

"Now you each have an application for voter registration," the main speaker was saying, holding up the piece of paper. "There's nothing to be afraid of. It's just as if you apply for a job. It's just a questionnaire. What is a questionnaire? Nothing but a series of questions. You take an oath. What is an oath? A sworn statement, and you don't have anything to be dishonest about. Your residence address. What does that mean? It means where you live. Length of residence. What does this mean? Not how long your cabin or house is but how long you have been living where you live."

"I do believe," the next speaker was saying, "that somebody out there is spyin' tonight. I don't care, whoever you are. The Uncle Toms are the people we got to understand. They are scared, and we got to feel sorry for them."

"As you may be aware," said a gray-haired man, standing up off to the right, "I can't see. I went down to register, and I can read and write Braille, but the registrar can't read Braille. So I was asked one question. That's all. Then I got the paper in the mail, and it said I failed."

"All right, then. You should write to the Justice Department and tell them what happened."

"Yes, sir."

"Now, be there tomorrow, all that can, and don't be ashamed and don't be afraid. You got nothin' to be ashamed of, and I know that people in Lowndes County just don't go to mass meetings, because it just ain't safe. You're here tonight, so I know you're not afraid."

Hayneville is a quiet farming town, its streets tree-shaded, its older homes white-painted, its newer ones red brick ranch types with white trim. The old, two-story, peaked-roofed, red brick jail sits on a mound at the edge of town.

"Now I wanta tell you," said one of the registrars, in a dark-blue suit and white shirt and dark tie, standing on the front porch of the jail and looking down at the more than fifty Negro faces sweating in the sun and looking up at him, "that I welcome you here, because you have a right to be here."

"Yes!" they said, all in one voice.

It was nine-fifty in the morning, and some of them had been there since seven-thirty. They had come with their children packed into their cars, and some by truck, and most were wearing Sunday clothes.

"Now you have a right to make your application for registration," the registrar was saying. The other one, in a brown fedora and green zipper jacket, was standing up on the porch with him along with the deputy sheriff, and nodding. "That's the law, and we live by the law here. If there are any outsiders here, from Selma or anywhere, they're not gonna help you a bit. You don't need 'em, because we're here to respect your rights. Now, there are only two of us here, and we're gonna process you as fast as we can. How long it takes depends on you. We had one here last time took an hour and forty minutes. That's not our fault."

"And if any of you have a record," the registrar in the brown fedora said, "if you've been in the pen, forget it. You're wastin' your time and our time. That's the law."

"I'm a sergeant in the United States Army," a Negro said. "Can't you get more people to make the registrations? I mean, you only got two. . . ."

"Look," the registrar in the blue suit said. "We don't get paid much for this job, and I have to leave my own business, and I'd much rather be there. I'm here because you're here. . . ."

"But some of these people been here since seven-thirty. They got work to do too. When does this start?"

"It starts," the registrar said, "when you're finished askin' questions."

They registered them four at a time at two tables in the bare, damp, fifteen-by-fifteen-foot room with the three barred windows and the steps leading up to the gallows on the left. One of them was Mrs. Fannie Robertson, who is white-haired and wears glasses and was born in Lowndes County seventy-six years ago.

"Now that's the oath you take," one registrar was saying, pointing to the paragraph on the paper. "Be sure you read it before you sign it."

"Yes, sir."

Mrs. Fannie Robertson had seven children and nineteen grandchildren and two great grandchildren. She read slowly, following the words with the index finger of her left hand, her head nodding with each word.

"It were hard," she said later, standing outside with the others, "but when they say everybody can vote in the county, I thought I better try it too. I pays my taxes and everythin'."

"Right," somebody else said.

"It were hard," she said later, "but when they say everybody can vote in the county, I thought I better try it too. I pays my taxes and everythin'." (Bruce Davidson/Magnum Photo Library.)

Just west of where the road from Hayneville joins U.S. 80 at Lowndesboro, the country is gently rolling and, where the marchers had come, one hill looks like another. Already it was difficult to find again the spot, at the right of the highway leading toward Montgomery, where Mrs. Viola Liuzzo was shot and killed the night of the last day of the march. The wheel tracks, left by the car where it went off the road, had weathered and become indistinct, and the grass was growing in them again. The four-strand barbed-wire fence, straddled by the car, had been put back up again, but where the wheel tracks ended someone had placed in the grass, under the bottom strand of barbed wire, a bouquet of now faded pink flowers.

After eleven years, U.S. 80 had changed. We were driving east, and hurriedly to get home, and where I thought Trickem Fork should be, the road is now a four-lane divided highway, and scanning the countryside off to the left, I could not find the two oak trees and the Rolen School and the Mount Gillard Baptist Church.

"Excuse me," I said, "but do you know where I might find Jesse Favor?"

We had pulled up to the two self-service gas pumps in front of the new market. The sign on the front read: "Favor's."

"Jesse Favor?" one of the two white women sitting inside said, the other shaking her hand. "I never heard of him."

Outside a middle-aged black man was at one of the pumps, putting gasoline into his car.

"Excuse me," I said, "but I wonder if you know a man named Jesse Favor?"

"Jesse Favor?" he said, thinking. "No sir."

"And Trickem Fork?" I said. "Can you tell me where Trickem Fork is?"

"It's around here somewhere," he said, gesturing back down the highway, "but I'm not sure."

Heading east again, and as we approached where the road from Hayneville links up with U.S. 80, I searched the fencing and the green farmland rising to the right. I saw no evidence of that place where Mrs. Viola Liuzzo had been shot and had died that night, no monument nor marker.

255

The monuments of the Selma March of 1965 that publicized and set the moral climate for the passage of the Voting Rights Act, are not, of course, in stone. They are in the registration since of more than 2,000,000 new black voters in the South, in the more than 2,200 blacks who hold office in the eleven states of the old Confederacy that, before then, had fewer than 100 black officeholders, in the black sheriffs, and, throughout America, in black mayors, city council members, and members of Congress.

(*Wide World Photo.*)